The Keys to Freedom

Kaden Lebray

DEDICATION

Dedicated to all those people who are transforming the world by being a living example of their words. Always empower others towards greatness. As quoted by Robin Pate (my old man) "always do the best you can and if that's not enough, then do what you got to do." Always treat others how you want to be treated and life will bring you a debt for your actions. Keep in mind that being wealthy means someone has acquired good debt.

CONTENTS

Dear Poverty,

I have known many who have judged you harshly and speak so badly about you, myself included at one point in my life. I have seen many who blame you for their bad experiences which were only created as a result of them not truly understanding you or knowing your nature. I stop trying to understand you or figure you out and when I did, it became clear to me the truth of you, which this letter unfolds.

I thank you because you represent the momentum that inspires me to improve my quality of life. The growth and expansion of humanity are inevitable, but what you represent is the basis of discovering what I deserve. When we met, our connection was a time of GREAT AWAKENING.

You are what has inspired me to travel through life, the world thought it was my VEHICLE. When I was young, you were the guidance system that motivated me to move through life, only to discover that no matter where I traveled, my conditions stayed the same. But I thank you for building the inspiration within me to discover my true GPS (GOD).

You have given me lessons that assure me that no matter what challenges life throws my way, everything will always work out for me. You have helped me develop stability within myself. You have kept my imagination active and inspired me to make a lot of money. You have shown me that I can experience freedom without an abundance of money. Through appreciating the abundance of you, it led to the abundance of friends, which led to the abundance of disappointment, which led to the abundance of fear, which led to the discovery of God, which led to the discovery of FAITH, which led to inspired action, which led to freedom, which resulted into me becoming a BILLIONAIRE.

I release the feeling of ignoring you and I choose to free myself from the negative thoughts of you that I have been dragging around by yielding to your appreciation. I token you to be the inspiration that led to my freedom, the discovery of the newness that I have been seeking and for the adventurous reality that I call life. You have allowed me to learn a little more and more about myself over time.

As an honor to you, I will create the basis whereby the entire human family will benefit from our struggles. We have spent years together and it's an honor to have gotten the opportunity to know you. "I am worthy" is the answer to all the unanswered questions, so you've shown me through our relationship. You have shown me that accepting the goodness and potential of myself is much more life-giving than an intellectual conversation, a relationship with another human, or even money itself.

This is my personal acknowledgment that you have shown me that there is nothing I cannot be, I cannot do or cannot have. Freedom has played a huge part in being, doing and having. You have inspired me to always focus on better thoughts. You have inspired me to accept myself. As a closing to this letter, I want to say, "POVERTY I love you, unconditionally."

Foreword

My name is Jeremy Milburn. I am a business owner, and friend who has had the pleasure of getting to know Kaden for the past 4 years. We met while he was playing professional basketball for the Moncton Miracles in New Brunswick, Canada. Our initial meeting was over one of his previous books, Lost and Found: The Dark Testament. We became very good friends throughout that season and have kept in close contact ever since. Throughout our friendship, we have both shared our life experiences both positive and negative and our love for the Lord.

Kaden is a very honest and spiritual man who I respect greatly. He puts the same energy and focus on his writings as he does his basketball and every other aspect of his life. He has studied and applied his research to his own life to become successful and happy. His love for God is displayed in his work and his compassion for others. Kaden is a good friend of mine and he wishes to share his experiences and knowledge to help others better their lives as he has his own.

I'm honored to be writing this foreword. I believe this book can help each reader achieve their goals and to live a richer, fuller life. I hope you enjoy this book and find it as helpful as I expect you will.

Jeremy Milburn

Chapter 1

It begins with a Thought

(Thoughts are Things)

"Thoughts are energy, powerful energy at that, when channeled with intention, strategy and an unadulterated desire to express them in a form that serves the greater good of humanity."

The benevolent discovery of the power of thought became crystal clear in the life of Corkney Taylor. This discovery did not come about from watching the discovery channel. It came about in years of experience and a mere desire to know why her circumstances in life were not favorable. Corkney never knew exactly why things in her life were not favorable but was absolute in her pursuit of gaining clarity to the why questions of her life. She wanted to be a nurse, not she desired to be a nurse. Notice how she went about transferring her want into reality through gaining awareness of the key principles in this chapter.

When the thought of becoming a nurse flashed into her mind, she deviated from the idea because she didn't feel the need to act upon it. Her mind was clouded by the difficulties she would have to face. She did not have enough money to become registered as a nurse. She didn't have the necessary education, or she felt no support from her family because no one else in her family ever stepped foot in a college classroom except her. Her ten-year-old son was misbehaving in school. She didn't have a job to financially uphold her apartment. Every two weeks her car would break down which would require her to spend money that she didn't have, but she had faith. Faith without works is dead. All her difficulties were adequate in the sense that they were true, but with her thinking being clouded with her difficulties, even FAITH would have a difficult time operating in her life (BE FROZE).

Although the road to her goal wasn't clear, Corkney knew she had to start somewhere. She was determined to move forward with the process of becoming a nurse. She had the type of determination that wouldn't settle for DEFEAT. Throughout the week, she would spend countless hours wondering what steps to take towards her goal. The more she wondered, the more her mind seemed to be clouded by her difficulties which always left her in a state of discouragement. Finally, she got her first break. She was informed by a confidential source that if she took a written test and passed it, then it would make her eligible to become a nurse. She had all the study materials for the test. The test was very similar, if not a match, to a test she had taken in her previous years. When Corkney was shown the information in the form of study materials that were on the test, she felt a surge of confidence. Within her mind, she felt like SHE KNEW IT ALL (BE FROZE).

The test was weeks away and Corkney was confident based on the study materials that she would pass the test effortlessly. So confident that instead of preparing for the test by studying, her preparation was guided by her "Know it all" belief that led to the idea that she didn't need to study at all. There are 336 hours in two weeks. The test consisted of five sections and each section had 20 questions. Of the 336 hours, she knew if she spent at least 70 hours studying, then she would reap her desired outcome but when it was time to study, she would be distracted by this thought in her mind that said: "I already know the material, I don't need to study."

"If you fail to prepare then you prepare to fail." Even though she knew the importance of studying, the ideas of the "know it all paradigm", crippled her from doing what she knew was important for her to do. It hindered her from acting in a manner that favored her greater good.

After two long hours of testing, she was given test results that were extremely unfavorable in her eyes. She FAILED and her test scores were lower than her self-esteem became after viewing her test scores. It may have not been seen in her physical appearance, but she became very depressed. Her mind became fueled by why questions.

- Why did I fail the test? Why should I keep trying?
- Occasionally the WHY questions gave birth to HOW, SHOULD, WHO, WHEN, WHERE or WHAT questions.
- What's the point of trying? Should I even become a nurse?
- Why am I in so much pain?
- What am I doing wrong?
- When will I get good luck?
- Who is going to hire someone like me?
- Where and how will I make money?

If the ideal truth within her experience could be effectively interpreted to everyone that reads it, then there is no need to read the remainder of this book.

Her circumstances convey the importance of knowing that your thoughts are far more important than your appearance, words, and actions. In fact, your thoughts are what creates and dictates your words, actions, and appearance.

Crippled but not defeated by her outcome, with perseverance, she moved past the discomfort created as a result of not passing her test. She made the choice to FAIL FORWARD. Although her physical body was moving forward, her mind was even more clouded due to the energy vibration created from failing the test. Maybe Corkney did not know at the time, but the presence of the unfavorable thoughts in her mind were the keys to the door that locked her away from achieving her own endeavors. Her own thoughts were just like watchdogs in a prison and she was the inmate searching for freedom. The truth is some inmates are freer than citizens. Her vibraction (vibration, actions, and attraction) wasn't in harmony with her own goals. She continued her search for answers to the why questions of her life, totally unaware, that within her mind she is searching for solutions, but her mind was the biggest problem.

Opportunity still came to her life. The opportunity didn't present itself in the same form that it did when she first began her path. It still came in a manner that was different than what Corkney expected. That's one of the facet characteristics of opportunity. It has a tendency of showing up unexpected and often unrecognizable in the form of DEFEAT, challenges, or periodic setbacks (BE FROZE). This suggests why so many humans are unsuccessful at recognizing opportunity.

An opportunity was offered for her to pick up a day job at McDonald's. This wasn't her career pick, but she figured McDonald's was a formattable pitstop until she reached her destination. She thought to herself, "I guess I will work at McDonald's until my opportunity comes to be a nurse and when the opportunity comes, I will accomplish it no matter what it takes." Her persistence was very admirable, although often perceived as "Stubbornness." What a different story human would have to tell if we knew the importance of intentional persistence with respects to staying on purpose.

Corkney was not very enthusiastic about the job but was more so moved by the chance to work. Monday through Friday, between the hours of 8 am to 4 pm, she would quietly crawl in and out of work. A consistent paycheck was an awesome asset of McDonald's but hidden behind the smile her facial expression displayed on payday were thoughts of the misery she had to undergo just to get MONEY.

Perhaps money is worth more than happiness. When asked the question, is money more important than happiness, most of the time the response is NO. When compared to the substantial value of human happiness, money holds no power. Although the mouth expresses an easy-going attitude about money, the words of the mouth are insignificant when compared to her thoughts about money. "I need money because I got to pay bills, my car needs gas, I need some new clothes, my son needs clothes, I have to get my hair done." Because these vibrations, in the form of thoughts, exist in her mind, when transmuted into its physical counterpart, it creates a vibraction of neediness. Neediness tends to create a low vibraction, driven by impulse, desperation, emotion or misery as Corkney identified it.

After three months of work, Corkney found herself without a job and again, began to wonder why? Her outcomes were becoming the same and, in her mind, she was caught in this downward spiral. She still had faith but compressed under all her unfavorable thoughts, but her light of faith was as dim as a lamp covered with shades.

How much happiness did Corkney experience? How much money did she make? Perhaps it brought her the satisfaction of saying I have a job and the short-term joy of receiving MONEY that had to be spent just as fast as it was earned.

She wondered why her outcomes remained the same despite her desire to persevere and strong faith. Corkney thought herself out of opportunity without acquiring the knowledge or awareness that the itch of a thought can be transformed into its physical equal by the application of the law of vibration.

She thought herself out of fulfilling her own endeavors. She did not have an "I quit attitude." She had faith and believed in God. She had an education. She always smiled when people spoke to her. She had influence, but she didn't have the awareness that the invisible energetic forces, known as thoughts, ideas, and beliefs dictate human vibration, action, and attraction (vibraction).

Now let's explore a different situation and examine a woman who possesses all the qualities of what we classify as a "good person" but always found herself in bad situations.

Good Person-Bad Outcome

One small positive thought can transform your entire day. And so, it is with negative thoughts.

Sharon Eagles, who became one of the most successful Family Physicians in the country, was caught in the busyness rush days and it wasn't visible to anyone in the outside world. Because Sharon, just like most, spent more time mastering things outside of herself than inside. After years of golden achievements, she discovered things about herself that would appear as a lie to the untrained eye. She had never been exposed to the saying that "What glitters may not be gold and even wolves may smile and fools will be led by promises to their deaths." Although she had a naturally golden image, the very thoughts compressed behind her shining smile led her to unfavorable outcomes.

After years of hard work, she earned the honor of becoming one of the most highly paid family physicians in Canada. Her success was so magnetic that within a mere week after launching her business, she needed staff to help her serve all the clients that her golden image and ethic were luring. She would train her staff to follow in her exact footsteps because she believed her process was relative to her success.

Sharon was a beautiful woman who was marked by her positive attitude, magnetic smile, ability to overcome obstacles, channeled focus, rich personality, and not to mention, her reflexive natural blue eyes. Her presence carried an energy that was so powerful that it could not be mimicked and could only be felt when she entered the room. A presence so strong that it could drive out negative energy with the single utter of a breath.

"She never met a stranger" because she was always caring, loving, and welcoming to anyone whom she crossed paths with.

If you were to describe her using five adjectives: creative, loving, detail-oriented, sensitive and humorous would paint the best picture of her identity.

Although her image appeared confident and fearless, all to no avail, her true image of herself was the exact opposite. Her true thoughts were compressed within the smile she displayed to maintain the high achiever's image, in which people act the exact opposite of what they feel to uphold an image.

Sharon could sell an image. She sold her image all over the nations. In fact, she sold it so successfully that no one could see past her efforts to suppress how dissatisfied she was with her body. Despite years of financial success and independence, Sharon discovered that life became distasteful because she didn't have the ideal body weight and shape.

This feeling of distaste crept up on her out of nowhere. The pressure of looking good and upholding the golden image snuck up on her like a thief in the nighttime. Only to leave her with a deeper damaged image of self (BE FROZE). Maybe high achievers wouldn't chase this perfect image if they were aware that it leads to deep pools of insecurity influenced by the desire to uphold the status quo.

"Thought suppressing lead to stressing and constant stressing leads to depression."

Beneath the layers of her golden image were severe depression and self-esteem insecurities which were the natural side effects of dealing with "the pressure to look good." Her supporters always showered her with compliments. Sharon, you are so beautiful, I wish I had your eyes, you are hot, I wish I could be you for a day. Sharon would always respond with expressions of appreciation and gratitude, "oh thank you, you're so sweet, I appreciate that, BOOMERANG". All the while, her mind was overtaken by unfavorable thoughts. I am so fat, I have serious issues, I hate myself, I disgust myself, I need to lose weight, etc.

Sharon developed an eating disorder. The thought of upholding the golden image mixed with her unfavorable thoughts created a self-image that drove her to become skeptical about herself. Her skepticism reached a level that she became desperate to lose weight, even if it meant she wouldn't eat. It wasn't difficult for outsiders to notice Sharon losing weight but because of the respect people had for her, they were afraid of the potential consequences of questioning her about her weight.

Even after losing weight, she still carried a mind clouded by unfavorable thoughts. This overlap of negative thoughts, although never physically spoken or expressed, led Sharon to attempt SUICIDE.

Practically humanity waits until someone dies to turn their thoughts inward. Why is it that we wait until cataclysm occurs before we make the necessary changes? Sharon later lost her business and had her physician license legally suspended. Losing everything she worked for in a time span that seemed quicker than the blink of an eye, left Sharon in a state of depression that grew so strong that it led to her lashing out and making more suicide threats.

She was still an awesome lady. She was still beautiful. She was still extraordinary. If you were to describe her using five adjectives, they would be: creative, loving, detail-oriented, sensitive and humorous.

The Golden Image is a magician. It is a false truth that may captivate an audience. Consequently, it creates a mental race for perfection. Chasing perfect left, her in a pool of dissatisfaction because she was chasing a goal that she already obtained but wasn't aware of it. Perfection exists within, that is why it is called perfection (perfect-in). The only thing you can do perfectly is be yourself.

The fortunate family physician, unfortunately, became a doctor patient driven by the thought energy produced by her brain because she was under the illusion that one can have thoughts and if they are not spoken or written, then they don't affect your actions.

After six months of research concerning the discovery of how thoughts transmute into our physical reality, Sharon decided to take her life back into her own hands. Sharon vowed to herself that she would no longer be held prisoner to her own thoughts. Each thought served as the symbolic bars. Because of this truth, it isn't farfetched to concur that some inmates are freer than citizens. But favorably for Sharon, the awareness of the influence thoughts had on her vibration, actions, and attraction served as the keys that freed her from the confines of her own mental prison.

While serving the LIFE SENTENCE in her mental prison, Sharon lost her business, lost weight, lost herself, and even attempted suicide. After failing suicide, Sharon expressed an important discovery that she made.

She pointed out that "the worst day of life isn't leading up to suicide or when you decide to kill yourself, it's when you wake up after failing your attempt and have to clean up the mess you've created."

She believed angels were protecting her because in every suicide attempt, she made, it failed. Many people have short-lived thoughts of death and they don't necessarily always attempt suicide. On the contrary, not many plan suicides, and remain physically alive to tell the story. Sharon was blessed to be alive to be able to tell her story, but there are thousands of phenomenal successors throughout the world who were led to their grave by suicide due to the emanating power of unwritten or unspoken thoughts.

Stories like Corkney's and the good-person bad outcome will be read and told countless times by those who live in a physical body and co-exist with this material world. To all these people, the suggestion that each story wishes to offer is this: All actions and outcomes stem from thoughts and if you knew how powerful your thoughts were, whether favorable or unfavorable, then you wouldn't ignore them.

Life has its strange ways of ushering in higher knowledge and greater awareness. Traditionally they are compressed in the crevices of experiences that offer discomfort. Corkney's and Sharon's experiences have a common root that's so simple, yet profound as it holds the keys to their destiny's in life. Both profitable in character, ambition, the knowingness of purpose, and active pursuit of their desired outcomes. But neither had the awareness of the power of thoughts, how thoughts influence actions and ultimately how to transform unfavorable thoughts into favorable outcomes.

In enhancing awareness of how to do so, this book was written.

As you read this book, the answer to your long unanswered questions, prayers, discoveries that you've been seeking, and ideas that left you in a state of wonder will be found. The answer may be revealed to you in the form of a renewed or refined idea, strategy, or plan that shapes the purpose leading you to your destiny.

"As it only takes a small seed to uproot a gigantic tree, it only takes a small spark of awareness to start the fire that lights the guiding torch of the one seeking direction."

When you begin to examine how thoughts are transmuted into actions, you will witness that thoughts create a state of mind. The nature of thoughts, whether favorable or unfavorable determines actions. Actions are merely the results of thoughts being converted into physical reality and thoughts create an invisible magnetic field (vibraction) around the human body that attracts experience to us based on the nature of the thoughts we practice in our own minds. For example, if a person's thoughts are negative, their actions will be negative, and their vibration will carry negative energy which will ATTRACT negative experiences, and their perspective of reality will be marked as NEGATIVE.

Without the findings gathered from years of observation, the answers to the previous questions would remain unanswered. Shift your attention to this universal truth. To some degree, every member of the human family is unfavorably affected by thoughts, regardless of whether they are thoughts we believe or thoughts we've been programmed to believe. Have you ever taken a second to ask yourself, "where do my thoughts come from?" Unfavorable thoughts typically lead to a life marked by struggling, depression, poverty, and suffering due to the Golden Eagle Syndrome.

Golden Eagle Syndrome

The story unfolds how Eagles are trained to fly. Most golden eagles try to fly before their wings are strong enough. Their eagerness to do so is fueled by watching their parents fly. After constant trial and error, some golden eagles give up on trying to fly.

Even when the eagle reaches the age where their wings are fully developed and possesses the power to soar the winds freely, it becomes mentally crippled by the failures of the past. It becomes lazy about utilizing its natural ability to soar at higher levels. The eagle, as a species, is a universal symbol of power, freedom, and dignity. Despite the great things the eagle symbolizes, the creature still allowed thoughts of its past failures to cripple its present capabilities, which is the underlying ideology of the Golden Eagle Syndrome.

There is a Golden Eagle in everyone, waiting to hatch or maybe has hatched but not flying as high due to being weighed down by thought energy. As soon as you give yourself permission to be freed from the Golden Eagle Syndrome, which will only occur through mastering the fundamentals of this ideology and commence to following the rubric to implementing those fundamentals, you will experience the energy of freedom and your quality of life will improve. Is it possible? Give yourself permission to find out.

One of the primary beauty marks (beauty marks refers to a quality marked as unfavorable) of humanity is that the average person tends to undermine the power of negative or unfavorable thoughts. Negative thoughts, when transmuted into our physical reality, is typically expressed through our human mouth in the form of disallowing statements. I can't do it, it won't work, I want to but..., I think I might be able to, I won't make it, I wish I could, etc. The human family knows all that cannot be accomplished. This book was written for those who have been searching for the Keys to freedom, success, wealth, and abundance and are open to building themselves upon the fundamentals of those keys.

It took many years for me to become a conscious thinker. Immediately afterward, I changed the music that I listen to, the people I spent my conscious time with, my diet, my habits, my phone number, my career path, and I even went a step further and legally changed my name. It would be inadvisable for you not to do the same.

Keep in mind that freedom within this human template comes to those who are conscious thinkers. For Example, you will only live abundantly when you are abundantly conscious. Defeat and non-fulfillment come when you are failure conscious.

Being limitation conscious is another phenomenal beauty mark that we commonly see in the collective members of the human family. Habitually, many people measure their outcomes, realities, and capabilities with their own thoughts and beliefs. Many will read this and think that no one can be freed from the confines of their own thoughts. They are unable to consciously comprehend LIFE in terms of wealth, freedom, abundance, perfect harmony, and fulfillment because their habitual thoughts have been saturated with limitations: (Resentment-Anger), (Agony-bitterness), (Intimidation-fear), (Neediness-wants needs), (Boastfulness-pride), (Omission-grief) and (Worthlessness- guilt and shame).

The purpose of this book is to assist all who believe in Miracles and would like to engage the miraculous process of transforming their minds from limitation conscious to abundance conscious.

Many of us look at the achievements of celebrities and "stars" and wonder why their lives emanate richest, fortune, blessings, or whatever is credited for their achievements. Not surprisingly, two of every two hundred thousand know the "keys" of their success and all human souls who are aware of the "keys" are simply too humble and flashing to verbalize the "keys" because the keys are so asinine. An intellectual undertaking will make plain "The Keys".

The Busyness Rush

When Robins Williams, a highly credited comedian and actor, decided to become more success conscious, he rose to fame. Quickly he chose to establish careers in comedy and in filming, which later proved to be formidable decisions.

What makes a good actor? What makes a good comedian? What power must you possess to exceed expectations? The answers to those questions will be found in the story of Robin Williams. His lifestyle contains details and instructions on how success isn't stumbled upon.

Although obtaining a net worth of over $50 Million, observe how Mr. Williams was swept by the invisible forces of the busyness rush. The busyness rush is marked by a mental state in which one stays busy or relies on unfavorable outlets to escape the problems or pains that stem from their thoughts.

As far as his design, growing up, Robin was merely a boy who had an unadulterated desire to make his mother laugh to get her attention. Robin always credited her for his sense of humor. He wasn't a very talkative kid because he was shy. Apparently, shyness faded away throughout his high school years as he was voted "Most likely to succeed", "class clown" and the "funniest" by his peers

"What was your first impression of Robin Williams", was later asked to Chris Reeves. William's "brother from another Mother, Chris said, "He wore tie-dye shirts with tracksuit pants and talked very fast. I'd never seen a person who had so much energy. Robin was like an untied balloon that had been inflated and immediately released."

Robin and Chris were students of the great Edith Skinner, known as one of the world's best leaders in vocalization, impersonations, and dialects. Skinner had no idea where to place Mr. Williams due to his uncommon combination of skills. Shortly after the death of his close friend and soul brother, Chris Reeves in 2004, Robin decided to begin his standup comedy career. In the mid-1970s, after a series of Revolutionary Standup comedy performances, Robin caught his first break.

When George Schlatter, nationally known television producer, observed Mr. Williams, he instantly knew the phenomenal impact Robin could have in show business and thereby invited Robin to his showed titled the Laugh in Show. Although the Laugh in show didn't bring as much fortune to Robin's life that he assumed, Mr. Williams now had a "television appearance on his resume" and an even stronger desire to polish his impersonation, vocalization and dialect skills, which he saw as the keys to achieving his goal.

By the 1980s, shortly after the Laughing Show, Robin landed an appearance on Richard Pryor and suddenly his career began to launch. Within the blink of an eye time span, Robin became famous and got caught in the busyness rush. Opportunities were coming so rapidly that Robin could barely fully engage one opportunity because he would be distracted by the incoming traffic created by others.

The comedian got his big break when casted as Mork, the alien, in the hit television show Mork and Mindy. Mork's presence in the show is attributed to the success of the sitcom. Mork, as a character, became so popular that it was highlighted on t-shirts, coloring books, posters, toys, lunch boxes, and other featured products. Mork and Mindy would weekly reach a pinnacle of roughly 60 million viewers and is reputed as the show that turned Robin Williams into a "SUPERSTAR."

The success of the Mork and Mindy show landed Robin Williams on the cover of Time Magazine, which was the leading news magazine in the United States of America and a position on the cover of the Rolling Stones Magazine. Williams was beginning to reach a broader audience in ALL areas of his career. Especially in his standup comedy, including the start of three phenomenal HBO comedy shows titled: An Evening with Mr. Robin Williams, Off the Wall and The Spectacular "Robin Williams: Live at the Met."

He became a regular guest on talks shows such as Late Night with David Letterman and the Tonight Show starring Johnny Carson. His comedy, marked by hilarious impersonations, provisions, dialogs, and behaviors made him the Comedian of Hollywood. Robin was so consistent with his craft that by the year 2004, he became listed as #13 in the list of top "100 Greatest standup comedians of ALL TIME."

Actor

Robin may have never personally been exposed to the slogan "Success creates more success," but his life surely resembled how true it is. Because with an upscaling comedy career, at this point it was effortless for Robin to gain favor in his acting career. Mr. Williams performed as the character in the show Popeye, leading role in Survivors, and The World According to Garp. In William's mind, these weren't the ideal jobs that he imagined in his vision for success, with respects to his acting career. They merely allowed Robin a channel to broadcast the acting skills that he demonstrates through his comedy and previous television appearances.

Those performances served as success pitstops until he caught his first major break. Favorably for Robin, his acting skills were just as magical as his standup comedy skills. In 1987, which was seven years after performing his role in Popeye, Williams was nominated for the Academy Award for Best Actor for playing the starring role in the hit film Good Morning Vietnam. The cameraman noted: We would just cut the camera on and Robin would just create.

This section shows some of the movies Robin was fortunate enough to feature in, the year the film was made and how much money he profited from every MOVIE:

Movie Features	Profited Salary
Jumanji (1996)	$15,000,000
Hook (1991)	$1,000,000
Aladdin (1992)	$100,000
Crazy Ones (2013)	$165,000 per episode
RV (2006)	$1,000,000
Robots (2005)	$100,000
Flubber (1997)	$10,000,000
Jack (1996)	$15,000,000
Man of the Year (2006)	$1,000,000
Bicentennial Man (1999)	$20,000,000
Patch Adams (1998)	$10,000,000
Mrs. Doubtfire (1993)	$1,000,000
Good Morning Vietnam (1987)	$500,000
Mork and Mindy (1978)	$35,000 per ½ hour episode

Robin Williams was happy and successful as spoken by the voice of the golden image. And even though numbers don't lie, the numbers weren't accurate indicators of Robin Williams' true thought condition. Hidden beneath the facets of his golden image and golden smile were suppressed truths that became visible through the reading of a news Headline titled "Hanged."

Strangely after enduring years of success in his acting career, Oscar winner and magnetic actor, Robin Williams ended his life by hanging himself with a belt in his home in Paradise Bay, California. His story is very unusual to tell because I never predicted his story would lead to his outcome. An outcome that cannot be expressed from the source because scattered ashes are all that remains of Mr. Williams on Mother Earth.

While on camera or on stage, Robin captivated large audiences with his unique style and contagious smile but behind the scenes or backstage, he battled with stress and depression. He started using drugs early in his career. The standup comedy was a competitive and brutal field. "Often the thoughts would get me worked up, drugs would mellow me back down, and performing would bring me back up. You become obsessed and you lose the focus that you need," as stated by Mr. Williams when describing the complex nature of being a standup comedian.

Why is it that we try to escape our thoughts instead of facing them? "EVERYONE DOES IT." Running away from yourself in this manner leaves the human mind in a state of dis-ease that occurs so much that we've collectively accepted it as "Normal." Maybe we are not aware that a "thought" knows no boundaries and the desire to escape thoughts impacts ALL branches of life some way. Desire is a magnified thought impulse and the amount of pressure put on one to be successful in their work environment and relationship compels the desire to escape our thoughts on a day by day basis.

All problems or pain stems from thoughts. Many do, but not all use drugs and/or alcohol to escape their thoughts. For those who are willing to admit the areas of life in which they are trying to escape, ready to face the favorable or unfavorable thought realities and looking for the keys to do so, this book was written for you.

The keys to doing so may come in this chapter or may appear in your mind in some following chapter. Potentially the key could present itself in the form of a calling, plan, or strategy. Subsequently, the key may provoke memories, traumatic events, haunting feelings, and produce some type of tutorial to reclaim ALL the power you've forfeited through discomfort. For you are a student and everything that happens to you is your instructor. The key is to listen to the voice of your own instructor and be taught by it.

The birth of his son Zak served as the primary motive to quit drugs and alcohol. Williams described the birth of his son as a huge wakeup call that motivated his sobriety. In the year 2003, after his son's birth, Robin started drinking again. In a later interview, Mr. Williams confessed that he never sustained sobriety, but he didn't use cocaine anymore.

"No. Cocaine – paranoid and impotent, what fun. There was no bit of me thinking, ooh, let's go back to that. Useless conversations until midnight, waking up at dawn feeling like a vampire on a day pass. No."

How do we end up living this way? Why do we do this to ourselves? Why do we know we are human beings but shun the significance of being human? How can we engage the joys of being a human being if we are too busy?

The busyness rush of success disallowed Robin from living an examined life and from dealing with his thought emotions. His friends would ask him, "How are you doing?" He would look up with a lowered voice and weepy expression and state: "I'm so busy, I have so much going on." Momentarily after, another friend asked him how he was. Once more, the same expression, same tone, and similar response, he would state: "I am ok, just busy. I got so much going on and so much to do." The tone expresses dis- ease, overwhelmed, and life fatigue.

The story of Robin Williams may not be expressed with day to day accuracy, but the outcome and core of it is correct. Gather from it, the fundamental qualities of thoughts that dwell within our minds: instigate us, in favorable and unfavorable ways, even the more when thoughts are converted into physical reality.

Those who are seeking the keys to freedom, you do not have to look very far. The key has always been with you and will always be with you.

A Success Pit Stop (Action Plan)

Here are some techniques you could use to reform your thoughts and transform your LIFE.

PRAYER: Power Recharger and Your Energy Recharger

Positive Affirmations - "Repetition is the God of learning and programming." Through repeated positive, personal, past, present and future tense quotes, phrases and statements that can override the unfavorable thought that has already been programmed. Repetition of these positive affirmations will allow renewed channels of thinking, behaviors, and attitudes because the body is designed to act in-formation with the mind. For example, the repetition of "I am designed as a winner" can transform a mind that's failure conscious. Also, be very conscious of the usage of negative expressions such as "I need to exercise." Instead say, "I desire to exercise."

See the Bigger Picture

Our Fallen Stars

"Happiness doesn't result from what we get, but from what we give"

When Presidential Candidate, Ben Carson wrote the far-seeing quote, "Happiness doesn't result from what we got, but from what we give", he should have informed us that the reason happiness results from what we get, but from what we give, is because the concept of giving relates to our thoughts.

Mr. Carson should've informed us that the medium in which Mother Earth spins, in which we travel and exist in, is a model of energy in motion at an unbelievably rapid rate of vibration, the medium is filled with a form of Universal power at which remodels itself to the nature of the thoughts we store in our minds and sways in natural and supernatural ways to convert our thoughts into their physical counterpart.

If the Presidential Candidate had told us of his universal truth, we would know why happiness doesn't result from what we get, but from what we give. He should've informed us that this universal power makes no attempts to differentiate between favorable or unfavorable thoughts. In fact, this universal power will impel us to express into the physical reality thoughts of Agony, Resentment, Intimidation, and Neediness just as fast as it will impel us to respond to thoughts of wealth, abundance, Unity, and fulfillment.

Also, Mr. Carson should've told us that our brain becomes magnetically fluxed with the direct thoughts we store in our minds. By means that most are unaware of, these "magnets" attract to us, the natural elements, the people, opportunities, and conveniences that are in harmony with the nature of our direct thoughts.

Mr. Carson should've made us aware that to experience happiness, we must magnetically flux our minds with an unadulterated desire to pursue what makes you happy, then we must pursue the desire until we develop a clear strategy to create that desired reality and most importantly, continually ERASE negative thoughts, and REPLACE them with thoughts that are in harmony with "being happy."

Despite Being a Superstar under the influence of the busyness rush, Robin Williams always made time and exemplified the art of giving. Regularly, he donated to different "causes" around the globe ranging from Women's Rights, Literacy, Charity for Children Promise, Red Cross, and St. Jude Children's Research Hospital. Despite how much money, time, knowledge, insight, or laughter he gave, his thoughts wouldn't give him a chance to live and see the many fruits of his own labor.

The subsequent series of events leading to his success proved that his success wasn't a mistake. Mr. Williams' thoughts were far more important than his success. It was his thoughts that gave birth to his success, but it was also his thoughts that drove him away from life itself.

Robin Williams is one of our many "Superstars" who despite failing forward was hindered by simply overlooking the thoughts that are stored in the mind. This section briefly articulates on the "thought" causes and unfavorable outcomes of some of our nationally known and forever remembered Falling Stars. These are some of the shining stars that you may have been an adoring fan of.

Iconic figure Marilyn Monroe, a powerful sex symbol, committed suicide by overdosing on barbiturates. Those close to her noted that she had a lot of fears and constant depression.

Kurt Cobain, the famous Frontman of American Rock band, committed suicide at gunshot in his home after suffering from years of drug addiction and depression. Alongside his body, a note was discovered that he had written to his imaginary childhood friend named "Boddah", expressing how he no longer felt excited about the THOUGHT of creating or listening to music anymore.

19-year-old child actor, Sawyer Sweeten, known as Geoffrey Barone on the hit show "EVERYBODY HATES RAYMOND", took his life by a gunshot wound to the head. The young star closest sources say he constantly wrestled with the THOUGHTS of his fading career, financial crisis and unfavorable rumors concerning his sexuality.

Jovan Belcher, Kansas City Chiefs Linebacker, shot Kasandra Perkins, his girlfriend, nine times in front of his mother before he went to practice. When he arrived at practice, he then shot and killed himself in front of his coach and general manager. Before he shot himself, he said they didn't give me enough help. He was experiencing a lot of suffering and depression due to the unseen realities of being a Professional Football player.

Chris Benoit, one of the greatest professional wrestlers in the world, committed suicide by hanging himself after murdering his son, Daniel and his wife, Nancy.

Ernest Hemingway, a great American novelist, journalist and story writer, shot himself in the head with a shotgun. His wife, Mary, mentioned in an interview after his death that he previously attempted suicide.

Hemingway had depression and alcoholism problems.

Simone Battle, the 25-year-old American singer, actress, member of the pop group GRL and the X-factor finalist, took her life in September 2014 by hanging herself in her dwelling in California. Close sources disclosed that she suffered from depression due to THOUGHTS of her financial issue. Her death shocked her friends, family, and fans across the nation.

Christine Chubbuck, an American television news reporter, shot herself in the head during a live television broadcast in July 1974. She suffered severe depression at the expense of her own thoughts. While covering the news, as usual, Chubbuck pointed out "in keeping up with Channels 40's policy of bringing you the latest in blood and guts and in living color, you are going to see another first attempted suicide. She shot herself and was pronounced dead 14 hours later at Sarasota Memorial Hospital.

29-year-old Lee Thompson, the young actor known for his role as a lead character in the Disney Channel series, the famous Jet Jackson and Chris Coroner in Friday Night lights, died from a self-inflicted gunshot wound in August 2013. After his death, it was expressed that Young had severe depression issues.

Virginia Wolfe, an English writer, drowned herself by walking into a lake with large stones in her pocket to hold her down in the year of 1941. In her suicide note, Mrs. Wolfe wrote "I began to hear voices, I feel like I'm going mad again. I feel like I can't go through another one of those terrible times. I can't concentrate so I am doing what I feel is best."

Michael "Mike Awesome" Awesome, Professional wrestler, hung himself in his home in Tampa Bay, Florida in February of the year 2007. By the time his friends discovered his body, he had been long dead. Close sources say that before his suicide, Michael was released from jail for physically assaulting his wife after she expressed her desire to get a divorce. Thoughts of his new criminal charges and loss of his family led him to his death

Don Cornelius, the creator of the dance and show "The Soul Train", television show host and producer, committed suicide by a self-inflicted gunshot to the head in February of the year 2012. Don's son mentioned that before his death, his dad had to undergo an operation to fix deformities in the cerebral arteries of his brain. The effects of this operation left his dad in a lot of pain. Before his dad's death, he would always mention that he didn't know how much longer he could take the pain. He knew the thoughts of the pain were reaching unbearable stages, but never did he assume that his father would commit suicide.

Freddy E, Seattle rapper, died from a self-inflicted gunshot to the head in January of 2013. Before taking his life, Freddy's last post on his Twitter page were these lyrics "If there's a God then he is calling me back home. This barrel never felt so good next to my dome. It's cold and I would rather die than live alone." The thoughts of losing his long-term relationship with Honey Cocaine, his ex-girlfriend, left the rapper depressed, stressed and heartbroken.

"To every beginning, there is an ending and to every ending, there is a beginning."

Just as the power of thought commands your success, so it does with your fate. All the phenomenal legendary superstars begin their careers with a single thought. "I believe I can be a successful rapper; I dream of being an NFL Football player, I believe I am beautiful, I want to be the best guitar player in the world, etc." On the contrary, all their legacies ended with thoughts. "I'm fed up, I feel like I'm lonely, I can't live this way anymore, take these thoughts away from me God, etc." To every reader, there is a shining superstar that dwells within you.

Although their stories may not be expressed with day to day accuracy, the outcome and core of it is correct. Gather from it, those who are seeking the key to freedom, you do not have to look very far. The key has always been with you and will always be with you. It can be found through conscious awareness of the influence thoughts, whether they are unwritten, written, spoken or unspoken, have on one's vibration, actions and point of attraction.

The time has come to examine one of the MOST IMPORTANT fundamentals. It is imperative that you BE FROZE and uphold an open mind and spirit as you explore this key section in this book of awareness. Keep in mind, that the fundamentals compressed within this book were gathered from people of ALL colors, cultures, and creeds varying in financial status, gender, race, religion, and educational background. Because these fundamental truths are universal, they can now be utilized to serve the greater good of you. You will find a renewed joy and excitement in this process which will make it fun to engage.

Before you continue your journey of discovery to the upcoming chapter, I would like to inform you that it pertains to credible information that can TRANSFORM your entire life so as it does for anyone whose "willing to give themselves enough of a chance" that they are courageous enough to apply it.

The discovery of this Key fundamental came about through stupendous experiences and observations that I could not token my life without. In fact, life would just be a four-letter word without this key fundamental. This fundamental is the key to all the doors.

Chapter 2

Eager Desire for TRUTH and FREEDOM

(Universal Keys to ALL FREEDOM)

"The Truth Shall Set You Free"

When Robin Williams entered college, by his classmates, he may have been marked as "strange, weird or crazy by his appearance and energy, but his thoughts were those of a mighty pharaoh. As his career catapulted, his thoughts remained active. As he excelled in his standup comedy career, he never lost sight of the image of himself being a big-time "film actor." He envisioned himself on the television fulfilling what became one of the most favorable consuming passions of his life, which was a desire to become a successful film actor.

Robin's desire was not an aspiration. It was not a momentary feeling of ambition. It was more so a personal decree or expectation that he had out to himself, which surpassed everything in the world. It was unmistakable, specific, and precise.

The desire was not discovered when Robin began to experience success in standup comedy. Robin's desire governed him for a very long time. At the birth of the desire, it probably was or may have been wishful thinking, but when you combine desire with wishful thoughts, they transmute wishful thoughts into the physical reality.

The dream that influenced his life became a physical reality. Those who are unaware of the commencing power of thought transmutation may feel resentment or jealousy towards him because of the idea that his outcome was based on "good luck" or because he was given a better opportunity than the next member of the human family.

Robin became successful because he chose a "thought" at which he converted into an unchangeable goal, placed ALL his energy, impulses, and power into manifesting that goal. Robin did not accomplish the goal when he got his first "acting offer" but he was satisfied and cheerful to begin in the lower levels of work, for as long as it offered a favorable window to take another step towards his devoted goal.

Years may pass before the opportunity you desire to obtain reveals itself. During these years, not a single thread of design, not one practical plan towards achieving the desire may be visible to you. To everyone, except you, you may appear as "strange" only because you are the only one that sees your desire. You are the only one who has your vision (BE FROZE).

It is phenomenal to know that you are the one chosen to give birth to the magnitudes of greatness compressed within your desire. No one else has your desire. One must give birth to their desire by feeding it with projections, time, strategies, actions, money, emotions, and even tears so that it will be born through you.

One of the primary perfect imperfections of humanity is to "quit" or "give up" on their vision because their family doesn't support it, did not have a clear plan or got fed up with being cast out as "strange." Stand by your desire, because the only reason they can't see it or understand it is that God only made it for you, to manifest through you (BE FROZE).

Robin's story is a profound revelation of the capability to pursue a desire. He even created a strategy by which would be the roadmap towards his destiny. He supported his desire until it established mastery over his life, going from a thought to a possible, then to actuality.

When Robin engaged his acting career, he did not utter to himself, "I might get the opportunity to act in some film or it's impossible because I already have a bust standup comedy career", he said, "I desire to become a successful actor and so he did."

Robin did not say, "I will try and if I do not get support then I will quit and look for joy elsewhere." He did say "I am willing to accept my success pit stops as long as they lead to my destiny." He was willing to do anything it took if his efforts or circumstances ushered him towards the manifestation of his desires. He did not turn his attention to another career path. He had a "Plan A" and didn't make a "Plan B", because the time and thought energy put exerted into making Plan B could be utilized towards actualizing "Plan A."

He was ready and prepared to forge his entire life on his capability of getting what he desired.

There is a huge difference between being ready to receive a thing and being prepared for something. No one is prepared for a thing until they've acquired the formidable thoughts to obtain it. Preparedness is merely a state of willingness to construct and ready is a state of mind marked by being immediately prepared for action. In other words, he prepared himself to be ready and then when the opportunity presented itself, he was prepared and willing to take the necessary actions to obtain his desired outcome.

He left no room within himself for the doubt that followed Plan B or option two. He left himself only two options, overcome or be overcame. That's the moral of the story of Robin Williams's phenomenal earth contribution.

Desire is a supernatural, meaning exceeds the natural, enhancer. The impulse of mere desire offers power and strength that allows the users' capabilities to become stronger, indestructible, and faster than others and oneself without the presence of desire. Desire unlocks the SUPERNATURAL capabilities related to the manifestations of one's purpose, goals, and destiny.

The FLU Game

It was a moment that marked the legacy of one of the most phenomenal pioneers of the century. A well-timed, legendary basketball player solidified his legacy in a victory that secured his success on the basketball court. The stage was set for Michael Jordan and the Chicago Bulls to take on the Utah Jazz in the 1997 NBA Finals.

Around 2 am on Tuesday, the day before the game, Michael phoned his trainer to come to his hotel where Bulls Leader laid on the floor weakened and outrageously sweating. Michael barely had the strength to walk and was experiencing a lack of energy, exhaustion, dehydration, and more FLU-like symptoms, which led Jordan's trainer to make the inconceivable decision that Michael can't play in the championship game the next day.

The morning after the unfavorable news, which was GAME DAY, Michael wasn't fully recovered from the flu but was thinking to himself to will his way through the victory. He felt weakened and vulnerable by his condition, but his supernatural desire could overcome any challenge that was presented if he was led by his burning desire to win. The series for the Chicago Bulls and the Utah Jazz series was tied 2-2 leading into Utah for a pivotal fifth game. Michael Jordan reached a final decision that flustered the media when the news emerged. The news was the final decision made by Jordan to attempt to play in the game anyway, despite being extremely sick and affected by illness.

It was a moment in sports history that will never be forgotten. It provided fans with one of the Greatest Playoff Performances in the NBA history. Michael Jordan and the Chicago Bulls defeated the Utah Jazz and later went on to become the 1997 NBA Champions. Michael will powered himself to 38 points, 7 rebounds, 5 assists and 3 steals for a final score of Bulls 90, Utah Jazz 88. Not to mention Michael Jordan played 44 minutes of the game despite being visibly sick.

"Most people that have the Flu or even Flu-like symptoms suffer from diarrhea, vomiting, body aches, fatigue and dehydration noted Michael's doctor. By adding the intensity of playing an NBA Championship Basketball game and the additional fluid loss from sweating, his performance was impressive. I wonder why he didn't pass out".

After the game, television analyst, Ahmad Rashad, interviewed Michael Jordan after his phenomenal performance.

Michael Jordan: "It was ALL about the will. It's all about desire. You just must come out here and do what you got to do. We wanted it really bad and me as a leader, I had to come out and do my best and hopefully, the team could rally around me and make contributions."

Ahmad Rashad: "Never any a doubt down the stretch, I mean how weak were you?"

Michael Jordan: "I was really tired and very weak. At the half time, I told Phil to use me in spurts, but somehow, I found the energy to stay strong. I wanted it really bad."

"It was probably one of the most difficult things I've ever done," Jordan said. "I played myself into passing out just for a basketball game." Michael's coach Phil Jackson said, "This was a heroic effort, another to add to the collection of efforts that make up his legacy."

Conversation of the Inner Voices

Every person who stands up for the emanating power, willpower, within them called desire, accomplished extraordinary endeavors. When the going appeared hard, the voice of his trainer echoed in his mind saying "Michael you have flu-like symptoms or maybe food poisoning, you CAN'T play in the game", the voice of his family " be smart and give yourself time to recover ", the voice of doubt spoke and said, "there is no way I can perform under these conditions." During all these voices, there was a very small voice of desire that echoed "I want to win, we can do it."

The easier thing for Michael to have done would've been to listen to all the other voices. Jordan forged himself into the leadership of that small voice called desire, which did not recognize failure. Michael decided to say HELLO to his desire. And said GOODBYE to any voice that didn't favor his desired outcome, which was to WIN. By saying YES to the voice of desire, Michael gave himself permission to be successful.

If you are ready to say yes to your desire, this book was written for you. One of the primary keys to converting our desires into physical reality is to free yourself from the forces of the unseen voices that dwell in the mind.

It is very important to recognize the voices of the mind. It is especially important to follow the voice that favors your desired outcome.

You may have been programmed to believe it's not possible "to be misguided by the voice echoes spoken by the mouth of he or she whose limitation conscious." It is easy to convince yourself to believe that this dynamic of the human mind, with respects to its standard operation, does not apply to you. To a human soul who is not aware of the SUPERNATURAL working fundamentals of the human mind, this idea may be assumed as farfetched.

Consider it favorable, to all who are unaware of the power of the human mind, to know that "thoughts are always bouncing back and forth, hitting the walls of the mouth like Playing Tennis. In the mind, thoughts travel in the form of voices and will continue to go back and forth until the choice is made to throw down the tennis racquet and walk away from the tennis court. Hence, stop the thoughts (voices) and get out of your mind.

Every human was born with a profound life purpose and destiny that will only be interpreted and understood when one is pursuing their desires. Hoping, day-dreaming, and wishful thinking ALONE will not transmute your desires into physical reality. By adding conscious time, energy, effort, thoughts, strategy, and fuel to "a single desire", backing it with action, and exerting a strong magnitude of perseverance that sees ACHIEVING FREEDOM as the only option, our life circumstances will be transformed.

The practical strategy to free yourself from the voices that intentionally foreshadows the voice of desire when it speaks is articulated in this SUCCESS PITSTOP.

Universal Keys

1. Recognize the Voice - Whether the thought is positive or negative, you must recognize them. Without recognizing them, you are consequently accepting them and allowing them to continue to manifest in your mind. Recognize the emotion behind the voice. For example, Johnny tells Whitney that he doesn't think she should try out for the basketball team because she may not make the cut. Johnny is speaking from the emotion of DOUBT.
2. Ask Yourself Questions - Ask yourself formidable questions and ANSWER them to the best of your ability. Am I going to keep being controlled by my own thoughts? How do I stop it? Am I going to follow the voice of my desire? Does this information allow me to operate in-formation? How is the voice evident in my behaviors?
3. Initiate Forgiveness - "The mind believes whatever it is programmed to believe." The voices that echo unfavorable thoughts become unconsciously programmed and can only be gotten rid of when one forgives themselves for allowing themselves to be influenced by the programming of the voice. (FORGIVENESS EXERCISE)
4. Nurture the "Desired Voice" - Feed the favorable voice "thought" with ACTIONS, INTENTIONS, FINANCES, AFFIRMATIONS, PRAYERS, ATTENTION, STRATEGY, and PLANS. Feed the favorable voice "thought" until it becomes an all-out obsession, so much that through you, the desired "voice thought" becomes visible.
5. Be One - "Whatever a man thinketh, so does he become." Become harmonized with the favorable voice. Become ONE with FAITH. Become ONE with your greatest desire. Be the desire instead of having the desire.
6. Walk-in Freedom - Reap the fulfillment of being energetically, spiritually, mentally, and physically detached from the negative seen or unseen energy chords of the unseen voices.

His mind interpreted the voices based on his state of conscious awareness. Michael Jordan was an obsessive winner. In other words, he was win conscious. Was it true, that he was sick, Yes? Was it true that he needed to recover, Yes? Was it true that Michael could win? Yes.

Favorably, Michael Jordan said yes to the voice of desire. And by overcoming the challenge, he freed himself from the energy of fear and doubt that came with the other inner voices.

The human mind tends to make situations more difficult than they are. Hence, the importance of being able to recognize the nature of the voices because the unfavorable "voice thoughts" will convince you that freedom from the voices is IMPOSSIBLE. The goal is to be so harmonized with the voices of desire that you persuade yourself that it will be obtained.

Those who become 'desire conscious' become freed from the unfavorable recognitions of the UNSPOKEN voices. Desire conscious implies that the mind is charged and thoroughly soaked with the desire that you can foresee yourself achieving your desired outcome.

The sensibility of the information displayed in the Universal Keys reflects the practical thought patterns of dreamers, Entrepreneurs, Investors, Way-Pavers, CEO's, Leaders who can, were willing, and is willing to put their highest aspiration into action. By using these fundamental keys, many went from rags to riches merely overnight.

It may be helpful to know that the Universal Keys suggested here were well-examined. They are consented to not only being the keys to freedom, but also for the achievement of any goal. The keys do not require "hard work." They do not ask for credentials or a resume. They do not demand an advanced level of education. But favorably the application of these Universal Keys does request "yielded" desire and an active imagination that allows one to witness that freedom is not obtained by mere coincidence, possibility or luck. One must be aware that those who have been freed from the voices of failure did an undeniable amount of wishful thinking, dreaming, desiring, strategizing, and exercising FAITH before they gained their FREEDOM.

Also, consider it favorable to make you aware that every leader, regardless of their color, culture, or creed was an idealist, dreamer, and partial rebel with an active imagination. If you do not envision freedom in your conscious imagination, you will never experience it. With the continual re-occurring shifts in society, life isn't going to present a better time than NOW for the dreamers to show themselves and let their lights shine. Every member of the human family seeking freedom should be made aware that this energetic world is constantly requesting NEW inventions, NEW laws, NEW healing techniques, NEW Medicines, NEW cures for diseases, NEW Computer Programs, NEW books, and NEW modus operandi, to all areas of life. To usher any form of newness or improve the quality of "the already existing" one must have a conscious desire to be free, that is backed up with undeniable motivation, awareness of what one would like to obtain, and have a contagious desire to obtain it. The simple application of action to a favorable thought is and always will be the most standardized approach towards being set free from unfavorable "voice thoughts." Whoever desires freedom should always keep in mind that the Captains of the world were always those who utilized, through practical application, the abstract power of the invisible energies of possibility and good fortune. They would transform the invisible energies of possibility (voice thoughts) into Multi-Millionaire Dollar Corporations, Mansions, Cars, Businesses, and other forms of agriculture, which adds to the human quality of life.

Patience, awareness, and understanding are mandatory for the leaders of today to possess. Whoever is closed-minded or has a fear of the NEW, are ill-fated from the beginning. Everyone is gifted with ideas and the gifts are in the present. Therefore, there is no better time than NOW to share your gift with the world. The world is becoming more and more expanded which requires NEW trends and constant refashioning of the trends that are already in place.

During periods of mapping out your strategy to obtain your freedom, disallow unfavorable influences to deter you from the voice of the dreamer that rest in your mind. In order to do extraordinary things in this dynamic world, one must seize the energy of the great fathers and mothers of history, whose thoughts and ideas have created channels that allow society to continually grow and develop in remarkable ways. The single ability to channel thought energy presents a lifeline in our individual world, our collective world, your success, my success, and our freedom.

Keep in mind that many of our great leaders in modern-day society have stories of being "overcame by difficulty" but became an "overcomer" when discovering the truths about themselves. In doing so, freed themselves from the voices of doubt injected into their minds by other people or human conditions. Making the choice to free themselves from the voices of doubt and consciously pursuing the voice of desire is "the key."

Remember Oprah Winfrey, the great American proprietor, talk show host, actress, a philanthropist, who plotted herself into the televised world and was fired from her first job because she was told that "she was unfit for TV." She also got terminated from her position as the co-anchor of the 6 O'clock weekday news on Baltimore WJZ-TV after the show's ratings were steadily decreasing. Mrs. Winfrey described these moments as "the first and worst failures of her career."

Years later, Oprah got relegated to the morning TV and found her VOICE. Soon after, it created what appeared as a domino effect of success. She started "The Oprah Winfrey Show", owned her own channel called OWN Network, a part in the 1985 film, the Color Purple, to now having an estimated net worth of roughly 2.9 Billion. Oprah could no longer be cast off as "unfit for TV" in fact, she is known, honored and praised for her earthly contributions, thus confirming that freedom conscious allows no unfavorable thoughts and limitation conscious permits excuses.

Albert Einstein, cast off as dyslexic, schizophrenic, and autistic by an advance number of experts, was self-assured about the genius he possessed even when circumstances didn't favor him. His parents died at his birth and growing up without them affected Albert's functionality, in terms of what's classified as being "normal." In his early years of education, Albert was always picked on by his peers and his teachers.

When he began elementary school, his teachers told him that he would never amount to anything, that he was wasting everyone's time, and he should leave the school immediately. Albert won the big stakes because, despite the many voices of difficulty, his circumstances planted into his mind, Albert was able to discover the voice of the genius, and broke through the bondages and invisible barriers created by the echoes of his conditions and his elementary teachers. Einstein later became nationally recognized as the genius who transformed the face of modern physics.

JK Rowling. Her life may appear as phenomenal based on her ongoing success in selling the Epic novel, Harry Potter. Let's not forget that before selling the novel, she was suffering from depression, putting forth her best effort to raise a child on her own, going to school, and writing her novel at the same time. She was challenged and impacted by the voice of "worry" and "uncertainty" which made JK feel as if she would physically breakdown and hit "rock bottom." Her conditions became so unbearable, Rowling relied on governmental welfare to survive. Within a timespan of spending five years of listening to the voice of desire, JK Rowling was able to "breakthrough "the invisible restraints that her "circumstances" had on her and became one of the richest women in the world.

If the goal you desire to accomplish serves your greater-good, as well as the collective humanity, then give yourself permission to do it. Put all your energy, efforts, and focus into it and don't be dismayed by the echoes of that unpleasant voice of failure. In fact, give yourself permission to respect the voice of failure. Failure is likely unaware that when you give yourself permission to respect failure, with that comes the opportunity to get something out of failure that will allow you to succeed.

The BEAUTY of Failures and Breakdown

Life is full of failures and defeats that are designed to cause breakdowns, only to give birth to a breakthrough moment, which offers the opportunity to surplus our experiences. The voices of failure speak from different directions, in different tones, and the volume of the voice of failure typically gets louder at a different time than assumed.

Having achieved its goal, the voice of failure leaves us in an unfavorable mental state called a "breakdown." The simplest things to do in these moments are to accept failure and ACCEPT defeat due to what feels like a physical, mental, or emotional lack of vitality.

Before freedom comes to most people, they are faced with breakdowns. Those who go on to live and be freed from the echoing voices of breakdowns are those who persevere beyond the point of brokenness and allow themselves to see the TRUTH about breakdowns.

One of the unseen truths about BREAKDOWNS is that they offer us the opportunity to experience breakthroughs (BE FROZE). The breakthrough marks the turning point in our lives for those who choose to be introduced to that higher version of themselves that can only be born through crisis.

Maybe at your time of crisis, you were unaware that your breakthrough was hidden within the crevices of the discomfort revealed in your breakdown. The key is to discover the voice that magically breaks through the thought barriers created by the voices of failures and defeat. Most humans ACCEPT failure and ACCEPT defeat. Perhaps that is the reason it has become such a challenge to discover the symbolic golden breakthrough that rests in the depths of your human body.

When Walt Disney first created Mickey Mouse, the image popped out of his head and onto a sketching pad. Walt noted that "business fortunes of him and his brother Ray were at their lowest before creating the idea for one of the most successful and nationally idolized corporations in the United States of America. The Walt Disney Corporation is one of the most dynamic enterprises, possessing theme parks, an extraordinary film studio, and various television networks.

Steve Jobs became one of the richest men in the world after creating the iPod, iPhone, and iPad, faced misfortune because he was a college dropout, didn't have business success, and was fired from his tech executive job. Later Steve explained, "the heaviness of being successful was replaced by the lightness of being a beginner again. It freed me to enter one of the most creative periods of my life".

Elvis Presley began as a no-name performer. After being fired from his first performance, Mr. Presley discovered the voice that lived in his mind. Elvis went on to become the second bestselling artist of all time.

The voice of disaster smothered Bill Gates during his early years as an Entrepreneur. However, Gates' disaster didn't hold him back from his desire to discover new opportunities. Bill Gates, years later after forging a new path to success, created the Microsoft product and forged a new path of freedom.

I am sure you have heard of Hershey's Chocolate, but when Milton Hershey began his candy construction career, he didn't initially experience success. Milton was fired from his job as a printer and as a result, created three different candy related enterprises and witnessed them all FAIL. In his final attempt, Hershey structured the Hershey's company and found enormous success. By continually following the voice of his dreams, despite his countless failures, Milton Hershey became one of the wealthiest men of his time with a net worth of $683,423,000.

Hershey's passion, creativity, DETERMINATION, and willingness to follow the voice within him that favored his higher capabilities, allowed him to be freed from doubt and disbelief.

Practically, the fear of getting hurt or experiencing disappointment over "love-based relationships" has an effect that disallows freedom. "You cannot allow your ex-relationship to stop your next relationship." The voice of fear and disappointment disables the ability to convert the most powerful emotions into dreams of a favorable nature.

An appreciable humanitarian quoted this universal truth that is revealed through these lines:

Don't ruin today's good Mood
By remembering yesterday's
Bad one
Feeling such Heart Break
In the moment
Speak to the Heart Break
And tell her
That she only exists for the greater Good of God's plan.
Which is for all Colors of the rainbow to live in
freedom,
with dignity and unconditional love.

Lisa Nichols, the founder and Chief Executive Officer of Motivating the Masses Inc. credited her success to the discovery of "the champion" that slept within her. Lisa's determination and dedication gave her permission to set her champion free as she quoted. Lisa Nichols is NOW one of the world's most highly sought and requested Motivational Speakers, whose CEO's a global organization that has reached and served nearly 30 Million people nationwide.

Her breakthrough began at the age of 27 when she discovered herself being held captive to the disallowing voice of her difficulties: Single mother on government assistance with less than $12 in her bank account, raising a child whose father was in prison, grew up in a rough area of South Los Angeles, that marked the split between territory of two warring gangs.

Lisa proclaimed: "I felt rock bottom and I realized I have to do something." Nichols reported. "I have to be on my own rescue. No one is going to rescue me."

Lisa didn't make excuses for her circumstances, instead, she found a mirror, looked herself in the eye and spoke to herself saying: "I am designed for greatness, my light is meant to shine and my job is to let it shine. I've prayed the prayer, I've done the work, I've said YES. Now I am going to set my champion free."

Lisa gave herself permission to walk it as she talked it. In doing so, she applied one of the most phenomenal keys to freedom which is to believe you are worthy and deserving of healthy, whole, and Complete Freedom.

Evidence of the Efforts of these Way-Makers of Civilization

Martin Luther King is another phenomenal example of someone whose desires over stood the echoes of the inner voices and eventually became the most profound dreamers that barely missed the chance to witness his dream become a reality.

Born as Michael Luther King, but later had his name changed to Martin, as a child with more than a typical dream. Martin had a dream that required a catapulted amount of RESPECT, Altruisms, Integrity, Neutrality, Bliss, Obedience, and Wholesomeness to follow. Dr. King saw his dream as the precious gold at the end of the rainbow.

Martin was not the typical dreamer. He started as a man who BELIEVED that his dreams and goals would be achieved. Eventually, it transformed from "I BELIEVE it can happen" to "I KNOW it's going to happen." Although he didn't live to see his dream come true, if you are reading this book in the United States of America, then your present reality was created and envisioned in Martin's dream.

Knowing is marked by firsthand awareness through experience. Anything KNOWN to mankind is absolute, definite, and unchangeable. Believing is a state of mind identifiable by its constant interchangeability. Constantly we choose whether or whether not to accept or deny what we hear, sense, or read. In a state of mind marked by mere BELIEFS, the choice faculty considers the voice echoes of second party beliefs and ideas.

By believing, you are committing to an idea without FULL awareness. Millions of people fall one step short of freedom because of their beliefs or beliefs they've been programmed to follow. Perhaps one person in every hundred thousand knows that the key to freedom is to achieve a state of knowingness that will silence the voice of uncertainty and indefiniteness that beliefs indelibly carry.

Without transcending our beliefs, we will never be "free." Beliefs separate us from the TRUTH of who we are CREATED to be. Martin transcended his beliefs and entered a state of knowingness, that didn't allow, fear, doubt, and limitation and as a result "the DREAM CAME TRUE."

He had a dream and followed it with the spirit of knowingness. Although the odds didn't appear in his favor considering that he was being judged by the color of his skin, Martin stayed available to the voice of desire within himself that uttered the four words "I HAVE A DREAM."

Dr. King didn't say to himself "I will follow this until my family supports me or I don't have any support, so what's the point of trying." But what he did say to himself "I will accomplish this dream, even if it takes the remainder of my life." If you are living in the United States of America, you are the living representation of the story Martin Luther King didn't live to tell.

Martin Luther King was an African American minister and activist in the 1950s, during the Civil Rights Movement, which was a terrible time for African Americans in the United States of America. Martin was commonly recognized for his involvement in the furtherance of the nonviolent approach towards ending racism and segregation.

The racial harassment and behaviors committed by whites to assure separation were nothing short of unnecessary. Day in and day out, African Americans were victims of hate crimes committed by whites who intended to refuse their human rights. Here are some of the rights that were taken away from them: They couldn't walk on the same sidewalks as them, they couldn't attend the same churches, were not allowed to drink from the same water fountains, they couldn't eat at the same restaurants, couldn't ride the same buses, or couldn't order food from the same type of menu.

The crisis Martin faced was quite enough to have deterred a lot of people from their own desires. Martin was so determined to find a way to manifest his desire for the well-being of our character and unity amongst the human family. The pursuit of his dream did not come with the answers to the who, what, when, where, and why questions. It did not come with a step by step manual. It came with a man who with a desire so unobtainable, that he was willing to sacrifice and risk his life to get it.

Below we list the voice echoes that Martin Luther King was facing during times of detrimental triumph. Plus, some categories that each voice was expressed from, which ultimately indicates what outcome will be created if Martin follows the impulse of the thought.

Resentment Agony Intimidation Neediness Boastfulness Omission Worthlessness Desire

_R_ They already don't respect our churches. They only respect white power.

_A_ I give up, no matter how hard I try it is never enough to get people together.

_I_ I am worried that someone will try to kill me because I'm black. I may fail; therefore, I will let it go, it won't work.

_N_ I need support. I need to be appreciated for my efforts because I am the one making the sacrifices.

_B_ I dare these whites to disrespect me. They don't know who I am or where I am from. They can't disrespect me and get away with it.

_O_ What's the point of trying? I've tried over and over. I can't force them together.

_W_ No one will respect me as an African American. I am just a regular person.

_D_ I HAVE A DREAM

Dr. King possessed a single desire, so strong that opposition, crisis, doubt, and unfavorable beliefs would forfeit to it. For most of us that weren't physically alive during his time, his story may appear as a pretty painting, fairytale, or folklore of the imagination. We would never know freedom, as a human family, without the heroic efforts of Martin Luther King and his willingness to pursue his desire.

Although the story is paraphrased, the content of the story is exact. So, for all of you who feel "torn and worn" down and are struggling in the pursuit of their desires, remember the words of Martin Luther King "I HAVE A DREAM."

I HAVE A DREAM, I HAVE A DREAM, I HAVE A DREAM

No one is guaranteed to see the ending results of their work and efforts to pursue their desires. Martin died as one of the most significant Americans of the 20th century and later became only the third American whose birthday is commemorated as a federal holiday.

In 1963, Martin spoke the precious words "There are those who write history....there are those who will make history...I don't know how many historians we have in Birmingham tonight...but you are certainly making history...and you will make it possible for the historians of the future to write a marvelous chapter..."

There is so much one can learn from this man. Martin devoted his life to serving the greater good of his community. He was willing to fill the leadership role despite the unspoken voices of fear that his circumstances spoke into his life. Like any great achiever that lives in freedom, he didn't allow himself to be overly discouraged by the cataclysm of the unseen voices. His goal was not to be the highest-paid minister in the world. In fact, Martin Luther King died with a net worth of only 250,000 dollars. Remember it requires knowingness of self-value to rise above the mental archetype that sees money is worth more than freedom. Because of his efforts, along with other great historians, a NEW chapter has been written in American Awareness marked by the presence of freedom.

Before you move to the next chapter, ignite a renewed flame of Awareness, Faith, Unconditional love, and Bulldog courage, in your mind. If you've already established these mental states and are willing to actively apply the fundamentals illustrated, all your greatest desires will come to you when you are prepared for them. Benjamin Franklin stated by "failing to prepare then you are preparing to fail".

There is a huge difference between being ready to receive a thing and being prepared for something. No one is prepared for a thing until they've acquired the thought pattern to obtain it. Prepared expresses willingness. Being ready is a state of action. Prepare yourself mentally to be ready for the golden abundance, wealth, and prosperity that come with FREEDOM.

Imagine yourself free: Create an image of yourself living a life in freedom. Envision the person you desire to become. Put aside conscious and intentional time each day to be alone and free from distraction.

Give thought to previous breakthroughs. Every breakthrough, be it micro or macro, is evidence that you can achieve more freedom. Celebrate each breakthrough. Remember it when you begin to be unable to find faith in yourself.

Position Specific Strategy - Create a clear strategy that allows your desire to be alive and fully expressed. Be consciously aware of when you deter from your strategy and take the necessary steps to reposition yourself on the favorable path.

Stay Open to Positive Energy

Cultivate a positive self-image and attitude. The manner at which you project yourself, including your actions, responses, and decisions are completely within your control.

As a formidable peak of this section, allow me to introduce you to one of the most influential people I've ever met. I've known him since the day he was born. He came into the ordinary world with an extraordinary desire to play professional basketball, but he suffered from many conditions that the Doctor said would not allow him to make his dream a reality.

He challenged the doctor's opinion. He had the right to do so. This gentleman was and always will be my "BEST FRIEND". Before he passed away, Kason Cheeks vowed to himself, a commitment that he spent his life on Earth rendering. The commitment was not openly expressed, but the echoes of the unspoken voices of this commitment dwelled, restlessly, in his heart and mind. Kason vowed to himself that his dream would come true. Doctors could prescribe him with as many medications or inject his mind with as many false truths as they chose. In his mind, he knew his desire would become his reality. Assured that there must be a way and if he looked within himself, he would find it.

As quoted by the Rainbow Warrior "Every shoe has a sole, but you are the soul of every shoe, just take a step, walk in faith." He chose to surrender to the voice of faith that was smothered beneath the doctor's opinions. We all must learn to surrender to the voice of faith within us. The guidance may lead to avenues of discomfort, but by facing discomfort, we shall experience the FREEDOM.

Kason Cheeks desired at an unmatchable level to become a professional basketball player. As I observed him, I never thought it would become a reality. After spending countless years witnessing him, I knew he was compassionate, but I was certain that he would fall short to the voice of limitation.

I spent hours with him in the gym practicing to achieve the unseen. Even though he had not achieved the goal, he practiced as if he was already on a team. Surely, you have been taught that you must see it to believe it. Kason believed "you have to be it to believe it." He couldn't always answer the who, what, when, where, why questions about the way the dream would be converted into physical reality. Somehow, he knew that eventually, he will find a way if he surrendered to the voice in his mind that stood up for his ignited desire.

From dawn until dust, Kason would spend conscious time nurturing his desire with hopes that as a mere side effect of his commitment, he stumbles upon his goal. These types of thoughts occurred in his mind and he didn't express them to anyone except me.

As an observer of this relentless pursuit, I noticed something very unusual about him. When he arrived at a point of knowingness, no attempt to deter him from his plan would be workable. Although you couldn't always decipher this truth about him based on his words, you could always hear it in the voice of his actions. That observation served as true even at the moments that doubt seemed more convincing.

Kason was offered an opportunity, to play professional basketball in United Arad Emirate. When he became aware of the news, he immediately reported to the post office to pick up his passport, which is appropriate to have to play professional basketball in another country. On his way to pick up his passport, SOMETHING HAPPENED.

The occurrence was entirely unexpected. Kason got into a car accident that left the vehicle totaled and left him with various soft tissue injuries in his muscles, tendons, and ligaments. The car flipped in the air and was high enough in the air that it went through the surface of the ground when it landed. The accident was very critical but despite critical conditions, after being wheeled away in the ambulance, "I desire to play professional basketball" is all Kason could think about. He would always repeat the phrase "Let not your heart be troubled if you believe in God, believe also in me". The relevance of those words didn't become clear until years ahead.

He soon spoke to the doctor after being in the hospital for what seemed to be long hours, to receive the doctor's instructions and description of the accident. Shortly after walking into Kason's room, the doctor proclaimed: "You will need to be on bed rest for 3-4 months. You may not feel much pain right now because of your endorphins and adrenaline, but after rest, you will wake up sore. You will need to walk on crutches until the damage repairs. Also, we have decided to put you on blood thinners for the remainder of your life".

Having spent more than ten minutes listening to the doctors, Kason paused the doctor and asked, "When will I be able to play basketball again?" Immediately the doctor responded, "I'm quite sure you are not going to want to hear this, but I must be HONEST. You can't continue to play Basketball. You are having blood clots and playing physical sports while on blood thinners will put you at a high risk of getting an injury that can easily lead to death."

Certainly, these discoveries made by the doctor are naturally deemed as true and definite. That was the doctor's opinion, it was not the patient's opinion. The words from the doctor were not motivational, but by following his DESIRE supported with determination and dedication, it led to a favorable celebration. The doctor believed if that if he played in any sport that requires physical contact, then it would lead to death at a young age for Kason. On the contrary, Kason believed that when you find something that you are willing to die for, that's when you will be freed from anything disabling you from living at your fullest potential.

By the time Kason was checked out of the hospital, although physically weakened, his outlook was changed. The collision from the car left him physically weakened, emotionally drained, but spiritually brightened. He spent all his time and energy preparing to become a professional basketball player and as soon as he reached the finish line towards his goal, TRAGEDY STRUCK.

Overwhelmed by tragedy, Kason initially found it difficult to immediately transfer in his mind, the voices of his desire. Soon, I witnessed him discover the treasure buried deep within the pits of the heart that rest behind the walls of his chest.

"Life is a school; your experiences are your teachers and compressed in each experience is a lesson. The key is to sit at the feet of your own life and be taught by it." The significance of this self-discovery didn't become clear until years later. The significance was that lessons learned through self-discovery give you the keys that will open the unseen doors.

When he listened to the voice for the first time, it was not difficult to interpret the words he heard. Now standing in front of adversity, with a wounded body and mind clouded by the unfavorable voices echoing "YOU CAN'T PLAY BASKETBALL", "YOU ARE SUPPOSED TO BE ON BED REST FOR 4 MONTHS", "GIVE UP", "YOU WILL DIE IF YOU GET HIT BECAUSE YOU ARE ON BLOOD THINNERS AND BASKETBALL IS A PHYSICAL SPORT," Kason was forced to make a choice. The only options were to GO THROUGH it or GROW THROUGH IT.

Having determination, he would only attune to hearing the voice of his desire, GROW THROUGH IT was the choice he surrendered to. In every experience, whether they vary in degree or color, there is a gift-wrapped inside of it called "adversity". The gift is designed to plant into the mind that you are "MUCH MIGHTIER" than any affliction that life can offer. But your MIGHTINESS can only be discovered through adversity and once discovered, adversity becomes one's greatest asset. The discovery of this mightiness presence will only be activated by choosing to GROW THROUGH IT instead of GOING THROUGH IT.

Perhaps the doctors were clearly educated and advanced, which I emphasized to him. I must confess that I viewed it as very ignorant not to follow the guidance of the skillfully trained doctors. I continued to emphasize to him the importance of listening to the doctors, hoping that he would allow my words to settle into his mind and create comfort within him.

Logic and reason spoke plainly to me saying "there was no adequate condition to shun the philosophy of the doctors". My mind was so wrapped around the programmed beliefs about doctors, that when the time came to hear anything that opposed my programmed thoughts, I would summon the voice echoes of reason and logic to protect and comfort my embedded thought system. However, as I continued to observe Kason, it appeared that he had super-natural hearing because despite how much reasoning and logic, I projected onto him, he would only subject himself to the voice of desire. And the more he professed the choice of GROW THROUGH IT, which will incontrovertibly happen by surrendering to the voice of desire, adversity seemed to be pushed away in any sense where it was disallowing.

In retrospect, he did not listen to anything I told him. I told him that he should TRUST the doctor's judgment. I pitched to him the idea that the doctors possessed a level of knowledge that he didn't. The doctor knows what's best for you in ways that you don't know for yourself.

Proven to be true, the human mind will program itself to believe ANYTHING one wants it to believe. One can continually be in a state of dis-ease but if they continually reinforce to themselves otherwise, eventually the mind will become saturated in the nature of the reinforced thought. Ultimately, this will disallow the voice echoes that are in harmony with dis-ease to manifest.

However, as he continued to follow his voice of desire to become a professional basketball player, hoping he would discover a specific plan or strategy to serve as the way-shower to his obsession to become a professional basketball player, it made sense as to why mere desire is an important mental faculty for creating favorable outcomes. The dis-ease of his condition created many reasons to question himself regarding his capabilities. Regardless of what those reasons were, the voice of desire that rested in his brain always gave Kason the advantage over his circumstances. While recovering from the car accident, I observed how cooperative he was to his voice of desire. For example, although he was physically weakened, the voice of desire viewed him as a "SUPERNATURAL BEING." As a sign of cooperation with this burning desire, he did not allow anyone to show him any special attention, grief, or accept sympathy. People always did and always do feel bad for you when something unfavorable happens. He saw this car accident as an opportunity to discover, at that time, what appeared as the unknown part of himself.

Despite being unable to physically walk, he wouldn't allow his own mother to help him walk around the house. When his friends came to visit, he would not allow them to remain in his company if they were crying instead of celebrating. I asked him, what is there to celebrate when you see one of your loved ones suffering, stretched out on a bed with stitches in his knees, blood on your shorts, particles of glass stuck in your skin, sore from the colliding ricochet of a car collision, bruised, and tormented by the recording voices of fear that people project on him. PLEASE TELL ME, what is there to celebrate?

He showed evidence of the power within his mind by his response. "I have been granted a renewed 24 hours of life today. Wounded only so I can be healed. I bare my crisis in a state of knowingness that my obedience to my suffering is essential to giving birth to a greater version of myself. Instead of allowing the outcome of this matter to be dictated by others, I choose to take this time of suffering to learn obedience to the voice."

For several days, I would contact him to check-in and get updates on his condition. I would always ask him, how are you feeling? He always responded, "I feel free."

One afternoon, less than two weeks after the accident, I received a call from Kason informing me that he was invited to a basketball game. Before the accident, he signed to a Semi-pro team in Jacksonville, North Carolina called Big Texas. Still physically weakened from the growing pains of the car accident, Kason decided to attend the game and give his moral support to his team.

After arriving at the game on crutches due to his weakened and recovering body, Kason sat on the bleachers and suddenly something very miraculous happened. After barely being able to balance himself without crutches, he had a strong desire to play in the basketball game. He never communicated this desire to anyone, instead, he found himself in the lobby restroom praying to God, asking for the physical strength to play basketball after being on bed rest from the accident.

Certainly, we are aware that "there is power in prayer." But the phrase alone doesn't tell us that prayer alone has enough capacity to transmute our desires into the physical reality. It didn't mention that the influence of prayer mixed with an unadulterated desire is the recipe for Miracles.

He loved basketball so much that he was willing to risk his life for it.

Through what seemed to be impossible, I witnessed Kason drop the crutches and despite having weakened legs, he STOOD by his decision to follow the road within himself. He gave himself permission to play, so he did. During those forty minutes of the basketball game, Kason scored thirty-five points and his team won by one point. This moment marked the most important turning point in his life and as an observer, I wanted to know, how was he able to push himself under those conditions? Where did you find the energy to perform after being on bed rest for about two weeks without practice? When are you going to listen to the doctor? What were you thinking to even attempt to play in a basketball game while on crutches? Who do you think you are?

Humbly I asked and meekly he replied: "I am the young man that got into the car accident and was told I could never play basketball again. I am the young man on blood thinners, who's discovered something within myself that tells me to climb every mountain that stands in my way. I've found something within myself that accepts obstacles as an opportunity to spread its wings and fly at a higher altitude. I have welcomed the resourcefulness that comes with truly stepping out on faith. In doing so, I've discovered the voice of desire that lives within me.

Later events subjected the substance of this small part of Kason's life.

When his older brother proclaimed as an eyewitness of watching his recovery from the day of the accident up to watching his little brother play in a semi-pro basketball game. "Perhaps he didn't have enough sense to believe he shouldn't have been doing what he was doing." While he was in fourth grade, attending Hannah Caldwell Elementary school, he tried racing me down a steep hill on bicycles and went so fast that he rode into a parked car. The impact left him unconscious in the middle of the street. During this time, the doctor gave him the order to stay home and rest every day. He had torn his ACL and suffered internal bleeding which disabled him from even going to school.

Although he was supposed to rest, every day when our parents went to work and our other brothers and sisters went to school, with both legs wrapped in a cast and crutches, he would walk to the neighborhood Park and attempt to shoot basketball. He was certain to arrive home before our parents returned from work because if they were aware that he was going to the park, he would be in BIG TROUBLE.

As he grew older, I began to take notice of his determination. When he played in the basketball game, it reminded me of when we were children. As an observer, I was convinced that my brother had a supernatural desire. I could tell by his actions that once he attunes to the part of himself that says, "You can do it", he will instantly develop a greater capacity of operation.

Through what seemed as merely impossible, I witnessed my brother arrive at a gymnasium on crutches and a cast because he could barely walk, to as if by a single stroke of supernatural phenomenon, not only playing in a basketball game but adding thirty-five points after being on bed rest for two weeks. His performance was a blessed MIRACLE".

Do you believe in Miracles? Every day God is using humans as the template to perform miracles through. "God moves in mysterious ways, with many miracles to perform." Kason found himself stuck in the seventh heaven, due to the changed perspective that had been conducted to him through his hearing of the voice of desire. He didn't rush to the telephone to call his friends and share with them the miracle. For the first time in his life, he could converse freely with God without the distractions of other people.

Following that day, he spent conscious time thanking God and pouring out his appreciation for allowing him such a humbling experience. In the most heartfelt manner ever experienced in his life, the voice of desire expressed itself into the physical reality in the form of a Miracle. Undeniably, he had encountered a moment that would take guardianship over his entire life as well as those who bared witness. By not being willing to accept humankind's belief in something untrue, with enduring DESIRE, he prompted humankind to rectify that untruth, through the most reasonable method readily obtainable.

Desire had begun to come into physical being through Kason's life, the success and freedom were just beginning. Kason had to configure a defining and useful method of communicating his miracle to the human family in a manner that would serve their greater good.

Barely recognizing the magnitude of what he had already experienced, but fully saturated with the fulfillment of the discovery of his EAGLE self, Kason Cheeks, wrote a note to himself describing the renewed motivation that he felt. Hidden between the crevices of this new motivation was a regenerated FAITH about his dream of becoming a professional basketball player.

Once he arrived at a space of restored inspiration, instantly all his greater aspirations zoomed into his mind. It was the current of his greater awareness which transmuted dis-ease into a tool bound to produce a gain in both fulfillment and freedom to every member of the human family.

The entirety and significance of that current of thought spoke to him and expressed this: It transpired in his mind that he could still fulfill his dreams of becoming a professional basketball player. He hoped to play professional basketball and create a way to help the millions of other people in the world who lost HOPE in their journey. If he could find a way to express his story it would be useful at making the world a better place.

Soon after he declared a decision to devote the remainder of his life to freeing the human family from the voice echoes of doubt, that creates HOPELESSNESS. He professed to write his story in a book that will compact all his experiences that it took him from what he called "a sinner to a winner." For a month and a half, Kason devoted the entirety of his day to doing in-depth research. He reviewed the whole networking system of the International Basketball League and developed ways of marketing and showcasing his talents all over the world.

Once properly marketed, he signed his FIRST professional basketball contract to play in Kosovo, Gjilan Europe. During his basketball season, he would set aside conscious time every day to write his book, which was a part of his design in his strategy towards freedom. Consciously aware, that he was in route to restore Hope and Freedom to millions of people who, without assistance, would have viewed HOPELESSNESS as inescapable.

By and by, after the ending of his first season as a professional basketball player, Kason registered the idea that he had accomplished his goal of playing pro-ball and therefore it was time to get his book published. He had no clue as to what steps to take to achieve this goal but knew that in due time, he would know the way. He had a plan that disclosed anything that didn't favor his desired outcome. He employed the same concept; I have used many years since his death.

"When you give, you give yourself the opportunity to get something out of failure that allows you to succeed."

As if he had spun the wheel of fortune, Kason landed himself a publisher in no time. By making the simple choice to GIVE. Practically humanity links "giving" to only material objects and money, which is one of the greatest mistakes I observed about the human family. Totally overlooking the importance of giving things such as your ATTENTION, TIME, ENERGY, KIND WORDS, and TRUTH.

When he did not know the way or reached a space of uncertainty, he made the choice to give. The local Boys and Girls club was hosting a Community Event called "Never Give Up" and looking for someone formidable to do some motivational speaking at their event. They had hired someone to be their keynote speaker but discovered that they hadn't raised enough money to pay for the service. Once they informed the speaker, he departed from the speaking position. The organizers of the community event rendered doubt as they were constantly denied in their attempts to hire a new speaker for the event. There is no doubt in my mind that MONEY is nothing more than a tool, often perceived as a necessity, used to create freedom and independence in various ways. Money also makes people lazy. When one learns to treat money as a tool instead of a necessity, money can be used as an instrument, not a stairway, to the top.

The organizers of the community rendered a state of FAILURE because they didn't have a speaker. Kason decided to use this moment to give birth to the unborn opportunity created by being present.

Having already mastered the art of transmuting his desires into physical equivalent, Kason decided to ACCEPT the motivational speaking offer. The organizers asked him "how much do you charge?" He replied "I am here to give. I charge you nothing." Perhaps he had enough money, that he didn't need the organizer's money. Maybe he was afraid to ask for money that he desired. Quite frankly, Kason knew that "true giving is giving without any expectations of receiving."

Kason decided to give his testimony at the community event and the outcome turned out phenomenal. The crowd was not huge, but lives were touched by the power of words and substance packaged in the story. As Kason walked to his car to exit the premises of the Boys and Girls club, a gentleman approached him and handed him a business card. As he handed him the card, he spoke: "That was an awesome testimony. You should write that in a book, I am a publisher. Give me a call when you are ready to put that story in a book."

As if some strange miraculous coincidence, there was a publisher in the crowd watching Kason's speech. Because he chose to serve the community in the form of giving, it gave birth to the unborn opportunity to becoming an Author.

Desire proved to be stronger than failure. Within three months, Kason Cheeks published his first book titled "Lost and Found: The Dark Testament", which summarized his journey by which he was being led by that quiet voice echo in the depths of his mind, called DESIRE. The same voice that even in times of adversity, which appeared as failure, instructed Kason in a manner that gave him the opportunity to get something out of failure that allowed him to succeed.

In all my years as a Life Coach dealing with women and men of all colors, cultures, and creeds, I have never eye-witnessed a single case that emanates the power of desire, more profoundly. Up until the day of his death, Kason Cheeks was able to be a prominent pioneer in the process of implementing concepts such as, It's possible, they say the sky is the limit but how can the sky be the limit if there are footprints on the moon, and Never Lose Hope. Commonly writers express stories and experiences they have but they project them in an exaggerated, superficial, and unimaginable manner. The astounding outcome was hard to describe, but nothing short of true. And if miracles can happen for him, then they can for you.

It was such a phenomenal experience to witness the physical incarnation of the voice of desire through my own best friend. Every step of the way, he maintained a humble attitude and nature marked by humility. He lived as a physical representation of what it looks like when one chooses to follow their desires. If becoming the embodiment of a Miracle happens as a result of pursuing desires with a bulldog obsession, it is sensible that miracles are REAL. In fact, miracles do happen ALL the time. We are unaware of the methods by which, every thought, every condition, every choice, influences our ability to give birth to the miracle within us. One day we shall discover the Key. He planted into his mind a desire to become a professional basketball player. That desire became a reality before his death. In addition, he planted his book on Mother Earth, used as a tool to serve the greater good of millions of people nationwide.

It requires supernatural awareness to lucidly explain how he accomplished such great results. It required DESIRE backed up with these other key components. First, DETERMINATION, by choosing the outcome at which you desire to see manifest. Second, DEDICATION, vow and be committed to your desire through your actions in every measured way possible, with over-flowing perseverance and intentional effort. Third, CELEBRATION, give credit for your daily victories that lead to the big CONGRATULATIONS. Hence, the" I knew you could do it moment".

Several years after the death of one of my most favorite people in the entire world, I discovered a powerful revelation. It came at a disturbing time, just days before Kason was lowered into the ground to begin his life in heaven. Days before I took my last look at him, in total honor of bearing witness of his fortitude and purpose-driven life. He always told me that even if he physically died, he would leave something on Earth that will show people how to live again.

He has planted many life-changing lessons in my mental garden. I was once asked the question "if you had to choose one lesson out of the many learned from Kason, which one would you say is most important?" ALL are important, but if I could choose one, that would be difficult to choose. The answer to the question can only be answered using this short story. I wish to convey a practical summary of the keys to freedom, despite your conditions, paradigm, or nature. These keys will be discovered in this summary of THING 1, THING 2, and THING 3.

THE TRUTH SHALL SET YOU FREE

Thing 1: The Over-comer

Thing 2: The Over-comer

Thing 3: The Under-achiever

Thing 3 told Thing 1 and Thing 2, "I can't do it." Thing 1 and Thing 2 instantly replied "that's not true, that's a lie, you've been programmed to believe as truth. The truth is that YOU CAN DO IT, ANYTHING IS POSSIBLE." Thing 3 insisted, "you guys are just trying to be positive. I respect your positive energy but let's be realistic I can't do it."

Was it true that Thing 3 couldn't be an over-comer? No, well according to him, he was being honest. Thing 1 and Thing 2 obtained a state of awareness where they believed ANYTHING is possible. In their reality, "I can't do it" is never the truth. Truth varies based on one's state of conscious awareness. For example, if someone is failure conscious, then "I can't do it" is perceived as truth. If someone is success conscious, "I can't do it", is an illusion.

As an author, I am intentional in implementing that all must desire conscious of something specific, kindle this consciousness with an unadulterated certainty that rejects phrases such as IT'S IMPOSSIBLE, YOU CAN'T, and does not consent to FAILURE. Because the TRUTH is that FREEDOM is only found on the path that the voice of DESIRE takes you.

To experience FREEDOM, one must be truth conscious because, without truth, there is no freedom. Without freedom, there is no truth. What is freedom, if there is no truth? And what is truth, if there is no freedom? Just an illusion because they are inseparable in nature. To have one without the other will always lead to suffering because when a truth is not given complete freedom, freedom is not complete.

Chapter 3

Determination:

The Art of Hoping, Persevering and Having FAITH

"You can't stop the rain, but you have the power to predict your own weather." Kason Cheeks

There is a road in the hearts of all of us. This road is hidden in seldom travels and it leads to an unknown sacred place. We are taught to SEEK outside of ourselves for the guidance and roadmap to this journey. Perhaps that's why it takes so long for the seeker to find because the truth is that the answer is within you.

The human body stores an inner presence that provides us guidance. Your ultimate responsibility is your ability to respond to this inner presence and adhere to the guidance. It speaks in a sacred whisper, uttering increments of guidance to you that can only be interpreted by the world, through you.

In pursuit of wonder about answers to life mysteries that reveal themselves in the form of the unanswered who, what, when, where and why questions, I had to honor to meet the Rainbow Warrior, who graciously shared his idea about determination. With my humblest gratitude, I share his words:

"There are many realities in life such as JOY and SADNESS, PLENTY as well as HUNGER, HEAVEN as well as HELL, WINNING as well as LOSING, IDENTITY as well as SHADOW, GOOD as well as BAD, FREEDOM as well as LIMITATION, LIGHT as well as DARK, HAPPINESS as well as SADNESS. But the one true reality is that life is a journey and sometimes we walk it in sunlight and sometimes in shadow. None of us asked to be born but we are here, and we must walk our journeys with our strengths and our weaknesses.Within all us, strengths and weaknesses exist because the human body is a huge molecular structure that transmits negative charge and positive charge, meaning because we are a molecular structure, whenever you have a positive thought, with that equally comes a negative thought. If there is the presence of Good, then there must be the absence of good called BAD, which is just the byproduct of disallowing Good. Within each of us is the will to live in freedom or to live in limitation. Or to put it another way, the determination to face life or the fear to turn away from it. Life is not always easy. There are difficulties, STORMS if you will. Storms that bring setback, loss, disappointment, sadness, dis-ease, and doubt that brings discomfort of every kind. But if the choice is made to sit at the foot of storms and difficulties and be taught it, you will discover that every storm and difficulty is designed to teach us to be strong. To learn to be strong, we must stand and face the storms and challenges that life offers us. It means crying when you need to, falling but getting up, making mistakes as proof of effort, but it means keeping SEEKING for answers and keep Hoping. It means to remain alive this moment, pull through the next moment, survive this moment, get through the next moment, make it through the adversity of the next moment, outlive the challenge of the next moment, and carry on until the darkness passes and the sun rises again, as it ALWAYS will.

Life's journey is like climbing a mountain, to reach the top, we must do it one step at a time. We should always remember that the smallest, weakest, or slowest step towards the top of the mountain, towards HOPE, is stronger than any storm, challenge, or difficulty. Keep in mind that when it storms, hang in there and stay strong because there's always a rainbow after every storm. Keep going, because your RAINBOW is on its way. And we should never forget that the key to determination is to keep going, no matter how exhausted, drained, or tired we may be. Above all, we must keep going.

Because although you can't stop the rain, you still have the power to choose your own weather. May you walk in freedom and may your eyes forever behold the red and purple sunset".

Determination is the way-shower of the mind. When determination is mixed with the vibraction of thought, the subconscious mind quickly interprets the vibraction, converts it into its intangible equivalent, and releases it to the Universe in the form of limitless awareness.

Determination, unconditional love, intuition, and hope are the most influential of all common emotions. When the four emerge, they have a "supernatural ability to cultivate the vibraction of feelings, thoughts, and emotions, in a manner that immediately enters the subconscious mind, then gets transmuted into its intangible equivalence, known as spirit, which is the only interior formation that generates a response from limitless awareness.

Unconditional love and intuition are two supernatural facets: associated with our SPIRIT presence. Determination and Hope are states of the MIND that are interconnected to the physical body's feedback. Combining or mingling the four of these emotions has the impact of allowing an unswerving course of dialogue between the mind, storing limited awareness and Unlimited awareness.

Determination is a characteristic of being willing to declare an outcome to the subconscious mind through the method of "GIVING yourself permission." The only real nation in the world is "the imagination", which will thoroughly be articulated in Chapter 7. The object of determination is to give yourself permission to transfer the thoughts from your imagination into the physical repeated through REPEATED AFFIRMATIONS or some form of repetitive thought reinforcement to the subconscious mind. By applying the guidance of "giving yourself permission" and Chapter 11 on the subconscious mind, you will program the subconscious mind to believe that you have the FAITH so that you'll receive what you desire or request. The mind will transmute that FAITH in the form of a vision, an idea, a plan, or strategy for obtaining your desired outcome.

The strategy whereby one develops determination where has not already been pre-decided is quite difficult to articulate: Almost as difficult as attempting to rollerblade backward up a slope. To those who are not aware of how the mind operates, this information may seem farfetched, but the meaning will be made clearer through the following quote. Stated in the words of a famous Motivational Speaker, "You can't stop the rain, but you have the power to predict your own weather."

This is identical to saying that, whether favorable or unfavorable, ALL thoughts carry a momentum and enthusiasm, which is constantly compressed onto the subconscious mind and is accepted and converted into action. The subconscious mind interprets the momentum and converts it into its physical identical by applying the most sensible process accessible. In relation to this, KEEP IN MIND that ALL THOUGHTS in the MIND DESIRES to be EXPERIENCED. THOUGHTS CAN NOT EXPERIENCE ANYTHING BY THEMSELVES. The mind is the activating agent of thoughts that are communicated through the body.

Once thoughts intertwine with emotions and feelings, they instantly start to transfer themselves from the mind into the body or physical reality to be experienced. In fact, the sentiment, feelings, or emotions segment of thoughts are the key essentials that FREELY transfer energy in the form of drive, motivation, momentum, and power to thoughts.

The emotion-momentum of determination, unconditional love, HOPE, and intuition, when united with the momentum of any thought, right away produces a more heightened amount of actions than any of these emotions can produce separately. This truth doesn't only apply to combining thoughts with the momentum of determination, this universal truth also applies when thoughts are united with any of the favorable emotions or the unfavorable emotions that enter and deceive the subconscious mind.

From this knowledge, you will realize that the subconscious mind will transfer a thought itch of a favorable or negative form, just as eagerly, as it will respond to thought itches with a favorable or positive form. Report this as the key to the questions of the reoccurring experiences that millions of people self-create mention as adversity, problems, disaster, failures, or storms if you may.

Many surrender to the beliefs that unite with thoughts that destines them to failure and scarcity because of mental faculties that they are completely unconscious of. They are conduits of their "failure" because of unfavorable beliefs compressed upon the subconscious mind and translated into physical identical.

Take some time and saturate your mind with the realization that you will undeniably reap from ANY thought that's compressed onto the subconscious mind. Regardless of the nature of the thought, the subconscious mind will transform the thought into a state of Expectancy and the physical transmutation will occur.

Determination influences the activity of the subconscious mind. Determination, the root word, determine, is when one pre-chooses, through the employment of their choice faculty, what thoughts they will allow to be projected into something tangible.

One of the most common human responses to adversity is to quit while in the pit. Every person in the world has given up on something or someone at some point in their lives. Strangely, the story of quitting in the pit has become common amongst the human family. Every time we choose to quit while in the pit, we disable ourselves from discovering the extraordinary power that can only be found in the pit.

Draw your awareness to a self-discovery encounter that appropriated Determination. Keep your mind alert to observe exactly what strange momentum showed up at the appointed time.

Road Trip Home

Doubtlessly, hundreds and thousands of college students across the nation await their spring break, fall breaks, and winter breaks because this time allows them a break from waking up early in the morning for class, relaxation, meet NEW people, experience wild parties, beautiful beaches, and many other forums of celebrating their youth through travel.

It is assured that no one wants to be stuck at their parents' house during their breaks from school, but in the case of Simone, spending the entire break with family was the plan.

The discovery of the strange power didn't come about at one moment. It came about bit by bit, shadowed by the decision to get home to her parents, on time. One of the essential qualities of the student's plan was that it was specific. She was determined to get home to her parents.

When the thought of visiting her parents for spring break shined into her mind, she was not in the appropriate mental space to move upon the thought. Her mind was clouded by the three disadvantages that sprinkled the enthusiasm of doubt and discouragement over any attempt to manifest the desire. 1: In the past 3 days, she had a total of 6 hours of sleep due to studying for final exams that were required before Spring Break .2: If she decides to go to her parents' house, she wouldn't get much rest because she would have to leave after her 9 to 5 work shift to make it home at a reasonable time. 3: It is a two-hour drive from school to her parents' house. These disadvantages were adequate to have disheartened a great number of those from their effort to manifest their desire. She was concerned about being overly tired and exhausted due to the unfavorable combination of all the disadvantages, but she had an extraordinary desire to see her parents.

She did not know what to do. She found herself stuck in between the gap of desiring a thing and merely giving herself permission to receive the very thing she desires. This gap is all about how much DETERMINATION you have. Determination in these moments gives the momentum and enthusiasm that influence the time that your desire will manifest and the course of you because if your doubt is equivalent to your desire, then the momentum doesn't move at all.

It becomes extremely difficult not to manifest unwanted things if your desire isn't stronger than your doubt. Doubt doesn't necessarily stop the desire from manifesting, it just slows it down. Surely her desire proved to overstand her doubt because after speaking to herself while stuck in the gap between doing and thinking about doing, she pledged to herself that she would get it done.

The pledge to herself was more than important because everything in life comes to you that same way. Every so often, as the thinker, we are not clear as to what we desire, which allows us to be emotionally carried away by contradictory energy. The pledge served as the thought energy that overthrew contradictory energy.

When faced with contradictory energy, draw your attention to things that align you with your desire. Find thoughts, practice these thoughts, feel the thoughts, and hold the momentum of the thoughts in a place of powerful expectation. Allow yourself to be swept by the momentum that the thoughts create.

As an observer of the human family, I noticed that many people settle for defeat while in this gap. She learned that to reverse that outcome, one must respond solely to their desired outcome, ACCEPT where they are, and never forget where they intend to be. This moment presented her with the opportunity to stake claims on her self-determination. Thereafter, allowing her to gain access to one of the keys that frees us from negativity and allows us to be energetically refreshed with positivity.

Having declared the choice of arriving at her parents' house no later than 7:30 pm, she decided to follow the momentum of the emotional inspiration created by pre-choosing the intended outcome. This emotional inspiration is very similar to faith. It is ALL that exists. Everything else is trumped-up reasons to create a disconnection between you and the momentum that leads you to achieving FREEDOM.

This instance may have appeared to have secondary importance. As it approached her final hour in her 9 to 5 work shift, the momentum of determination began to reveal itself because she had never felt such a strong urge to get off work and take to the highway. If the importance beyond predetermining her outcome is easily known to all humankind who have similar day to day encounters as this college student, there would be no need to continue reading this book.

What may have appeared as unimportant or a senseless moment, displayed the awakening of her becoming conscious of something that she previously couldn't see. By subjecting the energy of specifically stated ambitions to a task, which she verbalized in her self-talk and declared in her own mind, it created a momentum that combats the intellectual resistance created by fear and doubt. By persistently reinforcing the subconscious mind of that specific ambition, the energy of the reinforced ambition will carry you through adversity.

Driven by determination and the will to accomplish, she found herself cruising the highway in total acceptance of the momentum of determination. In totality, the drive was two hours. Within thirty-minute increments, observe the moments she was overtaken by the positive emotions and the negative emotions of the mind and how the momentum of her pre-determined choices created the enthusiasm to eliminate the negative emotions.

1st 30 minutes

During the first thirty minutes of the drive, her faith was at its peak. The radio kept playing her favorite songs, the windows were slightly cracked, allowing a fresh breeze and alongside her in the passenger was her invisible friend named determination. Philosophers have correctly said: "Begin with the end in mind." She was ready to see her parents. Moreover, she was determined to arrive at a reasonable time that would allow them to have supper and spend some highly anticipated quality time together. Having determined the outcome, she forged herself into this commitment and was not going to stop until she achieved what she was seeking.

Maybe she did not know at the time but, her determination was going to be tested. Because it was so definite, it had the power to rise above any unfavorable thoughts. Contrast momentum, thoughts, and emotions were destined to find her. It's all part of the variety of living in a physical body and corresponding to a material world. Her choice molded her into a place, that despite feeling the contradictory energy, she learned not to allow the negative momentum to carry her away.

What a different story this turned out to be because she employed an absolute purpose and stood by it until she became a living reflection of it.

2nd 30 minutes

After thirty minutes of driving, SOMETHING HAPPENED. She began to feel tired and exhausted. She began to say to herself "Ah well, what's the use of driving home. I knew I couldn't make it to my parents' house." The sound of the music was beginning to have a sedating effect on her, as well as the feeling of the wind blowing in the car. They were making her eyes drowsy. Perhaps the monotony of highways that all look alike, same songs on the radio, driving by herself on a two-hour stretch, especially after being sleep deprived was the condition of the second- 30-minute increment of her drive.

Her reaction time on the road was delayed by all the opposition in the form of voices in her head echoing statements, "Driving alone is too hard", "Pull over the car", "I don't have anyone to talk to", "No one is sharing driving duties with me", "no one is here to tell me if I'm drifting or nodding off on the wheel", "I think my best bet is to pull over and take a power nap", "after all, it's better to arrive alive, than to be late."

Just as trees offer the oxygen that gives us the ability to breathe, so will choosing one thought, feeling, or emotion give us the momentum to keep going. If you fill your mind with poverty, limitation, and doubt, the magnetic forces of thought momentum will take the spirit of disbelief and utilize it as a way-shower by which the subconscious mind will translate it into its physical equivalent.

She found herself catching the momentum of contrast thoughts and emotions. As every unfavorable thought spoke, she would feel her vibrational attitude changing. After stepping back and acknowledging that "it's all good", she was rescued from her pitstop by a wave of enthusiasm that showed up because predetermined thoughts don't allow itself to be swept by contradictory thoughts.

Take note of the words that have been used in her vocabulary and you will understand the abstract meaning beyond the language that contributes to the attitude of determination.

3rd 30 Minutes

While pulling over on the side of the highway, to take a nap, which would slow down the manifestation of her time-specific desire, she found herself completely surrendered to the energy of the thoughts that weren't in harmony with her desired outcome. As she sat in the car, she thought to herself, "It seemed absurd to be driving home under these conditions. I tried and I did not intend for this to happen, but I am not gone make it to my parents' house in time. I've set a standard for myself that I can't keep."

Whenever the opportunity is presented to use the power that God has put in us, we sprinkle our circumstances with POWERLESS words, which ultimately disallows or prolongs the manifestation of our greater desires. TRY is one of those powerless words that's habitually used when faced with the enthusiasm of misfortune, setbacks, or defeats. When you try, make an effort, or attempt for something, you are committing to suffering. Hence, the importance of committing to a specific thing.

It is imperative to replace the word TRY with, I WILL, or I CAN because by not committing to the positive outcomes then you are submitting to the negative outcome. Perhaps people didn't know that the word TRY attracts the energy of suffering because the word TRY shows empathy to struggle instead of empathy to determination. Therefore, for those who were unaware of this truth, the next statement will be deemed as farfetched that because you TRY to succeed, that's exactly why you fail.

She found herself distracted by the mastery of negative thoughts. The momentum of negative thoughts directly influenced the vibraction of her physical body in a manner that made her feel like she had been tackled. BUT SHE DESIRED TO SEE her family and arrive by 7:30 pm. Even while in the pit, she was reminded of this desire.

She was reminded that this desire was not something she wanted and hoped would happen. The desire was not something she wanted and believed would happen. This desire was not something she wanted and doubted would happen, but this desire was something that she knew would happen because she gave herself permission to make it to her parents' house at a reasonable time to spend quality time and have supper.

After pulling over for roughly ninety seconds, she glanced at the clock and it was 6:33 and she still had at least an hour to drive. In the plan to acquire her goals, she found herself under the influence of distracting thoughts. Distractions always lead to the wrong turn, as in the case of a car accident. See the human body is a vehicle, your mind is the engine, and your heart is your steering wheel. Once conquered by the influence of distractions, most never turn back. Fortunately, the outcome was totally favorable in the case of this college student. As she sat in the car, she began to repeat the words.

"I desire to make it home and I give myself permission to do so."

"I desire to make it home and I give myself permission to do so."

"I desire to make it home and I give myself permission to do so."

Following the momentum of those words, she decided to cut her car on and retake her position on the highway. Rising from temporary defeat, she found a new sense of eagerness. As she drove, she continually repeated those words to herself aloud OVER and OVER as she drove. The more she repeated the words, the more she amplified the desire. And as a side effect of synchronizing an amplified desire and the buffer of time, the manifestation of determination happened in a logical and sequential way. Determination showed up to bridge the gap between desiring a thing and acquiring a thing.

4th 30 minutes

Pioneered by the momentum of determination, the college student found herself about 30 minutes from home and totally swept by the enthusiasm of determination.

How is it possible for someone to go from tired and exhausted to enthused and energetically renewed instantaneously?

We should always remember that at the end of every storm is a rainbow. The lessons learned through the storms are as valuable to life as the pot of gold that dwells at the end of the rainbow.

"The easiest part of running a race is the end because you get more excitement as you get closer."

As she noticed herself getting closer to the goal, she kept her eyes on the prize which means remain focused on achieving her desired outcome, without being distracted by problems or setbacks. She discovered that setbacks are only the results of taking her eyes off of the prize because once she repeatedly reminded herself of her desired outcome through audible affirmations, the momentum that she felt at the beginning of the trip moved in, swept her, and just like a magic carpet, carried her to her destiny.

For generations to come and generations that have passed, philosophers, religious leaders, and false hope advertisers have recommended a suffering human race to have FAITH and NEVER LOSE HOPE, in this or that condition, or any condition they face in their human experience, but they are unsuccessful at showing people how to access and maintain a state of hope. They have not specified that hope is a state of mind created when one has pre-determined to prompt their mind by giving themselves permission.

In a manner, that serves the greater good of the entire human family, we will articulate the known method by which HOPE is discovered, in a place where it was not present.

NEVER LOSE HOPE in yourself. Have HOPE in your limitless capabilities. Before we proceed, allow me to remind you that HOPE is the invisible power source that gives vitality, endurance, and assertiveness to the momentum of thought.

This section of the book is worth reading aloud at least four, five, or six times. Hope is the new rocket that launches all of us to freedom. Hope lies at the root of all miraculous outcomes and all PRAYERS that we answer in ways that remain unexplainable by the laws of quantum physics.

Hope is the only natural medicine for favorable momentum when it is prescribed as Heart Open to Positive Energy.

The road will get rough, it will be difficult to find courage when the road is long. When you feel like you are going to let go, HOPE in the form of Hold On Pain Ends says, "when you feel like you are going to let go, tie a knot and just hang on."

HOPE is the conscious language which is expressed when determination is mixed with dedication, which allows one direct dialogue with the source that transmutes your circumstances into a celebration. Determination, Dedication, then Celebration.

HOPE is the component that converts ordinary thoughts, generated by the subconscious mind, into extraordinary spiritual experiences, in the form of Holiness Overpowers Evil.

Hope is the only internal force that storehouses the supplies by which makes life perfectly magical, in the form where the human body becomes the House of Perfect Eternity.

When all Hope seems lost in the wild, a fire will spark the much-needed HOPE to the torch that gives us a reason to keep going. And just as the spark of a match starts a fire that lights the torch of the loss seeking direction, so shall you be to a neighbor seeking freedom.

Every statement mentioned above can be proven true with evidence to support it. The evidence is plain and easily understood. It is enveloped in the fundamental of "Giving yourself permission." Let's channel our focus to the concept of Giving your Permission and discover exactly what it is and how it serves the greater good of the human family, with respects to wealth, abundance and FREEDOM.

It is nationally known to be true, that whatever one constantly repeats to oneself, whether favorable or unfavorable in nature, will be believed as "fact". Whether the expression is false or true, if one constantly repeats a lie over and over, eventually it will be accepted as the truth. Every human being interprets life-based on the domineering thoughts at which they permit to rest in their minds. Thoughts at which, by design, are in the mind and heightened by emotional impulses and blended with compassion, creates the inspirational momentum which influences and dictates their every motion, action, and service.

Now is the time to present a highly important statement of truth.

When thoughts are blended with feelings or emotions of any capacity, that blending creates electrifying momentum which attracts energy from the vibrations of the cosmos or other alike thoughts. The representation of what occurs when any single or multiple thoughts are charmed with beliefs and emotions can be symbolically demonstrated through comparing thoughts to a stick that starts a fire. By rubbing two sticks together, the friction grows and creates a spark, transfers the hot stick into your tinder bundle, blow your tinder bundle to keep it ignited, use the burning tinder bundle to ignite it and keep adding larger sticks to create a long-lasting fire.

The cosmos is a supernatural host of the invisible force of energetic vibrations. It is constructed of both favorable and unfavorable vibrations. It carts vibrations of all nature including scarcity, guilt, limitation, poverty, and equally carts vibrations of abundance, fulfillment, wealth, happiness, and freedom. Just as without a shout of doubt carts the sound waves of millions of human voices, animal sounds, musical tones, each possessing their own independency and pattern of verification through the reception and transcribing of frequencies.

From the warehouse of the cosmos, the human mind is always attracting vibrations which align with thoughts, beliefs, and ideas that possess the most influence in the human mind. Any thought, strategy, beliefs, goals, which one store in their mind attracts the vibration of the cosmos, summons this infinite power, and expand until it becomes the domineering, influential master of the person whose mind it has been stored.

Let's take a second and reflect from the beginning and clarify how a thought in the form of a plan, strategy, idea, or belief settles into the human mind. This information will be conducted in the simplest form. This explains why it is important to clearly define your goals, objectives, or highest aim, pre-determine your outcome, express commitment to the process by repeated audible affirmation, day after day, until these vibrations of traveling sound rearrange the subconscious mind.

Every human experience and human condition reflect thought vibrations, which our brains interpret and express through interactions with our environments and other human relations. Unfavorable environments always seem to build more thoughts of limitation, doubt, and poverty on your life order. Focus your attention on the mental faculties and chargeable aspects of the human mind that unfavorably affects the human family. The primary cause of humanic eruptions is the lack of self-assurance. This disability can be conquered and prevailed then converted into mightiness, through the application of giving yourself permission. This fundamental key may be exercised through adding momentum to positive thoughts through stating and continually restating thoughts with a positive impulse, writing and various mental exercises that work in favor of magnifying the enthusiasm of favorable thoughts until they become the captain of the mental ship known as the subconscious mind.

SELF ASSURANCE

A famous philanthropist quoted "self-confidence is the best outfit, rock it, and own it." Observe the words and ideology, which have been magnetized and you will discover the hidden meaning of self-confidence at which the philanthropist was attempting to convey.

Surely, confidence is important because it determines how much one can achieve in life because it directly governs the nature of your thoughts. Self-confidence influences the attitude at which you use to turn your thoughts into their physical equivalence. For example, when the voice echoes of people's opinions telling you "yes, no, you can't do this, you can't do that", self-confidence guides you through the disturbances of these echoes and holds you about in a manner that allows you to move forward and accomplish your goals.

One of the most profound self-discovered beauty marks about humans is their understanding of self. Humankind is not aware of how discovering "SELF" really works.

Life begins before a baby is born

In the beginning of time, we didn't know ourselves because we were inseparable from God. As baby's, we didn't have thorough wisdom, knowledge, or understanding of ourselves. Even after birth, a child does not become aware of themselves. It's natural that we become more aware of others and begin to define and identify ourselves based on the impression taken from others, including mothers, sisters, fathers, brothers, and more.

Gradually we learn to use our five senses. By using these sensory factors, we develop more awareness of others. Once it's realized that we have a nose, children learn to identify things and people by their smell. Once it is realized that we have hands, we identify others by touching them. When we discover they have ears, we listen to others. Upon discovering they have a tongue, we become willing to taste anything until we learn to distinguish between what's edible and what's improper to put in their mouths.

Through constant awareness of outside factors, we develop an understanding of SELF. This reflection is solely based on the understanding of SELF-created from the awareness of outside factors known as an identity. Millions of people spend their lives identifying themselves based on outside faculties. Unfortunately, people spend most of their lives mastering this version of SELF that they were persuaded to be instead of discovering the version of SELF that God created you to be.

We foolishly believe in this version of self that we've been persuaded to be as our true selves. Millions of people spend their lives perfecting this false version of self, surely unaware that this version of you accepts poverty, guilt, shame, and misery as reality instead of illusion.

Building self-esteem, self-confidence, and self-efficacies are extremely important tools for preparing yourself for freedom. Yet so many people struggle to find them but, those who do discover them, find it difficult to obtain. Those who lack self-esteem and self-confidence can find it difficult to experience freedom.

This book is written to provide answers to the forever unanswered questions. The awareness in this book is documented to serve as a way-shower of truth. Well as an author, allow me to ask you a few simple questions:

Have you discovered your true self?

How can you truly develop self-esteem if you don't know your true self?

How can you truly develop self-confidence if you don't know your true self?

If one is claiming to have good self-esteem and good self-confidence and they have not discovered their true self, is it true confidence and true self-esteem?

Someone will read this and has developed so much comfort with their false self, that they've persuaded themselves that their false self is their true self. They can't answer these questions in terms of truth, because they've saturated their thoughts and habits in this understanding of self they've been persuaded to be, and denial and suppression are the only tools that they can employ to assure their comfort.

Perhaps they are not aware that confidence is merely a state of trusting thyself. When you begin to trust thyself without "knowing thyself", you and every other person, develop an understanding of self-based on other's opinions, what other people think and otherworldly dynamics allows faculties outside of you to overstand your impression of self.

Whether intentionally or by virtue of default, the understanding of self-affirmed by factors outside of self always leads to negativity. Those who are unaware of this truth, the next statement may be deemed as farfetched that the reason you feel negative is because you have high self-esteem.

Take notice of this very significant truth: hence the importance of discovering your true self and becoming self-assured. Self-assurance is marked by a state of knowing thyself by its determination in pursuit of purpose and the understanding that knowingness surpasses beliefs. One person out of every hundred million truly knows themselves and those who do not know themselves are so engulfed in their misinterpreted understanding of self that they become to shameful, prideful or passive about speaking of it.

One's self-confidence can show in various ways, including your body language, how you speak, what you say, and your overall behaviors. Examine the following charts that show the lenses and language of self-assurance, determination, hope, and perseverance and compare them with the lenses of self-confidence.

Lenses of Determination

- Willing to take the risk and go the extra mile
- Do what you know to be true, even if others mock you.
- Congratulate yourself for your accomplishments
- You "know" yourself with respects to your capabilities and destiny

- Gives your thoughts permission to be transmuted into physical reality meaning you have control over your thoughts

Lenses of Confidence

- Stay in your comfort zone
- Spend time fearing failure and avoid taking on a big task.
- Wait for others to congratulate you.
- You "believe" in yourself and your capabilities with respects to your capabilities based on worldly dynamics.

Language of Determination/Language of Confidence

I will................................. I try

I choose to .... I should

I choose not................................. I can't

I allow myself to........................... I must, I need to

NO...MAYBE

I am going to....................................... I might but

I know I can... I believe I can

I can do it; I just can't do it with you........................... I can't do it

I am not certain, but I will know soon......................... I don't know how

I did it.. I wish I could

I am success... I won't achieve it

My challenge is only made for me............................ It is too hard

I am going to win................................... I don't want to lose

Your Civil Right

(Fill your name in the blank and read this every day)

I _____ profess that at some point in my life, seeds of limitation, doubt, and poverty were planted into my mind and truth be told it is not possible to experience complete abundance, prosperity, and wealth unless one is set free from these beliefs that pollute my mind. No soul will ever experience fulfillment, reach their fullest potential, become successful or develop unless they have the true freedom to express themselves, saturate in greater awareness, and then transmute their ideas and thoughts into things that serve the greater good of humanity; such as a business, cities, airplanes, automobiles, or NEW conveniences that make life more fulfilling. I _____ realize that earning money for the sake of using it to fulfill this task is pivotal.

I _____ profess that one can only be fruitful and expand by utilizing the freedom experienced by exercising the creative faculty in their imagination. And once discovering the creative self, the expansion, wealth, and financial abundance comes by giving yourself permission to have things. Therefore, we must be reminded about our civil right to have wealth, abundance, prosperity, which are natural side effects of Freedom. The object of all life is advancement, growth, and expansion. And everything that lives has a civil right to all growth it can acquire while dwelling on Mother Earth. Humankind's civil right to life declares the free and unlimited access to all things which may be utilized in favor of human expansion, mentally, physically, financially, spiritually, emotionally, or in other words, the right to be free.

I _____ am aware that freedom shall be spoken on in a literal way;

to be free does not mean to be normal or ordinary. There are many things in life one may be inspired to be, but normal should never be one of them, considering the marvelous capabilities we've been blessed with that will naturally allow us to experience more freedom when we share this gift. The purpose of life revolves around the buildup and evolution of the human family and every member of the human family has the civil right to contribute to the marvelous power, extraordinary creations, abundant outcomes, and things that contribute to the fulfillment of life; to find comfort or complacency in life with anything else is separate in nature.

He or she who gives themselves permission to own the freedom to accomplishing all the things beyond their wildest imaginations is one that can live in freedom. No woman or man can expand into the fullness of themselves without a state of freedom that will allow them to do so. Life gets so busy and we become so distracted that in order to live in a manner that allows the slightest level of happiness, a specific amount of freedom is required. It is our civil right to become all that we can become. The desire to reach a place of Heaven on Earth is built in every human being by God; we cannot get rid of the desire to be all that we can be. Freedom in life is choosing and becoming what you desire to be. You can manifest this desire only by using the civil right you have to utilize things around you and you have the civil right to utilize the tools around you until you expand enough within yourself to discover the freedom to create your own things. To fully understand the keys to acquiring freedom, the primary fundamentals are awareness, truth, knowledge, and wisdom.

There is nothing wrong with claiming your civil right to have freedom. The desire for freedom is really the desire for a fulfilling, peaceful, worry-free, and more prosperous life; and that desire is commendable, admirable, honorable, and because God put that desire in you, it is worthy to be praised. He or she who does not desire to live a life in perfect harmony and prosperity are ordinary, which incontrovertibly means he or she who does not claim their civil right to experience those benefits of freedom is ordinary.

Perfect harmony is experienced when we align with the complete truth of us, including no one person is better or more creative than the other, all are alike, and all were perfectly carved by God's hands. We all have the civil right to be alive, live life, and fully express ourselves even if others choose not to. It totally denies us the fulfillment of our life experience if we deny or do not honorably claim our civil right to be free.

I _____ acknowledge that if I have acquainted myself with conditions that are consequences of not embodying my civil right to be free, by signing this, I acknowledge that I will no longer deny my right to fully express all of that which God has put forth to manifest through the spirit that's created through the merging of my mind, body, and soul. I acknowledge that I am accountable for my own happiness, fulfillment, magnificence, and splendor which can only be experienced when one chooses to be true to their mind, respect and honor their body, and expresses every quantity of greatness that dwells in their soul. Whenever desires, aspirations or hopes remain unexpressed, unfinished or limited, it creates a natural dissatisfaction. I declare my civil right to pursue my desires, express them with determination, and operate in the entirety of my true self.

Humankind cannot thrive without the necessities including; food, warm clothes, and shelter. Mind Elevation and truth are the symbolic foods we must feed the mind in order to live in freedom.

As a member of The Human family, I profess that we cannot reach our fullest potential without feeding our minds in the form of reading books, study time, constructive dialogue, and opportunity to travel and expand our cultural awareness.

To live at our full potential, we must have an active imagination and must be willing to surround ourselves with people, objects, and things that carry the momentum that would be useful to our established emotions and feelings.

To live in freedom, one must have unconditional love and limitation rejects unconditional love.

Freedom is found in one's ability to love unconditionally: unconditional love finds its most supernatural and instinctive voicing through giving, offering, and contributing to others. He or she who gives themselves permission to give will fulfill their respective purpose in society, as an ultimate philanthropist of truth, awareness, and unconditional love.

Through utilizing the keys, the collective human family will discover that one's state of mind, directs the body, which dictates how the soul is expressed. It is therefore paramount to usher our minds into higher states of awareness.

I _____ declare perfect ownership of my civil right; which is necessary to live an extraordinary life.

I _____ declare ownership of my civil right of freedom, "knowing" that by doing so, I grant myself permission to activate my true nature.

I _____ will sign this document, commit it to my thoughts, and repeat it aloud once or twice a day, with HOPE and determined faith that it will influence my mind and actions so that I will become more independent and freer.

I surrender my trust and acceptance into this knowing, aware that contrary to popular belief, surrendering is the ultimate sign of strength and mightiness. Surrendering gives you permission to no longer feel pain and creates an openness to the unfolding of heaven on Earth. If I continue to avoid surrendering, I directly leave my destiny unintended, which will cause discomfort with God, my human family, and ultimately myself. The contribution made to serve the greater good of humanity will not be made through me without this declaration to better myself.

If you turn back to the earlier pages of this chapter and read again the story called Roadmap Home that lays out the experience of the college student, you will gain a clear understanding of the necessary steps towards being set free from contradictory energy including negative thoughts, negative memories, or negative momentum. To do so, it is imperative to form a clear and definite "knowingness" of what you desire: because you will not be able to transmute this desire into physical reality unless you, first possess it yourself.

You must obtain it and possess it before you can give it. Can you give a person one million dollars if you don't have it? No, many fail to take this same mental approach with their emotions, thoughts, or goals. And more than often, they fall short of manifesting their desire because they have themselves only an undeveloped idea of a thing they are inspired to do, become, or possess.

It is not enough to merely possess a general desire for a thing: everyone has that desire. It is not enough to just dream for a thing to happen whether it involves freedom, financial improvement, travels, etc. or not. Everyone has those desires.

Obtaining ownership of that which you desire, whether it is freedom, your mind, body, and financial abundance, wealth or prosperity comes as a result of specifying your desire and remembering: you are not designed to obtain anything solely for self-pleasure, recognition, or gratitude, to compete with others, to be famous, or to be rich. The human who lives for those moments alone will die alone because of those moments.

God designed you to experience freedom, so that you may be worry-free about what you may eat, drink, and a place to sleep when it comes to furthering ourselves: with hopes that you feed your mind, body, and spirit with infinite joy, travel the world, expand your cultural awareness: in order that you may learn to love ALL members of the human family unconditionally, fulfill your destiny, and be a reflection of the creator that creates things that will be used to help the world discover the TRUTH.

Always remember that there is only one truth and half-truths are no better than gratifying than dishonesty; both are unfavorable.

Release the belief that God desires for you to suffer or sacrifice yourself for others and by doing so, you will gain God favor. God desires nothing of that nature.

What God desires is that you become who you've been created to be, which will require you to see the difference between who you've been created to be and who you've been tempted to be. God desires to use you as a template that his vision will be born through. Therefore, you should make the most of yourself, for yourself, and the human family. And you can always serve the greater good of the human family by making the most of yourself, than in any other way possible.

Specifying details helps with the authenticity of teaching people practical ways to become extraordinary. Specifics direct your course of action and direct the course of action necessary to create favorable momentum and self-assurance. Specifics enable our ability to leap forward in faith.

Nimiq International Institute uses the Eagles strategic and goal setting method to ensure that objectives are Extraordinary, Attainable, Greater-good, Living-like, Energy-based and Specific. This section will display the benefits of adopting this method into your personal experience.

Extraordinary (Supersize what you think)

Extraordinary

(elevated, extreme, expanded)

- How amazing do you dare to be?
- How powerful do you dare to be?
- How inspirational do you dare to be?
- What can you do to transform the world?

Your goal should be so Extraordinary that it scares you. Otherwise, it is not big enough. Instead of supersizing your fries and drink, supersize what you think. Ordinary goals follow the belief that the sky is the limit. Extraordinary beliefs follow the quote "how could the sky be the limit if there are footprints on the moon".

Attainable (Resources)

(measurable, reachable)

- What are the daily practical steps that can be taken to accomplish this?
- How will I measure my growth and progress?
- What tools are necessary to fulfill this?

Greater-good (Motives)

(US, WE, the World, selfless, others)

- How can this contribution benefit the human family?
- Why do we desire to accomplish this?
- Why is it important to fulfill this?
- Is this goal about me or us?

Living like (Giving)

(allow, grant, permit)

- What will this give to the human family?
- What specific ways will be accomplishing this add to the quality of life?

Energy-Based (Compassion and Love)

(easy, effortless, excitement)

- Is this something I can do without getting paid?
- Does the thought of this excite you?
- Does this give you a purpose?
- Do you feel free when you engage this?

Specific (Time Management)

(Simple, strategic, sufficient)

- What exactly do we desire to accomplish?
- When are we going to work on this?
- What are the restrictions?
- When do we desire to accomplish this?

General Goal: I want to write a book

Extraordinary: I desire to write a best-selling book that's going to transform the world.

Attainable: I will work on the table of contents first, then my chapter layouts, and then I will fill in the text for the chapters.

Greater-good: Writing this book will help restore hope for many people in the world.

Living -like: I will give the first forty copies of my book for free. I give myself permission to rise above scarcity.

Energy-based: I will be excited because pursuing my passion is different than doing work.

Specific: I will spend twenty minutes a day writing. In those twenty minutes, I will write two paragraphs (10 sentences a day) for 10 months.

General Goal: I want to make money.

Extraordinary: I desire to earn a million dollars a year.

Attainable: I will find a skill I can be paid ten dollars to do. Then multiply that effort times ten, now earning 100 dollars. Then multiplying that effort times ten, now earning 1,000 dollars. And continue to duplicate until I reach 1 million dollars.

Greater-good: Money is a tool that's necessary in order to establish stability for my family.

Living like: I give myself permission to be better today than I was yesterday.

Energy-based: I decided to leave my 9-5 job and pursue my passion. It makes me happy to follow this path.

Specific: I will set a goal to make 5 dollars a day. Saving is important because once you become a millionaire, if you spend one dollar, then you are no longer a millionaire.

Release the idea that having a general desire is enough. Specifics are one of main fundamental keys you will discover in this book. It is true somewhere within your mind, resting dormant, lies the seeds of freedom, wealth and abundance which if properly harvested and cultivated into action, will elevate you to levels beyond your wildest dreams.

Remember the importance of claiming your desire, it must be claimed and specified in a manner that expresses that it is definite. The specifics, whether written or orally expressed, will be the magical power that puts your desire into action form.

See exactly what you desire, say exactly what you desire and PRAY for exactly what you desire. Go over your desires with yourself in the mirror. And just as a baby is born through a mother's womb, after hours of pain and discomfort, so will your desire be born through you after years of patience, commitment, and faith.

Specifying your desires helps you develop a clear mental picture of the vision in your mind, which is necessary as a captain of your mental ship. As you are moving closer and closer towards whatever you are sailing towards, it is necessary to keep your mind on your goal and never lose sight of it. There will be times that you lose sight of it, feel like you want to "quit", or give up. In the 1995-1996 NBA season, the Chicago Bulls set the goal of not losing any NBA games. That year the bulls set the record for the most wins in the NBA with 72 wins and 10 losses and later went on to win the NBA Championship.

It is a known truth that no one is perfect. At some point, you will make a mistake as a result of giving the best effort that you knew to give at that moment. Spend as less time possible giving thought to your mistakes and concentrate your mind on the things which require you to apply your effort and attention to them.

There's no need to take courses or classes in the area of concentration, isolate, nor overly judge yourself. All you must do is continually remind yourself of your desire enough so that it will stay in your thoughts and become your reality. The continual reminders serve as the fuel that drives you towards whatever your goal is.

It's never too late to achieve your desire. Poverty driven thoughts persuade us that our ability to achieve and be set free is influenced by age. Age doesn't determine maturity, attractiveness or when you have permission to achieve. The only time age determines maturity and attractiveness is with antiques, artifacts, and fossils, not with Humans. For humans, with respects to this book, age is nothing more or less than a reminder of how many years have passed, which serves as a reminder that there is no more time to waste on things that don't serve the greater good of humanity. There is no more time left to associate oneself with things that don't equate to a way-shower towards your destiny.

There are plenty of successors, who showed through action, that you may lose focus, not have all the plans figured out or be imperfect, but never lose complete sight of the unadulterated inspiration that comes with reminding themselves of their desire. It doesn't matter how young or old you are. What matters is the ability to transform the words "it's not possible or it is impossible" to "I'm possible because it is possible."

Harland Sanders, the commander behind Kentucky Fried Chicken worked as a gas station clerk, fireman, and insurance salesman before he began his career as a restaurateur at the age of 62. Martha Stewart might've appeared as if she's been free forever, but she didn't catch her big break until she was 40 at the expense of writing her first book. Years later Stewart faced imprisonment, along with other personal highs and lows, but is now worth more than $300 million.

Spend your time cultivating a clear picture of your desire. If you wish for anything and repeatedly add the emotions of unconditional love, then this will produce a supernatural state of mind known as FAITH. Millions of men and women spend their leisure time pressing towards discovering FAITH. Behind their many works, there was the emotion of unconditional love, whether from a woman or a man. This emotion is strong enough to carry the thoughts directed towards your desire through the unfavorable momentum caused by mental setbacks such as laziness and passiveness and allow them to work in one's favor.

For every great thing to happen, something more than possessing a desire is necessary. Specifically defining your vision causes it to press you towards whatever will bring it out in the tangible form.

If you are seeking to expand your awareness about the unwavering power of determination, Hope and Faith, observe the accomplishments of great women and men who have made phenomenal contributions to the human family as driven by these faculties. At the seat of those who projected the uppermost levels of these into the world comes the various symbols of God that exist on Mother Earth including Jesus Christ, Allah, Wakan Tanka, Gautama, Buddha, Krishna and more.

Religion, single-handedly, holds to be one of the most powerful faculties that influence the minds of the human family. The purpose of each symbol of God being the same, but their story slightly varying in degree, each divine being lived miraculous lives led by determination, hope, and faith. Regardless of how many people manipulated, tainted or misrepresented these divine beings, regardless of their reasoning, nothing can replace the great works that have been done in their names on Earth.

The nature and core of their teachings and accomplishments, which include "miracles" were nothing more nor less than a combination of Determination, Hope, and Faith. Unfavorably, many who follow these deities don't understand or exercise neither faith, hope or live their vision as guided by determination.

Your only part in exercising these three powers is to express our desires for a thing which serves the greater good of humanity, integrate that desire into specific steps that will be used to measure the process of attaining it, and then gradually forge yourself into the accordance as guided by God.

Living in the house of religion, mentally, causes the true meaning behind these concepts to be pushed into the realms of illusions. You do not need to pray to God repeatedly, for things you desire because God already knows what you desire. In fact, God put the desire in you to be born through you. This holds to be true because the answer to the manifestation of any desire is to behave according to faith not by talking, but according to faith while walking." Walk it like you talk as if your mouth has legs."

You will not transmute the desire given to you by God into the physical reality by establishing a specific day of the week, to tell God what you need, and not remember God for the remainder of the week. You will not excite God by merely spending hours in your closet, on your knees, or in a standing position praying to God, if you take no action towards the manifestation towards the instructions.

Praying is a powerful tool, that attributes to the unfolding of phenomenal outcomes, but prayer is designed as a form of communication to shed light on our vision and heighten your faith, but it is not your prayers that make your desires become tangible. To experience true freedom, it is imperative that we store this truth in the depths of our minds. Prayer is used to assure a grip of your vision, to manifest it into physical form and provide you with the faith that permits you to do so.

Transforming any creation into the physical form will require action.

From the moment you had the first thought of that which you desire strongly, in mind, spoke on this desire, whether with or without a clear strategy and went seeking for ways to make that come true, you've exercised determination, hope, and faith.   However, imagine the outcome of possessing a desire without the ability to take the necessary action that will allow you to receive what you ask for. There is only one force in the world that can transmute your desires into physical reality. That force is called ACTION.

In the pursuit of action, the directions on your journey become clearer. Surely, there are many symbols of God on Mother Earth, but how effective are any of them without ACTION. There will come a day when people of all colors, cultures, and creeds will see the truth. The entire world will discover the answer to the unanswered life questions that they've been seeking. Well if you are one whose been searching and seeking for the TRUTH, praying and crying aloud to God for answers and still haven't received a clear answer, this section is just for you. And if your reading this book and you are one of those people, just focus on this section, consider everything else a bonus. But the one truth in the entire Universe is that "Actions are our Savior." After holding onto your desire, feed it with time, feed it finances, feed it with building your leadership muscle, feed it with time, feed it with energy, feed it with risk, feed it with Action, after action, after action so that it can be born through you, and then the world sees it.

Lights, Camera, Action is a popular phrase that is used during cinematography, as a cue to the members of a film crew at the beginning of a take. Think of your vision as a mental movie with God as the film director. Somewhere in your makeup, there is a gift that will reveal itself in the form of a talent, hobby, or skill, which just like a LIGHT when it is switched on, it draws people to you and like staring through the lenses of a CAMERA, makes you more visible and affects the way people see you, whether favorable or unfavorable.   But with continuous ACTIONS, success produces more freedom, just as much as without ACTION, failure produces more limitation.

Let's do an overview of the unstoppable force created by Determination, Hope, and Faith as it is made visible through the life of nationally known people of all cultural backgrounds. Martin Luther King of Georgia, his story displays one of the most breath-taking stories known to mankind on the limitation that can be broken when one is under the influence of Determination, Hope, and Faith. Dr. King created more influence than any person on the planet at this time and he did this without having an abundance of tools, such as money, weapon, military forces, etc. Martin did not have a rich bank account, he did not recruit armed soldiers to strike against those who opposed his mission, but he had power and influence. How did he gain so much power and influence?

Power and influence were supernatural side effects of applying the fundamental keys of will power to the "desire" that was within himself. Through his constant effort to communicate that desire to the world, the efforts turned into millions of people around the world, following his message.

Martin Luther has achieved something phenomenal, through putting into action "a Desire" that NO President of the United States has ever achieved through abducting warlike tactics or merely being elected. He achieved the heroic accolade of pioneering millions of minds to move information, as one mind.

Out of experiences driven by Action, great leaders have risen and will continue to rise as leaders of all industries. Throughout history, there have been many more great pioneers who were driven by the wheels of action. Crazy Horse of South Dakota was deemed as a regular, Oglala Lakota, Native American until he forged his life into his vision and later went to lead Lakota warriors to victories against the United States Federal Government. Mahatma Gandhi of India did not own a home, did not have money, but he gained astounding influence and power by putting determination, hope, and faith into action.

The understanding of the term "leader" is due for refinement. The ways of measuring a leader, based upon the upper class, by using a combination of money and power to gain respect, will be replaced by the favorable fundamentals of Determination, Hope, and FAITH. Men and women who practice these concepts in action form will be recognized as TRUE LEADERS. They will not receive recognition based on the amount of money they've acquired, their level of education or the color of their skin. They will only be recognized as a leader based on their ability to give to the people of Mother Earth and do it without sacrificing their integrity, honor, and soul, at the expense of getting rich. They must reflect the difference between value and worth.

Perhaps one of the most significant things of all is to be leaders whose exercise and embody the same fundamentals utilized by Martin Luther King, Mahatma Gandhi, Crazy Horse, and many others. Only by this method will followers get from their leaders and vice versa the momentum of complete synergy in its purest and most extraordinary form.

Surely, civilization has produced a sufficient number of human beings who chose not to follow their vision. They will spread the same fear, doubt, and negativity on your vision as they've spread on their own. Despite the magnitude of paralyzing impressions, you must be willing to continue to walk alone. You must be willing to honor your desires to be free and willpower is necessary to do so.

If you are one of those who have wondered how the readings in this chapter will be enlightening, attune to the readings of this section. If you have any doubt that you can experience freedom, prosperity, perfect harmony and abundance, the awareness shared in this chapter should dispel that doubt, because you can obviously see in the story of these heroic way-showers, the fundamentals of this book described in action.

BE WILLING to have the Power

Following this path will leave you walking alone, but you must be willing to be the only one that sees your vision. You must be willing to do it by yourself. You must be willing to understand that your vision will not be clear to anyone except you. You must be willing to be your own teammate. Keep in mind, you must be willing to be your employer and employee. You must be willing to be the key and door. You must be willing to be the one that doesn't get support from their family. You must be willing to be the "one" that everyone calls, weird, abnormal, or strange. This period will exist just for a moment. That moment maybe a day, a year, a month or might be ten years. But you must be willing to "know that the reason your vision is not clear to anyone else is because it was only given to you."

The incredible fundamental of willpower over a desire holds to be an important feature of the remarkable picture that you see in your vision. To experience freedom, in an experimental way, do not concern your willpower with any forces that you can't control or dictate.

Release the habit of attaching your will power to a thing you cannot control. It is not favorable to apply your will power to others, women, and men, for the sake of getting them to do what you want or need to be done.

It is extremely unfavorable to pressure another by the application of mental force as it is illegal to pressure them by physical force. By captivating people by physical power to do things you want them to do lessens them to slavery; absorbing people by mental tactics fulfills the exact same thing: the only difference is the employed method.

If you are considered a force when your physically force to bondage, limitation, and hard labor, then you are to be considered a slave when you are mentally forced to poverty, force, constrain, limitation, doubt, and fear. There is no distinction in the concept.

It is not favorable to utilize your willpower on another, even "if you are trying to help, for you cannot truly help someone unless you've first helped yourself. It took a long time to digest this truth, but it became clearer when assured by an experience shared with a homeless man, concerning his daily routine and how he made his living.

He shared that he would arrive at the local convenience store every morning at 6 am and dress in a manner that appeared inconveniently ill. With him, he carried a hand-crafted sign that said, "I AM HOMELESS, HELP ME (GOD LOVES YOU)", and a glass jar to collect his payment from those who are willing to help him.

He was consistent in making almost $50 a day. He would reel people in with his sign and they would pay.

I asked him, "What do you do with the money you collect?"

(Suddenly, an extended silence came over our conversation)

He said, "I don't think I should tell, but I feel comfortable with you. I am addicted to heroin. So, I use my money to purchase my fixing."

How much did those people help him? Commonly we think that it is enough to act as led by good intentions, but don't know the awareness to match. Giving without awareness can be just as harmful as giving with negative intentions. Although their intentions in giving may be golden, did it really serve the greater good of the homeless man to give him the money? In fact, in your attempts to exercise your willpower through gestures known as help, without awareness, your outcome will oppose the reasoning beyond your actions.

It is not necessary to use your willpower as an influence to get things to come to you.

Those types of actions will over stand God's place in your life and would ultimately create pain and suffering and activate separation from who you've been created to be, which leaves you in a state of mind known as Separate in Nature.

It is not necessary to continually urge God to give you things. Use your willpower to improve that which you already have, and God will bring more things to you.

You do not need to use your willpower to defeat the name of another religious deity, being, or pray for and ask outside influences to participate in your doings.

God is friendly to ALL, including every color that makes up the supernatural symbol of the human family, known as the rainbow. And God desires to give you what you want, need, and desire. To experience freedom, it is important that you use your willpower on yourself.

When you are fully aware of what to call to mind and action, how to act and react, or what to imagine and reflect, then your will power is going to be a necessity to execute the favorable things. This is the most practical use of the will power in our day to day lives, which is necessary to foresee and transmute our desires into physical reality. Because our will power is what's designed to keep us on the right path.

Utilize your willpower to keep your eyes on the prize and behaving in a manner that's in harmony with what it takes to acquire that which you desire.

Make your best effort not to project your willpower or unfavorable thoughts into things or people.

Keep yourself in a space that permits you to move towards your destiny.

Create mental pictures of that which you desire in your mind and hold onto that vision with determination, hope, and faith and use your actions as the voice that communicates that you are staying on the right path.

The more Hope and faith are magnified, the more determination you will have to be set free because you will choose only positive actions as the solution to every challenge and you will not intensify or counterbalance your challenges with negative actions.

The thought of your desire, embraced with determination, smothered with hope and faith, guided with actions, and guarded by willpower creates the formula that will serve people of all nations throughout the cosmos.

As the momentum of this miraculous undertaking spreads through the cells of your brain, disrupting the negative thoughts that hold you captive, then gradually you will start to move closer towards the truth, as it relates to ALL. Miracles are real. All living things, all unseen things and all things imagined are used as platforms for miracles to be performed through. As you begin to attune to an energetic stance that allows miracles to flow into your personal experience, you will learn that everything in the Universe, whether good or bad is designed to work for you. in fact, Miracles are heightened when they are born through unfavorable conditions.

It is perhaps being unaware that all things, good or bad, are designed to work in your favor, which causes most who seek to experience freedom to give up. A negative thought, outcome or condition is designed to be the fuel that helps you move towards your positive outcome. Confusion, doubt, and uncertainty hold a significant place. It is by experiencing confusion, doubt, and uncertainty that we develop that mental state that allows freedom and abundance to move towards us. For those who are unaware that negative emotions are designed to be fuel, they will give unnecessary time and thought momentum to fears, doubts, and unfavorable beliefs. Every day you spend in negativity, every second your mindset rests in doubt, every minute you spend worrying, shifts you away from a state of alignment that permits the manifestation of miracles through you. All things are designed to work together in favor of the greater good of those who will allow them to do so. Notice how the word allow is used, which points out the reason we must use our willpower.

Complete knowingness holds a shielding significance, as your knowingness protects your thoughts and your knowingness will be measured, to a varying degree, by the way, you perceive things and how you respond. It is very important that you direct your awareness. In doing so, willpower will come in use.

Use your willpower to decide what things your awareness should be secured in. If you desire to become free, you must not devote your attention to limitation, poverty or resistance.

Each time you focus on poverty, the possibilities of freedom become smaller and thoughts of limitation become greater. For a moment, the only heartfelt proof of your progress will be your enhanced emotional state, but with each passing day, your momentum will continue to change until there is an obvious tipping point.

Things are not obtained by associating with their contradictory, opposite or inverse. Winning is never to be attained by thinking about losing. Losing weight is not to be promoted by stuffing your stomach with doughnuts and reading the recipes over and over. No one will experience freedom by studying contradictory thoughts and overly examining poverty and limitation.

Do not communicate about limitation, do not study it or even associate yourself with it. Regardless of what the causes are, detach yourself from poverty and limitation.

Focus your thoughts on the healing and curing of this condition.

Avoid spending time in sympathetic work or feeling bad for others. All sympathy tends to influence you to get attached to the feelings of others doing something for you that you are supposed to do for yourself.

I am not trying to convey that you should be close-minded, heartless, mean and deny offering support to the needy and less fortunate, but it is favorable to attempt to overstand poverty by using any of the ordinary methods. Divorce poverty by leaving it behind you and all that relates to it, engage the present by realizing the greatest gift is in the opportunities you create today and marry a promising future through "making good" usage of the tools you've been given to fulfill your calling.

Be set free; that is the most promising way to help those stuck in poverty and limitation.

We will not be able to hold the mental picture of freedom if our minds are filled with thoughts of limitation. Do not listen to music or watch television which gives circumstantial narrations of those who's found comfort in the mental confines of poverty, limitation, and so on. Do not read books or articles that fill your mind with the portrayal of wanting, neediness, and suffering. We will not be able to serve the greater good of the less fortunate by saturating our awareness in thoughts associated with these things, because the knowledge basis and awareness projected and reflected from these things does not teach people to rise above limitation.

The way to rise above limitation is not by associating your mind with thoughts of limitation and resistance but by allowing images of freedom, wealth, abundance, and prosperity into the minds shadowed by poverty.

You are not abandoning or turning your back on those overtaken by poverty when you disassociate yourself with things that fill your mind with images of suffering.

Mental restrictions will be done away with, not by increasing the number of people who pressed towards and think about mental restrictions, but by increasing the amount of less fortunate people who finds fortune with determination, hope, and faith to become free.

The less fortunate do not need welfare and voluntary organizations, they need empowerment. Welfare and voluntary organizations send them comfort in their survival state of mind or feed them a moment of happiness that makes them forget about their reality for a few hours, instead of providing them with the tools to living a better quality of life. Empowerment will cause them to elevate their minds out of poverty. If you desire to help the poor, demonstrate to them the tools to become free: prove that this work by getting free yourself.

The only way in which poverty will ever be dismissed from Mother Earth is influencing a huge and continuous number of humans to exercise the fundamental keys of this book. Every human soul who profess "life is a struggle", "if it easy, it isn't meant to be", "It's too hard", and statements of that nature as reality, will pave a way in which they have to put others down in order to rise up; but the human soul who experiences freedom the way God designed will pave a way that uplifts all and inspires others to continually uplift the people who make up the human family.

We must allow ourselves to be taught the way to experience freedom by choice, instead of being forged into it through unfavorable realities of being restrained. Freedom does not occur in one's life because of good luck, hard work, or favoritism. When we can accomplish the feeling of freedom before the physical evidence of your desires shows itself to you, the evidence must come and will continue to come if you maintain the thought pattern for the extraordinary thing.

In the absence of poverty, freedom is making its way to you. For a while, your only sign of evidence will be your improved emotional state of being. If you will let that be enough, taking no scores of miraculous signs, the miracle will show up. Let's allow ourselves to feel appreciation and eagerness for what's coming.

You have the power. Use the power that God has blessed you with. Use your will power to keep your mind away from music, readings, televisions or people that talk about poverty and limitation. You have more power than the button used to turn on the television. But it's difficult to keep remote control of yourself or tell-a-vision if you've hit the OFF button of abundance and the ON button of misery.

Chapter 4

Doing your First Job

(Make your Thoughts a Priority)

Doing the first job is a phrase that prioritizes the freedom and fulfillment which comes with pursuing your passion, aside from working manual labor. Stated another way "doing the first job" is doing the only thing you've been created to do. It is the business of action that exist between the part of the mind that's conditioned to ordinary and that which desires to experience life on an extraordinary plain.

Most professions, whether they offer a small portion or large quantities of money, confine or limit you to concentrate on and become an expert in one particular skill, but they don't make it a habit of realizing the relationship you have with your thoughts and fullest potential.

Although getting a job, before doing the first job will allow you to accumulate money, through continually engaging in things that interfere with the job you were created to do, whether through practical action or spontaneous volunteering ,you are putting a definite end to the accumulation that you are designed to receive by doing the first job.

Your job is not to make money, it is to earn it, through being yourself and mixing intelligence with organized faith, determination, dedication, and then celebration. The inability to interpret the beliefs that millions of people follow as truth or even those who speak as if they do not follow it, but they have not taken any actions that displays their desire to transmute the thoughts, humans are collectively unhappy. "You should go to high school, then work a 9 to 5 job and then retire at 65 years old", is a polluted belief that has unfavorably affected the human family. The truth is nothing of that sort. The truth will always have more power than a lie and if you're not fully aware of the one truth, then you are subject to deeming a lie as the truth.

Your job is to give your talent.

Thought is a creative force or the driving force which causes creativity to be activated. "Doing the first job" will bring freedom to you, but you must not rely, only on thoughts, disregarding the importance of action. That's always the bridge that most great thinkers and dreamers never cross; the negligence to connect thought with action.

God is the only being that can create directly by thought, without the use of mental processes or human labor. Humankind must not only think but their actions must be an add-on to their thoughts.

"I believe I can fly" would've been another good idea or thought had not the Wrights Brothers taken actions that propelled them towards it, instead of, like many, hoping, praying, wishing for a thing and believing that it will seek its way into manifestation. Wilbur and Orville later became the two inventors credited for building the world's first successful airplane.

Due to the underlying force that thoughts carry for you, it's important to make it your personal business that you must discover how to direct your thoughts toward you, you must learn to arrange your thoughts so that you are mentally prepared to receive "it" when it comes closer to you and as you move closer towards it. Thoughts give all things, constructive and destructive momentum towards transmuting your desires into a physical reality, but your actions may be that such they are disallowing your desires to physically reach you. You are not to take this matter lightly, nor deny it for the sake of assuring a comfort zone, but you must give your time and energy to your thoughts then your thoughts will exist outside of you.

You must discover the master within that can direct your thoughts. You only ascend as high as your thoughts, you can only elevate by being larger than your present state of mind and no one elevates past their present state of mind by not leaving unfinished, any of the work pertaining to the laboratory in their brain.

The world is developed by those who are willing to discover the master, which is included in doing the first job.

If any human acquires freedom, financially, spiritually, or emotionally, without doing the first job, you will see there will be a huge "going backward." Those who do not do the first job will smile and project a high-class image upon society as they work their highly paid government, federal, or local jobs, all along carrying a feeling of emptiness that makes them feel like a burden to themselves and the same to others.

The true meaning of progress gets tarnished by those who instead of doing the first job, belong to some form of manual labor. Although it may appear, as if they are "free" and fulfilled, when they are riding in their nice cars or cashing their checks, they really suppress the fact that they belong to a lower plane of life. And they spend their time keeping up with the image that manual labor projects instead of "doing the first job" and moving towards true freedom.

It has become common amongst the human family to take on so many responsibilities that eventually we lack the ability to respond to the voice of our desire that's intended to be born through us. This paradigm leads to much dis-ease amongst the human family as we find comfort in the misery of our work environment. This truth vividly reveals itself in the life of Allon McCoy, the highest-paid executive of Internal Affairs in the state of North Carolina. I was fortunate enough to land a personal interview with him only to discover the shocking truths. I opened the interview with the question, "How does it feel when you deposit your check in the bank knowing it has six commas?"

"I am an extremely well-paid man but, to be honest, I hate my job. Every day I battle with myself to continue to work there. Sometimes battling with myself leaves me with severe migraines and stomach pains from dreading the thought of going to work. My benefits package and compensation are the only reasons I am working because I owe my earnings to my two children including my six-year-old daughter and twelve-year-old son. If not for the benefits package and compensation, I would've been left the job. I often wonder why is it that despite making so much money, I am extremely unhappy with my life".

ANSWER: Place a check next to the statements that apply to you.

----- I don't like my job, but I love the MONEY.

----- My job situation will get better, I just got to hang on.

----- I don't like my career choice, but I'm pretty good at it.

----- Changing jobs would be more difficult than continuing to work here.

----- I doubt I will make as much money in another company.

----- I deserve better than these conditions.

----- I know it's not my dream job, but it's better than nothing.

----- My focus is more on the negatives, with respects to the potential of changing jobs, than the positives.

----- My family, peers and/or associates tell me I would be a fool to give up my job.

----- Work is made to be hard, so I guess I asked for this.

If you've checked just one of the above statements, then you've merely experienced a bad day. If you've checked two or more, then you've found comfort in MISERY which is the definition of peace with respects to the outside world, influenced by a desire to uphold the traditional ways of being, thinking, and operating. "Whatever you connect to is what you become." Therefore, by attaching yourself to a job that creates in the vibration of MISERY, then you become Misery.

All living organisms were created with more abilities and tasks than it could interpret in its root plane of existence, in order to manifest these greater abilities and tasks, organisms must develop a higher plane of existence which will lead to a transformation and emergence of a renewed organism.

Most people who fail to do or procrastinate about doing the first job, are or become, easily influenced by the opinions of others. They allow television (tell-lie-vision) and the voices of negativity to do the thinking for them. People's opinions are none of your business, but everyday people accept them as permission slips. If you are influenced by opinions, when you make a choice, you will not be successful in any commitment, much less in that of transmuting your desires from your mind into your physical reality.

If you are influenced by the opinions of others, you will not have any desire to pursue your own thoughts. Perhaps, people have delayed for too long in making the truth about opinions visible.

An opinion is called an opinion for a reason. Listen to how the word is pronounced o-pinion. When expressed, "opinions" are thoughts to help bridge the gap in making decisions. Commonly opinions are urged when one is experiencing doubt because they have not mastered their own mind. The truth is with accurate analysis, that most people in the world are closed-minded. As revealed in the word, an opin (open) ion is supposed to be expressed from an open mind.

An opinion (open) is only a true opinion if it is expressed from an open mind. Most have grown closed-minded as a result of lessons taken from their experiences and thereby that are not able to offer a TRUE opinion. What they are offering is a closed-minded outlook and if your mind absorbs this, which it will because innocently your mind is typically open when you asking for an opinion, you face the possibility of being dismayed from your truth because you are now deeming their false truth as true.

And when you listen to the opinions of others around you, be mindful of the thought pattern that their lifestyle reflects and how it relates to what you are trying to accomplish. In other words, do not EXPECT someone who's never played professional basketball to give you non-bias advice about how to become a professional basketball player. Have you ever had a decision to make and you decided you would pull from the opinions of the people that are close to you and every one of them gave you different answers? This one said to do it, this one said don't do it, this one said to do it but do it this way, this one said don't do it and don't do it ever and this one said to do it but wait for a few years, and they literally drive you out of your mind because they cannot give you advice that is beneficial to you. They can only give you guidance about you, which is beneficial to them. Because everyone must factor in how their desires for you fit into your life experience.

Everyone is selfishly oriented; you cannot help but to see through the eyes of self. For example, when you go to the car dealer and say to him "Which car do you think is the best for me?", he will respond by telling you which car is best for him to sell to you. He doesn't have the ability to consider all the struggles, sacrifices, obstacles, and conditions that led up to your discovery of what you desire. If you leave it to him, he will sell you what works best for him every single time.

When you go to the doctor, dentist, therapist, or anyone who has something that they are offering you, they cannot help but to factor in their relationship with you as they are helping you. And that's not a bad thing at all. Certainly, this truth is not mentioned to imply that they have negative intentions or are not meaning well in their efforts to assist you. What I am saying is that every time you interact with someone else, it creates a lot of vibrational thought interference because no one can guide you accurately. And when you ask them, even when they do their very best to guide you, however it turns out, you almost always end up resenting whatever it is that's shared with you because if you are not in vibrational harmony with what you are asking for, IT CAN'T COME. It doesn't matter how precisely you attempt to follow anyone else's advice. You will never expand your journey, you cannot get from where you are to where you would like to be by asking anyone outside yourself, what is the proper path. Religion cannot give it to you, your mother can not give it to you, or your job will not give it to you. No one can give you accurate guidance, but no one needs to because you have a supernatural built-in guidance system.

Anything acquired without Doing the First Job is generally unappreciated and dishonored. This suggests why we got so little out of our life experiences. The insight one acquires from the self-discovery of "Doing the First Job" bridges the gap between merely desiring a thing and acquiring that which you desire. If you are one that's stuck in that space, then make it a priority to practice the thoughts of the things you desire, and they will show up in your experiences. General education Institutes are highly successful at projecting the exact opposite modus operandi. General education requires payments and fees, after payment, it induces us to feel that we must finish the course, whether we are performing well or not.

The truth is you cannot lead from behind. If you are not in your vibraction, then you have nothing solid to give. Building relationships outside of your vibraction is as pouring from an empty cup.

Common causes not to do the first job

Cheating on your Own Thoughts

By not committing to your thoughts through making harmonious decisions and choices that support them. Take nothing into consideration in your decision making except your thoughts, truth, and the source of all creation. Do not follow the influence of other's opinions because their opinions will influence you not to be who you've been created to be, and you will spend your life seeking because you've fallen out of harmony with your purpose.

Family, Close Friends and Relatives

While not doing so intentionally, they typically disable one through cultural beliefs, opinions, and sometimes through sarcasm, which is meant to provoke laughter. Millions of men and women carry a sense of emptiness with them all through life because, some person who meant well or had good intention but was ignorant to the truth, compressed thoughts in their mind, that they begin to redeem as truth and it eradicated their self-esteem.

The NEED to Make Money

Most people who set out to accumulate money, do so without "doing the first job". Consequently, they get involved in manual labor without doing the first job. As a result, their minds become fixated by the opinions of their bosses, commitments to manual labor, and they permit money to think for them. You cannot make money; you can only earn it. Overly feeding your mind the thought that "you need money" is a direct sign that a person has not done the first job. After doing the first job, one will discover that you don't need money because you are worth more. What's necessary is the proper platform to share your gifts with the world, which will, in turn, bring money to you, instead of you having to chase money from day to day.

Not Using Your Mind

You were born with a mind of your own. The mind is the greatest power in all of creation. Many would say that God is the greatest power. I concur that God is the greatest power, but the mind is the greatest power in all creation; God being creator and mind being creation. Use your mind and make authentic decisions. If you need information, advice or facts ONLY take it from other people who have "mastered" the area of knowledge that you are searching such as a mentor, life coach, or an Awareness Psychotherapist. Make up your own mind, don't let people own your mind and make up your mind for you. If not, you will become a consequence of someone else's experience.

Improper Dependency (Depending on someone else for a thing that you are supposed to give yourself)

The characteristics of your mentor, life coach, or Awareness Psychotherapist may vary, but they all should do a qualitative amount of talking and listening. Keep your eyes and ears open and your mouth closed when you exchange dialogue. A genuine wisdom keeper does not teach you to rely on them for motivation, they don't display you have to go through them to experience God, or they don't give you just enough knowledge just to keep you coming back to depend on them. A true wisdom keeper does not give you just enough knowledge to keep you depending on them. A true wisdom keeper does not motivate, but they empower. They demonstrate practical skills and tools that can be implemented to remind you that you have the power. True Wisdom keepers serve to Cure, meaning you'll possess the tools to fix yourself and you don't have to continually see them after business affairs, but the common way shower teaches healing, meaning, you are momentarily fixed but you must depend on them in order to experience freedom.

Not Pursuing Wonder

The pursuit of wonder builds a genius. Have you ever wondered why you keep getting the same results over and over again? Have you ever wondered why you have the same habits as your grandmother, grandfather, mother, or father? Have you ever wondered why individuals, who have extraordinary levels of education, they have degrees coming off the end of the business card, are not doing very well, while others who have never stepped foot inside of a school, are making millions of dollars and building giant corporations, that are doing phenomenal, all around the world? These are all good questions. Those who don't pursue wonder, close their minds to discovering their true plan or purpose that is hidden in the answers of the unanswered questions. If you don't pursue wonder, you deprive yourself of many opportunities to acquire useful knowledge, wisdom, and freedom.

Do a lot of Pointless Talking

Every time you open our mouth, you display the lack of knowledge or your exact level of knowledge. Although the attainment of knowledge is important, the application holds to be just as valuable, if not more. Most people do more talking than taking action. Make it one of your personal decisions to do less talking and do more walking (take action). There is a reason we were born with two legs and one mouth.

When asked the common question, what's on your mind? You reply, "NOTHING"

That response is never true. In fact, we have an abundance of things in our minds. In that instance, we were focused on our past relationships, bills that we must pay, our dreams that we are not pursuing. and at that moment it gets stuck in our head. Even with the presence of these wondering thoughts, we still respond by saying, "NOTHING" because, in all actuality, we felt like it was not important or pointless to say," it wasn't something worth sharing. During this moment our thoughts were roaming from place to place without a fixed plan and we just happen to get caught during these times. Apparently replying with "all I can think about is how my dreams are going to come true, my bills, and my ex" isn't a favorable answer. Unfortunately, if you do not do the first job, then you will see the one-word response "NOTHING" as truth, which it never is. Deeming a lie as truth is a consequence of not doing the first job.

Before you can be assured about your ability to "Do the first Job", you will be required to know specialized awareness of the message, donation, and contribution which you intend to offer to people of Mother Earth. Perhaps another way to express that is to say you have to discover your true self, stay true to who you are, and never allow anyone to make you different or think differently about what it is you've been created to be.

Jesus Christ showed evidence that he personally did the first job when confronted by Pilate. He confessed that the primary purpose he had in life was to be recognized as a King (John18:37). He was not afraid of offending those loyal to Caesar. The special awareness, which he required was that things that controlled external culture had to be shifted for a true transformation to occur. He was able to raise powerful men of God, who alongside him, served as a bridge between the group of tough and strong: he demonstrated the aid of the "Mightiness Group."

Signs you are doing the first job

Willing to die for your Purpose

Life is not worth living if there is no GREATER cause equally worth dying for. To live a better quality of life, you must find something you're willing to die for. Meaning let go of what you've been tempted to be and surrender to who you've been created to be.

Motivated by Passion

Passion is a combination of love and hate. Any great leader knows that anything they are truly passionate about, there will be days they love it and days they hate that they love it so much, but the mixture of these two emotions creates an unconditional love that sustains and permits you to be great.

Run Towards the "Truth"

The primary purpose you have is to discover the truth and walk in it. Do not be afraid to walk in your truth. Understand that the way-showers of the previous generations had to discover the truth to attribute the efficient change to the human family. Furthermore, it is your turn to carry the torch that serves as a guiding light, leading those who seek direction.

Frequently Ask Questions

The best way to discover the answers to life's unanswered questions is to ask questions. In fact, one of the best ways to learn or be taught is by asking questions. When people answer questions, it reveals how much they really know, what's in their minds, their motives, and associates them in the process of the unfolding that enables them to remember and learn better.

Have Goals, Tasks, and Objectives

"Progress equals happiness." If someone has no goals or mission, they will never know if they've made progress or accomplished anything. If someone has no greater mission or purpose, they become clueless and unaware of what their destiny will be. It is imperative to operate with objectives and goals which enable you to fulfill the tasks and objectives with a day to day understanding of the who, what, where, when, and how to function.

Invest time in that which bears fruit

Wisdom, in decision making, is displayed by how someone invests their time. Invest your time, only in things that bear prosperity, abundance or wellbeing instead of spending time with the crowds. Investing time in that which bears fruit is an important part of getting the most results from your labor.

Confront Conflict

Conflict does not mean "attitude", "the Use of physical force", or "be dramatic" as a means of representing your heart through your thoughts. It is important to confront conflict as a means of keeping your inner being cleansed because avoiding conflict will result in an emotional buildup that will affect one's ability to rise in empowerment.

Marry yourself, then Engage the World

Traditionally, the world projects the standard of relationships in the order to get engaged, then get married. The consequence of this way of thinking has led us to a world where people don't "know themselves" instead they gain an understanding of self through experiences with others such as their husband, wife, or fiancé. Marry yourself then Engage the world. All your life, you've been and always will be in a relationship with yourself and in order to have a successful relationship with others, you must learn to have a successful relationship with yourself. Chaos is always the result of doing it, the opposite way.

Doing the first job requires you to differentiate between general knowledge and specialized awareness. General knowledge, regardless of the quantity or type it may be, is not beneficial concerning acquiring freedom. Colleges, universities, and schools, all around the world, practice every form of general knowledge. Most of the professors or teachers in the institutions have no freedom. Although they specialize in teaching general knowledge, they do not specialize in the application or usage of knowledge.

It takes specialized awareness aside from general knowledge, to discover ways to organize knowledge and distribute it amongst the human family through practical steps. Millions of people across the world falsely believe that "knowledge is power" or "knowledge is the new money." Neither statement holds to be true. Knowledge only declares "it's possible" to have power or money when it is structured into specific steps and directed towards a specific goal.

One of the biggest mistakes ALL education systems known to modern-day society will be discovered in the failure of educational systems to teach students how to structure ,retain, and apply the knowledge they acquire.

Many people amongst the human family make the common error of presuming that Bob Proctor had merely shreds of "schooling" because he is not a pioneer of education. Those who perfectly make that mistake, do not know Bob Proctor, nor do they fully understand the true meaning of education.

An educated person is not, automatically, created as the result of possessing a large quantity of general knowledge and understanding. An educated person is one who has "Done the first Job" of expanding the capacity of their mind in a manner that they may acquire anything they desire, think, express, or choose to permit themselves to transmute into its physical equivalence without disobeying the law or overstepping the rights of others. Bob Proctor is an exact representation of the true meaning of the term "educated."

The word educate is derived from the Latin word "educo", meaning to form, inspire, or extract from within. "Doing the first Job" is doing the work within yourself which will thereby make you ready and prepared when the evidence of Doing the first job appears in your physical reality.

During the 1960s, as appeared to himself, another high school dropout with a resume of dead-end jobs and a future clouded by debt. Bob was under the influence of those limiting thoughts until one book was placed in his hands - Think and Grow Rich - which planted the seed of hope in his mind.

In just a few months, along with the help of his mentor Earl Nightingale, Bob's life was transformed. Within a years' time, Bob was making more than $100,00 and soon surpassed the million-dollar mark.

Many asked Mr. Proctor a great variety of questions pertaining to how he was able to summon such miraculous conditions without having no form of education, no business experience, or without having a solidified supporting cast. All these people included psychologists, psychiatrists, behavioral scientists, and more in over 100 different countries all over the world. All of them who possess knowledge pertaining to life and general education deemed Bob Proctor as he was, in the mind, ignorant.

Bob Proctor would reply to such questions as the following: "Have you ever wondered why you have so many of the habits and idiosyncrasies as mom and dad has? Have you ever wondered why you are getting the same results over and over again? Have you ever asked yourself why individuals who have a phenomenal education, they have DEGREES, coming off the end of the business card, are not doing so well while others who maybe have never saw the inside of a school, are earning millions of dollars and building giant organizations, that's doing all kinds of good all over the world? If you really want to answer the questions you have asked or any of the other questions you have been asking me, let me remind you that "Seek and go find is good advice." If you're looking for it, you're going to find it without a doubt, there is solid reasoning to that response".

Now, will you gently allow me to expand on the allegoric meaning which this chapter is devoted to making clearer? There is a master that resides in you that's allowed to be summoned to your aid, at your will. This master knows the answer to all your questions concerning life in all aspects and can only be discovered by devoting time and effort to finding it or seeking (seek –in). Any person who possesses special awareness knows to look inside themselves to get knowledge which they need or how to apply the special awareness that the master possesses and how to organize knowledge into specific plans of action. This master can only be discovered by "Doing the First Job."

Through the aid of this Master, Bob Proctor had in his possession, the knowledge and specialized awareness necessary to allow him to secure a life of freedom; financially, spiritually, and emotionally.

Surely Bob Proctor was not the only one who had the sufficient capacity of "Doing the first Job."

Bob Proctor only had two months of high school during his pursuit of becoming a millionaire, motivational speaker, bestselling author, and co-founder of Life Success Publishing proved he did not lack education, neither did he live a life marked by limitation.

John D. Rockefeller Jr. dropped out of high school just two months before graduation, but he has managed to do well by himself, with respects to his freedom.

This specific section should rekindle a renewed flame of hope and inspiration to the human being who has the desire to acquire a thing but has not possessed enough of the necessary tools, education, money, or support to manifest such a thing that will require specialized awareness . We sometimes go through life declined by doubt that comes with not being educated, not having a faithful support group, and not having money to support your desires. The human who can structure and pioneer a mighty group of people who possess greater awareness useful in the gaining of our freedom is just as much a possessor of education than an educator in any group. Keep this in mind, if you feel declined by doubt because your education system has limited you.

Special awareness is compressed in the most genuine and priceless, gestures of gratitude that may be offered. Do the first job, if you do this, you become the storehouse of special awareness as well. You will also realize that you've always been a student because life is the greatest teacher.

There are millions of people, all over the country, who are interested in furthering their knowledge at colleges and universities, but they are unable to afford tuition, were not smart enough, already have a load of bills, and many more reasons. Now I stress the point to you that, the true education comes from the lessons learned from obstacles, pain, suffering, and challenges. These experiences are designed to mold you into self-mastery over your thoughts and feelings. Mother Earth is the one true classroom. Every human is here to obtain a master's degree in life. Once you've mastered or in pursuit of furthering the fundamentals of dwelling on Mother Earth, then you are considered "Doing the First Job."

Prerequisites of Doing the First Job

At first hand, configure the sort of knowledge you require and the reason whereby it's necessary because one's reasoning will always influence their reality. To a large degree, identifying your major purpose in life, the goal or desire towards which you are pressing toward, will help determine what knowledge is necessary, which will allow you to drive your efforts towards specifics. With those fundamental keys established, the next task is that you acquire valid information about the reliable sources of knowledge that are in-formation with the goal. The most significant of these include:

- Your own Personal experiences and education
- Intelligence, knowledge, and education learned through association with others (mentors, life coaches, and role models).
- Public Libraries (Read books, articles, and references in which you will find information that is in-formation with your desired outcome)

- Elevated Awareness Courses (through on-line, seminars, home study, or any form of awareness that caters towards your specific subject matter)
- Technology (Google and others makes it "difficult not to have access to knowledge")

As knowledge is obtained and expanded, it must be structured and put into practical application, towards a specific purpose, through practical strategy. "Knowledge has no power unless it's placed into application towards a task or because that serves the greater good of humanity. This is one of the reasons why "doing the first job" holds more importance than getting a college degree or any other higher forms of education.

If you are second-guessing or questioning whether doing more schooling, first configure the reason for which you are pursuing the knowledge you are pressing towards, then find out if this type of awareness can be claimed, from dependable sources.

Extraordinary outcomes, in all walks of life, require an everlasting commitment to knowledge. Those who do not "Do the first Job" make the common error of assuming that gaining knowledge is over when one graduates or finishes at an educational institute. Although earning a degree as a result of schooling is an extraordinary accomplishment: The truth is that schooling is just another representation of a path one can take towards acquiring experiential knowledge.

To every ending, there is a beginning. With this new dawn of civilization, which began as a result of the ending of the recession, came the mind bogging importance of "Doing the First Job." The goal for today is to do the first job. The astonishing emphasis of "Doing the First Job" is magnified by Professor Dweck and Colleagues, a Psychology professor at Stanford University. Particularly on the college level, student's beliefs about themselves influence their academic performance. The student who believes in their ability to learn and their effort, is active on the campus, interacts well with others, including people who have exceeded the standards in their studies as well as those who did not perform very well, and possesses a tipping edge advantage over the common academic student.

However, in departing or graduating from school, how will having great academic performance serve you in the "REAL WORLD" where job positions are more likely to be offered to those who display this tipping edge advantage.

It is often told that the student that makes the "A Honor Roll" will undeniably be there to get the great opportunity to get a job, but the truth is that most companies not only look at academic performance but community activities, character traits, and hobbies.

This truth is contrast to the mind of a student who's so focused on "proving" they can achieve, instead of "improving "the mindset of the self that is intending to be successful".

Students who don't develop this connection to themselves have a tendency of being overly concerned about their abilities when facing obstacles or challenges. This leads to unfavorable thoughts (e.g. I can't, because I'm not smart enough), feelings, and responses (giving up). On the contrary, students who develop this connection with themselves will interpret the exact obstacles and challenges from an entirely different understanding; merely an opportunity to learn a lesson. This understanding permits them to respond with favorable thoughts, (e.g. I must pay more attention to small details) feelings, (such as the thrill of a challenge) and responses (perseverance). This type of mindset is not taught in traditional educational institutions.

Jeremy Milburn, the business owner of one of the leading industrial companies, once quoted in a conversation we shared concerning tips for students that graduate from college and are looking for a place to work. He said: "Global Drafting is interested in women and men who can perform day to day tasks exceptionally well. For this reason, we highlight qualities of respect, integrity, and character much more than educational background when considering our employees."

Little by little, the truth of what's meant by "Doing the First Job" will unfold itself, as the fundamentals of the concept hold the key to the mastery over our freedom.

Self-expression, Abundance, and Prosperity are necessary to experience true freedom but there are some who will claim that the greatest level of freedom can be measured only by rights, obtaining American citizenship, by getting rich and things of that nature.

Maintain a spirit of open-mindedness and relaxed readiness; while doing so, make it a priority to replace thoughts of poverty with thoughts of abundance. In doing so, you will be "Doing the First Job." College and universities overlook the fact, that ALL manual labor today demands special awareness. One of the most dependable and reliable sources of knowledge available to those who DO the first job Is always available for free. Other schools and institutions give specialized training, ALL throughout the country, on subjects that vary based on cultural background. One advantage of Doing the First Job is that instead of just going to school, you are permitted to become the student and the teacher, you become the greatest athlete and your biggest competitor, you become the counselor, who has rightfully earned their position, but instead of looking for clients, you become your first client. Most schools carry with them fees of meaningless value when compared to the specialized awareness that comes with "Doing the First Job." No matter what color, culture, creed, social status, gender, or ethnicity you are, doing the first job is always free.

Make your thoughts your Top Priority

Expectancy is about simply having the awareness that "this" behavior, brings forth "this" experience. We would like for you to begin to expect the manifestations that come from the pattern of thoughts because that's how all things are created.

Before there is any manifestation, there are strong, constant and consistent thoughts about "it" which one desires. So, to be the intentional creator of your reality, which you are, you must master the art of directing your thoughts, which will inevitably quantify your journey. When you are directing your thoughts, your job is to discover the thoughts that are leading you in the direction of what you desire and what thoughts are leading you in the direction of what you do not want. Once these thoughts are discovered, then acknowledge and replace negative thoughts with positive possibilities.

Expect your life experience to reflect the fulfillment that comes from the pattern of your thoughts. In order to experience freedom, it is important that you accept the existence of this vibrational non-physical realm of creation. And it would be even better if you could see it as your Present-Day Creation. Therefore, when people say, "I don't see any improvement in your life, you can say," my improvement is not visible to those that are outside my vibration." Any they may say, "have you been to the doctor lately?" and you will say "there are no doctors in my vibraction."

The insight one acquires from the self-discovery of Doing the First Job bridges the gap between merely desiring a thing and acquiring that which one desires. General education institutes are highly successful at projecting the exact opposite modus operandi. General education requires payments and fees, after payments, it induces us to feel that we must finish the course, whether we are performing well or not.

I discovered this truth from over 15 years of observation of college students, before and after graduation. After completing five years of college education myself, remarkable discoveries of this awareness became more and more clear. I enrolled in a special training program in Quantum Physics. I finished approximately ten out of the twenty-six lessons in the curriculum until I found myself gradually fading away from my study habits only to "stop" studying. Although I stopped studying, the institution kept charging me and constantly sent bills regardless of whether I was acquiring knowledge or not. I figured since I'm paying for the course, then I might as well complete the course and reap the benefits of the money I paid. I felt obliged to finish school and I finished college and never used my degree, but I learned that a valuable segment of mastery was discovered in experiences where I was urged to pay for something. Although I never used my degree, my college experiences taught me that everything has worth but not everything has value. Therefore, just because it has worth, does not mean that it's worth it. Just because it has worth does not mean it's worth the value of your time, your money and your energy.

In the United States of America, we have what is known as one of the most impactful education systems in the world. We have raised millions of dollars to create buildings, we have provided iPads and laptops to substitute pencil and paper, we've even created online classes for students living in other countries, so they may attend the best education institutes. But there is one profound flaw to this education system; it is free. One of the astounding things about human beings is that they value only that which comes with a price. Anything free does not impress them because it's free. This is the primary reason why so many human beings do not do the first job and find it necessary to" quit" Earth class and join the Manual Labor group. It is also the major reason why it has become difficult to decipher from what stores value and what merely has worth. They have learned from experiences of such, to sabotage things that have value over things that have worth, but they are not worth it. In other words, it portrays that it is perfectly fine to jeopardize one's morals and values for the sake of upholding the status quo. This recognition is not pleasant in nature, but the discovery of it is an essential part of discovering the significance of "Doing the First Job" and experiencing true freedom.

There is one beauty mark that is a direct effect of us being deceived by the distinction between value and worth. It is the lack of making time for self. People, especially those in the manual labor group, who arrange their time to sooth others, typically get so absorbed in attuning to the well-being of others and building relationships with everyone else, that they never do the first job, which is to assure your general well-being and build within yourself. Their actions will open the way for phenomenal discoveries through experiences with others. They will habitually avoid confronting any challenges, obstacles or discomfort in their path, and they will gain the momentum to build relationships with only those who put them in the way of greater experiences, all while ignoring the becoming of who they've been created to be, by God.

The manual labor way of programming is a normal means of surviving for people who, after leaving school, seek to expand in the area of general knowledge and was not successful in their attempt to do so and could not find the time to "Do the First Job", which is to practice the thoughts of the thing they desire.

The ever-evolving economical condition that emerged as a result of historical events, such as "The Great Depression", "The Recession", and "the Advancement of Technology", have created more reasons for millions of people to find a sense of self-worth in manual labor, tangible things, and many other things outside of themselves, which incontrovertibly causes them to depend on things outside of themselves for happiness and reliance on material matters for a sense of fulfillment. For most of these human beings, the key to all the difficulties will only be discovered by "Doing the First Job". Once "Doing the First Job" many who are a part of the "manual labor group" will be required to change their occupation. When a man finds treasure in the depths of the ocean, he doesn't leave it in the ocean, where it would have no value. He finds a way to bring forth the treasure, through the depths of ocean water to the world to be used to help him meet his demands. Well, there is a talent, gift, or passion that dwells within you, that God placed in our body, to be brought forth to the world, through us.

Every person must make it their business and priority to "Do the First Job" and discover the inner prize. Although manual labor makes it their business to bring personal services and benefits to make their positions seem efficient to their merchants, if the services do not offer JOY and PEACE in return for your service, one must change their occupation, because the greatest benefit available that a job can offer is "one's freedom."

Dwayne "the Rock" Johnson entertained the thoughts of following the career of an NFL football player after playing defensive lineman on the University of Miami football team and briefly a linebacker for the Canadian Football League's Calgary Stampeders. He did the first job and discovered the inner prize within himself and decided to change his profession to Professional wrestling and joined the World Wrestling Foundation (WWF) at 24. The decision prepared him for the overflow of freedom that came in the form of occupations as an actor and a producer, which propelled him towards the "national spotlight" and declared him a life of freedom, prosperity, wealth, and abundance. Even though he did not have to, he completely deemed it to be tremendously valuable to pass on the old, as a sign of honor to the newness that was being born through him. And now, "the Rock" is an American icon who tokens his success to his willingness to take massive tons of actions and always being yourself (who you really are deep down inside your soul) can launch you to true freedom.

Arnold Schwarzenegger made not one, but two incredible career changes. Initially, Arnold Schwarzenegger emerged into the world as a champion bodybuilder in his 20's to an award-winning actor in his 30's, then Arnold claimed his place as the Governor of California in 2003 at the age of 56.

Anna Mary Robertson Moses, also known as Grandma Moses, started her extraordinary painting career at the age of 78. In 2006, one of her paintings sold for $1.2 million. Before pursuing painting, which came as a result of "Doing the first Job", Anna was a housekeeper and farm laborer.

Just to inform you and disallow the excuses the mind may be making in the form of thoughts that say, "I can't do it because I don't have support", "I am too old", "my conditions are worse than theirs", I will make you aware that Grandma Moses was well past forty and "atypical" farm girl when she decided to do the first job.

Investing her time in discovering this special awareness of herself that

Doing the First job permits, self-taught artist, Anna started paintings on postcards, painting her own scenes, to having her paintings displayed and purchased by art collections in New York. During her upbringing, doing manual labor as a "farm girl" didn't bring home the amount of money that equated to the labor. Well the time, energy, and effort most humans put into manual labor, without money, Anna was willing to pay the cost of putting the equivalent time, energy, and effort into herself, which paid off because it led to her discovery of who she really is and what true freedom really is.

Whether the seeds are favorable or unfavorable, all will always reap what they sow. It pays to reap the unmatching benefits of sowing intentional energy, time, and effort into discovering the gift that always has and always will dwell within the confines of the human body. It pays to "Do the First Job."

The human who partakes in school without authentically gaining their masters in the study of self is forever hopelessly doomed to conditions that disallow freedom. The way to freedom is through the continuous pursuit of special awareness learned through self-discovery.

Let us examine the story of Pam Newton who went from Corporate to Cupcakes.

CORPORATE TO CUPCAKES

During the recession, a successor in finance found herself jobless and in a state of uncertainty. Nelson was stressed because, for the first time in what seemed like a long time, she did not know her next move. Having some experience in baking cupcakes, she decided to open a cupcake shop with her friend. Starting with one cupcake store and the belief that she'd only be doing this for six months or a year. Six years later, Pam is still assisting in the operation of Butter Lane cupcakes, which has multiple locations in New York City.

Her idea was to only make vanilla, chocolate, and banana cupcakes and allow the variations to come from their icings. Nelson says "running the business of her own sweet shops is the most satisfying job she ever had." "It's great to have a paycheck coming in and I've worked in the corporate world and I enjoyed my job but there's some powerlessness in not knowing who your next boss is going to be or not having control over what your next project is going to be." Nelson says because of the choice she made "it allowed me control of over my destiny and freedom. Of course, it's on you to make the rent and payroll, but the freedom comes from knowing it's all yours".

Now Pam Nelson is a part of a phenomenal business with thriving services, all because she made a choice that proved equivalent to what money can't buy, at any cost.

Special awareness and creativity were the key elements that attributed to the creation of this phenomenal business. Years before the opening of the business, Pam was working at a job where initially she was earning much more, but the adversity of the recession taught her that although money has worth, her freedom and joy are more valuable. In fact, it is our efforts and energy that gives the money its value.

The beginning of this successful endeavor was a simple thought. I deem it an honor to have the opportunity of supplying favorable thoughts, which will be a pivotal part of each reader discovering true freedom. I now accept the honor of providing some food for thoughts which has within it the keys to human expansion; also, the opportunity of providing the practical tools to millions of people who desire freedom.

This truth was discovered by observation of the doctor who gave up his medical career and became a pastor. When the thought entered his conscience to become a pastor, he quickly denied the idea because he was attached to the "Title" Doctor. In other words, he felt he worked too hard to earn his position and based on the effort put into the gaining of the title, it was not worth letting go of that profession. In other words, at this moment, his title was worth more than the value of his future. Little did he know that one of the most important keys to freedom is to be willing to give up what you are for what you are becoming.

Because you know everything that's why you don't know anything.

Lowell never met a problem he did not KNOW how to solve, so he told himself. Lowell always knew how to get it done, whether, he was familiarized the problem arena or not. He always knew how to fix it or seemed like it. He was a smart man, very hard working, but he constantly found himself in a state of emptiness because his life was not turning out the way he expected. Despite having completed Medical school, despite training alongside a practicing physician, despite earning a master's degree in general knowledge, despite knowing how to take care of everything and everyone else, he was suffering from a sense of hopelessness and emptiness because he did not do the first job.

Amongst his peers, the doctor was known as the know it all. "Know it all's" actually suffer from low confidence and use their knowledge to prove others that they are smarter than they are, using intelligence as a tool to hide the "self-defeat" they experience in their personal lives.

Over the years, due to the increasing internet presence, people experience an overestimation of having acquired knowledge. We possess the feeling of knowingness, although acquiring very little knowledge. And quite often, we find outside sources which confirm what we already believe as truth.

Some professions are expected to know more than others because they require a higher level of education. Commonly when people connect to these types of professions, they get the know it all mindset. Although Lowell made himself and others believe he knew it all, this dishonesty with himself caused him to bypass one of the most important keys to freedom, which is "It's not about what you know, it's about what you do with what you know." The more he reinforced to himself that he knew it all, the more he finds comfort in being the storehouse of knowledge but equally, taking no actions towards utilizing his knowledge to serve the greater good of humanity. He might've been a smart man but relative to his great future, he knew nothing, while relative to his past, he knew everything. Therefore, what we'd like to say, as drawn from Lowell's experience, is that "Because you know everything that's why you don't know anything." What you know now, is nothing in comparison to the depths of richness and clarity that God desires to bestow in you, but the more you tell yourself you know it all, the more you disallow this clarity from flowing into your experience. And as that is happening, you will be wondering why things aren't going your way, why nothings changing, why are my circumstances getting worst. Totally naïve to the fact that it's your thinking that is creating your reality. And because you know everything about all the general knowledge in the world, you know nothing about the specialized awareness bestowed inside you.

This overestimated acquisition of knowledge creates an issue itself, which is necessary to be emanated. A "Know it all" may excel in the area of general knowledge and what they recognize as common sense. They may project themselves as experts on every topic.

So, this created an issue, which is necessary to be emanated. With the aid of some close friends and colleagues, who were well educated, financially stable, and who could prepare the doctor to reap the unmatching benefits of sowing intentional energy, time, and effort into yourself. One of his colleagues proposed to him an extraordinary question, which was used to instantly allow the freedom that permits newness to flow into one's experience.

One may not feel inclined to answer the question, "What's the reason why you became a doctor?" The question was straight to the point and triggered an emotional response because it dealt with a subject which assumed a large proportion of what made him feel significant, as it is with millions of men and women whose primary source of self-worth is the title they are upholding in their respective area of operation. The answer is to "make money." The idea of being driven by the thought to make money, the benefit of the moment helped him get the job, which he applied for, following and interviews, at a payoff created by others.

Moreover, he was unaware that your first job is to get to your inner-views and position your thoughts in a manner that when you APPLY them, they will keep you actively moving towards your freedom.

NO SELF LOVE

Self-love is not just a compound word. Self-love is displayed in one's willingness to release negative thoughts and judgments towards yourself and allow more loving thoughts to flow into your personal experience. Self-love is knowing that if another needs help and you sure up their weaknesses with your strengths, you help them not. Self-love is what occurs when one chooses to release all concerns about how others feel about them and focus only on what they feel about others because in doing so, you will unearth the true understanding of love and you will experience what true freedom really is.

There are millions of people, all over the country, who need motivation and ambition to do services for themselves that is necessary to sustain their general well-being. We KNOW how important exercise is to our health and development, but we NEED motivation to exercise. We KNOW the impact of healthy eating habits has on our body, but we NEED the Ambition to eat healthy. We KNOW that it's important to build a relationship with God, but we must be motivated by others to do so. We KNOW that the person is not treating us the way we deserve to be treated, but we always go back to that relationship.

Corporations flourish from providing services for those who excel in the arena of the adequate. The success stories exceed the largest employment and benefit from providing services for someone far greater to the customer than anything else that can be obtained from any form of employment service.

The idea of providing a service is necessary to offer platforms to earn money, but I say this with no intention to insult anyone's intelligence, but "Where is the brain-child that wonders why does it take motivation and ambition to do things that solidify your general well-being?" If it takes motivation and ambition to do the very things that solidify your general well-being, what does that say about one's love, value, and respect for themselves? It says that this only applies to the one that does not deem it valuable to do the NEW Profession, which will dictate the service they offer to the millions of people in the world.

Perhaps it suggests that most make the mistake of not loving themselves enough to cherish their well-being, just as Lowell Hunter, the great doctor, who was so attached to his previous career (the past) that he couldn't embrace the present (the gift of existing today) which led to the severing of his future. It is easy to move through life and put forth the best effort to hit every ball that life throws our way and to think we are "fine." Being so moved by the adrenaline rush of the moment and press forward to maintain that moment, until one finally stops and life creates a situation to direct your attention, not to your manual labor group, not to your corporation, not to your bank account, not to your boyfriend, not to your girlfriend, not to God, but to your general well-being including your health, mind, body, and life.

For many years we've taught ourselves to believe that "if we can give to others without making intentional time in life to fuel ourselves, then we are helping." One must possess that which they intend to give before they can give it. Can you give a million dollars if you don't have it? NO. In other words, if we are dissatisfied, on the edge of exhaustion, emotionally unstable or empty, it makes us stronger to silence this feeling with phrases such as "I'm just fine", "it's okay", or "I'm used to it."

We have been taught for a long time that if we are not constantly working hard or taking care of others, then we are being selfish. What we are not aware of is that taking care of yourself is taking care of others. If you do not, first assure your general well-being, meaning if you do not take time for restoration and relaxation, if you do not exercise your mind, body, and spirit, then you'll feel so empty, depleted, and burnt out that you won't be of any true help to anyone else, least of all.

Anyone who operates in this space and identifies it as "peaceful", have not found true peace. They've found contentment in dis-ease and satisfaction with emptiness. This contentment in a dis-ease state of mind recognized as peace ultimately becomes the reason it is deemed unnecessary to "do the First Job."

The United States of America runs their society like machines, overlooking the fact it's being operated by human beings. Doing the First Job includes developing a way of living that includes regularly fueling, by slowing down to enjoy the simple fruits of life. Doing the First Job could include watching the sunrise or sunset, burning candles, making a warm fire, drinking a cup of tea, wearing a pair of red heels just because, get your nails done, cleaning your house, setting aside time for laughter with friends and family, and more.

We've become more accustomed to the standard set by the busyness rush. Walk the dog, feed the turtle, cook dinner, tend to the children's needs, spend time with your partner, go do manual labor, and eventually fall into the bed at the end of the day. Does this sound familiar?

Doing the First Job is a beautiful outlook, which opposes the cluster created by the busyness rush. This beautiful outlook recognizes the importance of keeping your mind, body, and spirit in the restorative mode because this perspective recognizes and acknowledges the restoration and fulfillment that occurs when we appreciate the "natural" beauty that earth offers.

Now the list may seem insignificant at first glance. However, I declare that putting them into practice, every single day, which is "Doing the First Job" and allowing yourself to feel great.

- Start the day with ten minutes of meditation
- Treat yourself
- Cut your caffeine intake
- Read a good book
- Do All things for yourself without guilt
- Practice the art of Saying "No"
- Be of Service-give time, help friends, volunteer
- Compliment Someone today

- Break a good sweat
- Smile
- When your picking groceries say, "I am choosing this for my body because I love it."
- Try something new: exercises, hobbies, yoga, dance classes
- Invite your friends over for a night of fun
- Call your family members and tell them you love them
- Snuggle with your partner or pet
- Commit to a new habit for a week
- Always show gratitude; Say Please and Thank you
- Detach from Social Media
- Give yourself a day off
- Tell yourself "I love you; I forgive you and Thank you" while looking in the mirror.
- Hire a coach or counselor
- Dear ME, Journal Writing (Write it in the morning and read it before you go to bed at night.)

Dear Me,

First, I would like for you to know that you matter to me. I know that with you, I can fulfill the purpose of my life. Therefore, I declare my commitment to you, with sincerity, gratitude, and continuous, action towards the self-love that will allow the manifestation of our goals.

I realize the domineering thoughts of my mind, in due time, will replicate themselves into seen and unseen physical actions and slowly but surely transform themselves into the physical reality. Therefore, I will focus my time, energy, and efforts upon Doing the first job which includes figuring out who I desire to become and then practice the thought pattern of that person.

Through Doing the first job, any desire that I purposefully hold in my mind will eventually request expression through some form of workable means of acquiring the objective segment of it. I will devote ten minutes daily to committing to myself as an expression of self-love.

Even in times where the road towards my highest desire is not clear, I vow to continue to love myself during the seeking of the unanswered question, until I have developed sustainable self-love for myself.

I fully realize that I am no help or support to anyone else unless I've built myself upon truth and unconditional self-love. Therefore, I realize that by engaging in partnerships and relationships without loving myself FIRST, I won't be of TRUE benefit to all whom I engage. I will succeed by replacing negative thoughts with positive thoughts, which will allow me to attract positive conditions in my life. I will inspire others to be inspired to inspire others. I will remove resentment, agony, intimidation, neediness, boastfulness, omissions and worthlessness by first developing a love for myself that overflows out of me onto the collective human family. I know that love conquers ALL, but the quest for allowing love to conquer all begins with one's love for self. The reason this phrase had not been allowed to fully manifest in the world is that those who set out to express it get burnt out, feel empty, or drained, which are all effects of not refueling and remaining in replenish mode.

Through Doing the First Job, I will connect with my first true love, which is myself, because of that self-love, I will learn to love others and through self-love, we will learn to love each other.

I will sign my name to the vow, commit it to memory, and become it in my daily routine with full faith that gradually my emotions will shift until there is an obvious tipping point. Where I am no longer focusing on developing self-love, but I will become the embodiment of self-love, knowing that the true meaning of human success is to love ourselves unconditionally.

Best well to yourself

The thought of helping someone else when you haven't taken time to refuel self may appear to be fundamentally sound, but this thought pattern presents a huge challenge. Many of those who are left pouring from an empty cup, remains empty or they have a tendency of "carrying others pain." It should be remembered that all of life is about balance. The more self-awareness one gains about themselves and their capabilities, the more visible the impact of the imbalance created by pouring from an empty cup. Remember the outlook of working hard is not so exciting or encouraging. The thought of working hard has a natural proneness to kill off momentum. We call it "giving our best", caring for others and working hard which means that we accept "it's supposed to be hard" as reality and that daily thought pattern creates the habits that reflects the beliefs that "it's impossible, so we should just forget about it". I was once told "if it isn't hard it isn't meant to be" as if the degree of difficulty should be used as a determinate of one's capability. Perhaps this is one of the reasons many think great thoughts, but do not transmute their thoughts into physical reality because one's great ideas and aspirations are always followed by the voice echoes of the thought "it's hard" and the momentum that the thought "it's hard" creates is so strong that it interferes with one's ability to back their thoughts up with action. If you are one who possesses great ideas, but the crippling momentum of "it's hard" causing you to be hesitant in taking action or affects us in a way where it lessens our ability to take action, for this is another reason why it pays to start Doing the First Job. By doing so, one forms the habit of looking inside themselves, observe their thoughts, and learn how to embrace and maintain a state of existence that will keep them in a state of relaxed readiness.

TRUE PEACE

Those who've made it a habit to keep running while on Empty should remember what happens to a car if the gas needle is on E and the next fuel pump is twenty miles away. Collectively, we've done a splendid job at maintaining a sense of self during these times but identifying this state of existence as "peace" has had a long-lasting impact on the human family.

Observe this important moment in history known as SEGREGATION.

SEGREGATION

There was a time when the thinking of thousands of Caucasian males and females was swamped by SEPARATION. African Americans were not seen as humans, but as 3/5's of a person and during this time, because of the limitation put on their race, the likelihood of their living conditions improving seemed IMPOSSIBLE.

God has always seemed to see all humans as his children, but during this time in history, humans used "God as a way to shape the minds of mankind." Whites and Blacks were segregated and consequently, African Americans were not allowed to drink at the same water fountain, eat in the same restaurants, sit in the same seats on public transportation, or live in the same neighborhoods as whites. If you are wondering, the conditions of ALL things African Americans had access to, were of low quality in comparison to the privileges of the whites during this time.

If you are one whose elders or grandparents were alive during this time, honestly, do you believe that you'd be able to truly function during these times? When the African American elders, forefathers, mothers, and grandparents, that was alive during those times, tell the story, they've convinced themselves that they were at peace, but they are unable to perish all the unfavorable thoughts associated with that time. This is not true peace. True peace does not welcome unfavorable thoughts. True peace, in response to the demands of whites during this time, was merely a facet of the imagination, instead of a physical reality.

Generally, the idea we have of peace is not true peace. The true peace occurs when the momentum of a thought of peace impels actions, as driven by the faculties of the imagination. All scientists, historians, religious deities, philosophers, and more agree that we've become better at selling the image of peace instead of experiencing it personally. Those who Do the First Job, do not sell the image of peace because in doing so "you are making yourself believe a lie." In other words, by making yourself believe you're at peace and you're not, whether intentionally or by default, one is telling themselves a lie, at which one will begin to deem as truth." Consequently, the more one deems a lie as truth, it ushers them to a state of denial, which pulls them further and further away from discovering the truth of themselves and remember only the TRUTH SHALL SET YOU FREE.

Naturally, they begin to crowd themselves with so many responsibilities that it disallows their ability to respond to the call of their general well-being.

They become too attached to what they know, they make themselves naïve or move away from what they do not know because their space of knowingness declares their comfort (they call this peace).

Kaden Lebray is a phenomenal demonstration of what is meant by Doing the First Job. After his college career, he was a professional basketball player of the famous National Basketball League of Canada, when it was under the grounds of Commissioner David Magley.

Maybe David Magley's story inspired him to see that the sky wouldn't be the limit if there are footprints on the moon and long as one master the art of allowing their failures and disappointments to motivate them to succeed, as demonstrated by Mr. Magley's story, one will always be pressed towards their freedom. Anyhow, Kaden finished his 2016 season with incredible accommodations, at what appeared to be an extremely unhappy time, the moment in life which one chooses to surrender to the becoming of who they've been created to be, instead of who you've become as influenced by others. In other words, become the being that he was born to be instead of the being that he was tempted to be. In other words, being so integrated with the fullness of himself, that he can accept truth in the fullness of all that it is.

While exploring his inner views, meaning getting integrated with his own thoughts, he searched for job openings everywhere. After a period of substitute teaching and different volunteer services, he accepted the opportunity which offered the most sustaining benefits that he could acquire----working as the assistant manager of Burger King. Anyone could start off working "fast food" and Kaden was aware of that, but this job offered him something that later became the tool to help him acquire more freedom.

For over a year, he labored a job, which created distaste in his life, but he would not have elevated above his condition, had he chosen to do nothing about his distaste. He applied, at the job, as the assistant manager of the company and was hired. That one step forward was formidable because it was the assistant manager because it was credible enough to permit him to still see greater opportunity, but it also positioned him where he could be seen, by opportunity.

He made such a fine living playing professional basketball that Bob Reardon, the President of Sanlar Enterprise, was curious about that man, Kaden Lebray, who left Professional Basketball to take on a management position at the long-established Burger King. The business competitors of the cooperation would ask about Kaden. Surely, within months after the interview, Kaden was offered a position as General Manager overseeing the crew. To challenge Kaden's willpower, Bob Reardon would cut off all communications, leaving him to figure it out or fail in his new job. He did not fail. Over the years of playing professional basketball, Kaden abducted the spirit of "the overcomer that wouldn't be overcome by adversity." This spirit, alone, aside from his work ethic, inspired him to inspire every customer and employer at his job. "He was so positive", "I actually feel like he cared", "he inspired me", "he made my experience at Burger King awesome" were some of the comments of the customers who called the Corporate Office to make positive referrals about him. He put so much positive energy into his job that he was offered opportunities as the general manager. Burger King's in other divisions were pitching to him the idea of beginning his own Burger King franchise because they were inspired by how an opportunity most people would learn through selected years of obliged commitments, Kaden turned this opportunity into more opportunity within six months.

Consider it complex to say whether Mr. Reardon or Mr. Lebray is more credible for this phenomenal testimony, considering that both attributed their abilities to forge themselves into the momentum of their imagination. Mr. Reardon should be attributed to recognizing in Kaden a "determination" of meaningful perseverance. Kaden should be attributed to being willing to compromise playing professional basketball and accepting the challenge that came with the newly discovered part of himself, which is one of the primary points of emphasis in this entire chapter. We have much more control over our lives and outcomes, but we surrender the control of our own life to "facts" that are not even true. And then we begin to protect these false truths with "reasoning" that makes it seem truer.

We naturally become more defensive about IT and resort to logical thought patterns in order to sustain beliefs that are not in-formation with your desire.

We've done so well at surviving with NEGATIVE thoughts. "Everybody else thinks like this", "I don't have the money to do that", "I can't do it without money", "No one supports me", as you read, does this thought pattern sound familiar. It is pivotal that we understand, in our mind, facts are true. Therefore, if we keep making things that we do not desire to be true as truth, then we truly become more disconnected from the things we desire.

When doubt exists in the same thought pattern as desire, typically it causes us to give more attention to what IS or what was instead of What is to Be. Meaning we become so overly concerned about where you were instead of where you've been created be. We declare what was, as truth, totally unaware that Mother Earth, allows you to see what you give your attention to. For example, let's examine the phrase "I need to be in a relationship". Typically when people have those thoughts, they sever the relationship when it shows up in their experience because although they had a strong urge to be in a relationship, their mind was more focused on how long they've waited for it to happen instead of merely appreciating that it happened, which automatically brings unfavorable momentum to your experience such as desperation, neediness, insecurity. Commonly when we have bad experiences or experiences that we don't want, this naturally creates a path for the world to improve because it creates magnitudes of desire about what you do want which helps you become more aware of what you do want. There is a tendency, although we are seeming unaware, to overly focus on what we do not want, which will cause us to continually attract what we don't want.

We ARE GENERATORS

Think about a thing that you desire strongly. Whenever you WANT or NEED a thing, when you are claiming it, regardless of your word usage or verbage, since you've needed it for so long, then your awareness of how long you've needed it will play a huge part in your allowing of it to flow to you. Gradually, the desire will grow more and more mature, but if you're not energetically in-formation with that desire, then you do not allow yourself to be in the receiving mode and therefore you do not witness your thoughts turn into things. In other words, even though everything we desire is always flowing towards us, by beating ourselves up with contradictory thoughts, then you disallow yourself from being in-formation with the pattern of thoughts that generate the POWER for your desire to manifest through you. When you allow yourself to flow in-formation with the pattern of thoughts that generate a state of general well-being, you will naturally make yourself available for the path God created for you, with the steps already laid out, and you will bear witness of your true power.

HAVE YOU EVER felt like you needed motivation, HAVE YOU EVER felt exhausted, HAVE YOU EVER felt fatigued, HAVE YOU EVER felt like you lack ambition, HAVE YOU EVER felt passive or lazy minded about doing the very thing that you love or draws your attention? Well "Doing the First Job" gives a practical explanation as to why this emotional state occurs.

As a collective human family, we've done well at reminding ourselves and others through "Words" of our wants, needs, and desires. And almost every time, that desire doesn't become a physical manifestation because when we in these emotional states, we become less aware that the words don't teach. You must have life experience with the words, for true understanding to be born through words, but isn't it strange we offer so many words. Along with words we offer our knowingness and with our knowingness comes that lack of awareness that we've conditioned ourselves to believe as true reality, which is ideas and beliefs that we've accepted as our reality whether it holds to be true or not.

As humans, we are not naturally powerful. Power is not generated by the human body, rather it is created and generated through the human body, as influenced by one's thought pattern and focal point of attraction, which is a byproduct of the words, in the form of beliefs, stories, and ideas that are consistently compressed in our minds. Think about how a satellite picks up energy and uses it, well comparatively speaking, our minds pick up and receives thoughts and express the momentum of thoughts through the human body. In other words, if we consistently hold the thought in the mind "I am going to have a great day" then you will feel great, feel excited and motivated. That's not to say bad things won't happen but when bad things present themselves in your experience, if you speak and if necessary, continually repeat, the words "I am going to have a great day" bad things won't be seen as bad things because your thought pattern will permit you to only see the good in bad things, which will keep your mind in-formation with a thought pattern that assures your great momentum, keep you focused on good things, as well as attract good things to you.

In other words, have you ever had a person who likes to complain? And when you look at their life from the outside-in, your thoughts are "your life can't be as hard as you make it seem". _____ (Write down the name of that person). You may have been having a great day but after listening to them complain for however long, you feel drained, fatigued, and powerless. In truth, their conditions are never as bad as they make them seem and the only reason IT seems so bad to them is because for a moment, which could be ten minutes, two weeks, ten years or for generations, they've chosen to flow with the current of negative thoughts moving through their mind, which will cause their focal point of attraction to be negative, meaning they will have tunnel vision to NEGATIVITY.

You as the listener, or supporter, or shoulder to lean on, or ear, now become swamped with negative thoughts. And if you have not done the "First Job" you will be left feeling drained, absent-minded, lazy, and passive about doing the things that serve your greater good. Does this sound familiar?

The influence of these types of instances is now classified as moments that declares "love" in our present-day civilization. The understanding of true love has become strange because it is considered normal to love others before we establish love for ourselves, unaware that the more love we project into what object of attention we choose, the farther we are from discovery the unconditional love for ourselves at which we are created to spread to the world, meaning ANYTHING OUTSIDE of yourself.

STORY about love

Let us look at the magnitude of freedom this awareness will produce if one permits themselves to allow this expanded truth to flow into their personal experience. It has paid, and it still pays, to women and men all over the world who wonders the keys to building harmonious relationships instead of living a life that they mark as an overlap of bad experiences.

"Love" is now one of the world's most marketed solutions and answer to ALL, thus providing many with more of a reason to find others to make their true nature permanent. Hence, you get engaged and then get married, instead of "Doing the First Job" of marrying yourself then engage the world.

"Love" holds to be the primary cause of SIN, meaning Separate In NATURE. Because instead of connecting to our thoughts, we've adopted the nature of staying separate from our thoughts because we'd rather commit to another woman, man, cat or dog, which allows us to hide behind our thoughts. This leads us to staying mentally in-formation with the belief that others are accountable for our thoughts , instead of embodying the truth that ALL our thoughts are a reflection of how we were tempted to think, as influenced by family paradigm, aside from the thought pattern we were created to have as designed by "God".

Jesus ,perfectly, displayed true love when he died for our sins. Our greatest sin is being Separate In Nature from the truth that you and you only are accountable for your thoughts, feelings, and experiences.

This understanding of "Love" gives permission to maintain a focal point on one's intentions, even if their actions do not align with their words.

It has been used to bring fame and fortune to scores of artists, lyricists, and poets, who created, magnificent, works as a by-product of this pattern of thinking.

This understanding of love has done some powerful things.

All through the world, when women and men, face adversity in their relationships and they feel like quitting, they listen to a love song, songs to soothe their state of being in that moment, as if this moment will provide fuel to generate a thought pattern that permits them to progress.

Doing the First Job means understanding that if the concept of the song is love problems or romance issues, which is being told in a thrilling form of expression and we are feeding this music to our minds, through our ears, while we are in the same unfavorable state, the music will magnify the thought pattern that flows with the stream that creates romance issues and love problems.

Imagine your thoughts being like a fully blown balloon and you want your thoughts to go away or its power to be deflated meaning take the air out of the balloon. Well by stimulating your mind with thought patterns that reiterate that thought nature, it adds more air to the balloon. What happens to balloons once it has too much air? It explodes and the evidence of it is left scattered.

In other words, if you are having a problem with smoking marijuana and you are always listening to music "that consistently talks about getting high", the drums of music, the melody of music, the art of music will allow stimulation, but the thought pattern projected through the content of the music is the key that will influence our personal experience, with respects to your scope of the world itself.

A great spoken word artist revealed this truth symbolically through this poem titled:

Words Cast Spells

We could barely effectively pray and meditate
Because when we get in a saddened, vulnerable, or weakened state
We listen to music about sex, drugs, and alcohol
We listen because intrinsically we feel like you and the artist relate
We listen to movies about sex and wonder why we are struggling with the urge to manipulate, masturbate, cheat, and fornicate.

The songwriter is much appreciated in their contribution to allowing the phenomenal discovery that stores the keys to our freedom. It is through your headphones, television, (tell-lie-vision) and other forms of technological devices that strip us of our freedom whether it be for the better or for the worst.

Now that you are aware of the key to experiencing freedom, you as a reader should profess that the thought patterns your friends, your music, your association, your family, provided you with a stimulation that does not serve your greater good, which is important because what does not serve your greater good teaches you what does serve your greater good. Thereby, it serves your greater good to refresh the mind and feed it with the thoughts that will propel the reader towards fulfilling their destiny.

Whomever you are, wherever you are, whatever job title you possess, remember now and then, every time you hear or see words, that ALL freedom, wealth, abundance and prosperity, was born through "words." Not more so, the words we speak to someone else, but the words you speak to yourself. "Doing the First Job" means knowing that when you have a conversation with someone else, you're always listening. Therefore, you're always having a conversation with yourself.

Stop and think about that for a moment.

Remember words generate power as they flow through our minds and words are a key fundamental to experiencing freedom.

Re-read this section carefully. Give yourself a chance to discover what thought patterns added to constant experiences which caused the overflow of unfavorable momentum. Remember as you read this, that this is not a story that can be pulled from the Jerry Springer Show. Here you have a key, simple but made difficult, point of emphasis, which if properly implemented will begin to influence our freedom.

Because anything we focus our minds, feelings, and emotions too, becomes REAL because ALL Day our thoughts are channeling messages through the body in the forms of WORDS.

All our life experiences are VALID because experiences have been placed in order to help us consciously rediscover who we are. Every person on Mother Earth will have bad experiences that are designed to take them to a place of devastation, doubt, and fear because doubts create magnitudes of FOCUS about what you don't want, which helps you become more aware of what you do want. In fact, doubt is necessary because it gives birth to desire. Both doubt and desire are vital factors in "Doing the First Job", but it's up to us to sort through doubt and discover the thought pattern to permit doubt to be an asset that can never be measured in terms of money.

The influence of these types of instances is now classified as moments that declares "love" in our present-day civilization. The understanding of true love has become strange because it is considered normal to love others before we establish a love for ourselves, unaware that the more love we project into OTHERS, meaning whatever object of attention we choose to, the farther WE ARE FROM THE DISCOVERY OF THE FIRST TRUE LOVE, WHICH IS YOU.

The key is to deactivate contradictory thoughts. Find a way to deactivate the beliefs that don't align with your desires. Don't be misled to assume that unfavorable thoughts go away just because you say I'm not thinking about, because when a person says, I'm going to stop thinking about it, they are thinking about IT. Focus more deliberately on thoughts that are in-formation with your desire.

Re-Write Story - Your NEW STORY

Remember as you read, that your differences are important to the stimulation of new ideas, as well as to the expansion of the human family. Also as you read, keep in mind that within the key fundamentals described in this book, your freedom may present itself in the form of an idea, plan, or new habit, which presented itself as influenced by this greater awareness stored in the pages of this book. Keep in mind, the power of a single idea can create the path which stores your freedom.

This story proves the truth of that saying, "Whatsoever a man thinketh, so will he become." It was told to me by the Life Coach and Fitness Guru, the late Kaden Lebray, who begin his teaching career in the down eastern region of North Carolina.

While Mr. Lebray was going through substitute teaching at an Arts and Education School, he discovered many deficiencies in our educational system. Deficiencies that he knew he could fix if he were the head of an educational institute in which young men and women of all colors, cultures, and creeds would be taught to learn by "working smart instead of working hard."

He fixated in his mind to create a new education basis which would carry out his ideas without being disadvantaged by traditional methods of education.

He needed one million dollars to execute his project. How was he going to get access to such a large quantity of dollars? That was the thought that occupied most of the young successor's mind at the time.

But he couldn't seem to make any progress. Every day when he rose from his sleep and closed his eyelids to rest, he took his desire with him. His mind was so saturated with this desire that it became an all-out undeniable obsession to him. One million dollars is a lot of money. He recognized that fact, but he also recognized that it's not true when people say "the sky is the limit" because if the sky is the limit, then that means there's still a limit. No limit can be set to one's magnitude of achievement, the only limit is the limit one sets on their own mind. True freedom is experienced when one is free from limitation.

Being a motivational speaker as well as an author, Kaden Lebray recognized, as do all who live in freedom, that a definite desire to exceed ALL limitations is the beginning point from which one must start. He understood, too, that a definite desire for "freedom" created a path of wealth, fulfillment, prosperity, and abundance when assisted with an unadulterated desire to transfer that desire into the physical reality.

Although he was aware of these profound "golden nuggets" of awareness, he still did not know the answer to the who, what, when, where, and how with respects to the manifestation of ONE MILLION DOLLARS. It has become overly natural to "let it go, give up, or quit, by saying phrases such as "I want to build a school, BUT I cannot because I will never obtain the money to make the dream come true." That is exactly what most people have said. In fact, before this moment, those were the same things that Kaden Lebray said leading up until this moment where he decided to make a decision that proved to be the "key" to his freedom. What he chose to do and how he responded are so important that I now take this time to personally present him and allow him to speak for himself.

"One Friday night I sat in the office at Burger King thinking of possibilities and ways of acquiring the funds to execute my plans. For over six months, I had been wondering about, what to do but I had done nothing but wonder".

"I knew I had to take action, even though my directions were not clear, the moment where I take a chance, towards what's not clear, the closer I get to gaining clarity".

"I made up my mind, in that moment that I would get the required million dollars within two months." How was it going to happen? I was not focused on how. The most primary key was a conscious decision to get the money within a specified time, a strange idea popped in my mind, such a thought that I had never thought before. Something inside me seemed to say "Why don't you rewrite your story the way you desire for it to be told instead of the way it's been told in the past. For as long as you hold onto the past, the past will hold onto you".

"Once I applied the instructions, things began to instantly shift at a rapid speed. I rewrote my story, the way I desire for it to be told".

"I would begin with a Walk for Unity and Peace at which the starting point would be in front of the North Carolina Courthouse." The community would be gathered at this event. And at this community gathering, I would give a speech titled "WHAT WOULD I DO IF I HAD A MILLION DOLLARS."

I would share this speech immediately, regardless of the difficulties of the task. The spirit truth of this speech would draw the money to me".

"Long before three months' time, I will have acquired the money. I would read this story every morning when I woke up and at night when I went to bed. I tell you the more I read the story of the life I chose, instead of constantly remembering the story of the life chosen for me by others or remembering the story I created on the path of discovering my true self, the supernatural sense of assurance and momentum came over me. It was a weird feeling. It was almost as if I had already had the million dollars, just didn't have the physical evidence to match the momentum. But I could see myself in possession of the million dollars.

"One morning I rose after reading the self-written story of Kaden Lebray: The Guy who acquired a Million Dollars. I went to work on my speech immediately, but I must admit, even as I wrote it, it was difficult because it was different. But the pursuit of different allows you to make a difference.

After I finished writing my speech, I patiently awaited the day of the Walk for Peace and Unity, to present it. Leading up to that day, I faced very adverse conditions, but I was constantly in prayer with God "believing that this speech would catch the attention of someone who would supply the necessary money."

"While I was praying, strong feelings of excitement would come over me. And these feelings provided me with the assurance that the money is coming. My excitement outshined my judgment. Meaning I was crazy enough to believe that the story of Kaden Lebray would come true and beliefs would be felt by all who encountered me. The day had finally arrived for me to present my speech and I did not know how prepared I was to deliver this message to the people in attendance.

I didn't take any notes and contrary to what I once believed; I didn't need any. Instead, I brought faith backed with an unadulterated desire to transform the lives of each member of the human family. Before I spoke the first word to begin my speech, I closed my eyes and when I opened them, I spoke ALL my heart and spirit. I not only talked to my audience; I also allowed my audience an opportunity to ask me questions. As I spoke and responded to my audience's questions "I kept in my mind that God is with me and since that remains true, even when I feel lonely, I am never alone."

I told the people what I would do if a million dollars was placed in my hands. I described the strategy I had in mind for orchestrating this extraordinary educational institution where women and men of all color, cultures, and creeds would learn to do their first job which is to "discover their gift" and at the same time develop their minds.

As I approached the finishing point of my speech, I posed a question for each member of the audience. I asked them, how much is a human life worth, how much are you worth? The responses varied but they all were along the lines of "I'm worth a million dollars, I'm worth more than money, INFINITI, and no numbers equate to my worth." After allowing them to answer the question, I responded by saying, well do I have your active support? Do I have your active participation in the manifestation of this extraordinary Educational Institute? And they said, "YES, you do." I responded by saying, "therefore I have a million dollars because I have you and you are worth more than any numerical count." They believed I could do everything I said I would if I had a million dollars. To prove that they believed in me and my offering to the human family, in the form of an educational institute, they surrendered themselves and their support proved to be the tool that drew a million dollars to me".

Kaden Lebray hosted a walk for Unity and Peace and the million dollars was presented to him. With the money, he founded Nimiq International Institute Inc. One million dollars is more money than most motivational speakers, international basketball players, and authors have ever seen in the entirety of their career and lifetime. Yet in the case of Kaden Lebray, this reality was created in the young steward's mind in merely minutes. The moment that supported the idea that Mr. Lebray had been nurturing in his mind became magnified through constantly reading the rewritten version of his story.

We are always telling a story. This would be easy if you could understand that you are always telling a story and learn to discover the story you are telling. The way you feel, the way you move, your attitude, your vibrations, your focus, and your momentum tell a story.

"Doing the First" means find a way of thinking the thoughts of what gives you relief before the things around you can transform. You must begin telling a NEW story. You must tell the story the way you want it to be told before the story will actualize around the story of the way you don't want it to be. EVERYTHING that you feel, experience, or think is in response to the story you are projecting through your thought pattern, by which your actions are telling. The way you think, you feel, and your mood creates your point of attraction. If you desire something in your story and the way it manifests, you must tell the story in a way that shifts your momentum as you tell it.

TAKE NOTE OF THESE IMPORTANT FACTS: KADEN GOT THE MONEY WITHIN THREE MONTHS OF ALLOWING HIMSELF TO SURRENDER TO A PRECISE CHOICE IN HIS OWN MIND TO ACQUIRE IT AND SPECIFYING A PRECISE STRATEGY FOR ACQUIRING IT.

There was nothing different or extraordinary about Kaden thinking about how to acquire a million dollars and doubtfully hoping for it. It is quite common to experience contradictory thoughts or momentum, whenever we have extraordinary ideas. But there was something quite extraordinary and profound about the choice he made on that unforgettable Friday night, where he put the voice of doubt on the back burner and stored the voice of desire that said: "I choose to press towards acquiring one million dollars."

God will always show more favor to people who know specifically what they desire to do, especially if they are determined to do exactly that. The process which Mr. Lebray used to get his million dollars is still available. It is accessible to you. The keys are "free" and are just as accessible today as they were when Mr. Lebray applied them. This book articulates on the keys, chapter by chapter, that allows you to discover awareness that will propel you towards your freedom.

Kaden and every other successor have a common quality. They know the incredible truth that thoughts can be transmuted into their physical reality through the power of being specific, plus applying a definite strategy. But the way to discover your thoughts is by: "Doing the First

Job" meaning honor your first true relationship, which is your relationship with your thoughts.

If you are one of those who believe that others are accountable for your thoughts or experiences, honestly it is important to expire that thought. It is not true. Moreover, the truth is that you are accountable for ALL your thoughts and experiences. Freedom does not come from "blaming" or "denying." Freedom, when it is experienced at a peak level, is never the result of blaming or denial. Freedom comes, if it comes at all, in response to taking definite accountability for one's thoughts, experiences, and using this space of renewed awareness as the grounds to replace unfavorable thoughts with favorable thoughts, which will create a better-quality experience.

"Doing the First Job" is an idea that prompts people to acknowledge and organize their thoughts. Because in order to master themselves, one must be able to identify what thought pattern or patterns are creating their reality. Ordinary people do not know this. That is why they continue to "blame" their conditions on others, that's why they remain ordinary.

"Doing the First job" makes it a priority, a self-discovery to be made that is worth more than money can offer. Many people have desires or ambitions that their present thought pattern is not in-formation with. By merely, transforming the thought or thoughts that are disallowing you from moving towards your desire, you will begin feeling the excitement of your desires moving towards you and you moving towards it. You do not have to change your life in any way. More so, transform your mind by replacing thoughts that bear the momentum of doubt and limitation with new thoughts that are harmony with the thought pattern that permits the manifestation of your desire.

That is the key to acquiring freedom. As simple as it may seem, the human mind has a habit of making simple things difficult. This type of condition just shows that some simple thoughts in the mind overshadows the simplicity. Because the truth is "Life is Simple" and only unfavorable thoughts hinder the simplicity from being visible and heartfelt. Life can be simple and easy as you allow it to be. It is totally up to you, but in order to identify those thoughts, "Do the First Job."

The image the world paints of freedom is by all those who are imprisoned. Most women and men who didn't find the freedom to experience or express their thoughts on the "outside world", were able to discover their thoughts while in prison. Thereby prison yielded them towards true freedom when they were released from prison.

Bernard Hopkins knew little about professional boxing –prior to the time he served in prison, but he made use of the time in prison to face his thoughts and arrange them in a way that would assure him freedom and fortune.

Reasonably every great success story begins with the day when a person was mentally confined by limitations that presented itself in the form of doubt. Once they were able to rise above the voice echoes of limitation in their minds, it made them available for the freedom to pursue whatever endeavor they chose.

Hopkins spent his youth fighting against the poverty and limitation that surrounded him in the housing projects in Philadelphia. When Bernard was a boy of 18, he was sent to an adult prison on the outskirts of Philadelphia.

Millions of people have negative experiences or thoughts which they hope to escape or avoid, some have more than others. Perhaps it will provide momentary ease to avoid your thoughts, but the SMARTEST plan is not to depend on coping mechanisms that help you avoid your thoughts. It is favorable to know that "NEGATIVITY CREATES FOCUS, FOCUS LEADS TO WONDERING AND QUESTIONING and in that gap between wondering and questioning, you will find your FREEDOM."

It was favorable that Bernard Hopkins experienced negativity, as Hopkins attributes his time in prison for teaching himself discipline and the importance of utilizing every second in a day. Prison offered him the opportunity to FOCUS on his life and the opportunity to learn how to channel the same energy he put into crime; into a much more favorable CAUSE.

The opportunity to FOCUS is discovered by being willing to allow NEGATIVITY to create a focus and Bernard Hopkins allowed his negative experiences to wheel him to a state of channeled focus. At that moment, Hopkins discovered the key to freedom and achieving, that's required on any level of success. Millions of people have been prosperous by the discoveries made amid serving time in prison and much fortune has been gained through putting into use this idea. NEGATIVITY creates a focus that gives birth to a new beginning. In fact, it's only through NEGATIVITY that this supernatural focus can be developed.

When Hopkins made his discovery, did negative things stop occurring? NO. While in prison, he witnessed the murder of an inmate over a pack of cigarettes, but as he observed himself preserving through all his experiences, he discovered that there is a passionate "fighter" within him. It was no ordinary desire that permitted him to survive poverty. The thought of his brother being killed, being seventeen years old with nine felonies, and many other criticisms that created his disappointment. He had a supernatural desire to "keep fighting" which later proved to attribute to Bernard's legacy.

When Mr. Hopkins first discovered the idea in his mind to become a fighter, NEGATIVITY provided him more of a reason for that thought to remain alive because the contrast energy created more of a reason to focus on it. Over time, "the thought of becoming a fighter that was under its own control and it wheeled, motivated, governed, and freed me" as Bernard noted. Thoughts are exactly like that. Initially, you put time, energy, action, and effort into thoughts and then they take on the form of a force of nature which over stands all opposition.

Bernard Hopkins, a professional boxer, became one of the most successful boxers of the past three decades, having held twelve major world championships in different weight classes, including a long list of professional boxing accolades. Like Bernard Hopkins, Michael Vicks, one of the pioneers of the NFL that transformed the quarterback positions is a good example of "NEGATIVITY CREATES FOCUS." He was a sixth-year quarterback, with the Atlanta Falcons when he pleaded guilty for his involvement with illegal dogfighting.

Being the number one pick in the 2001 NFL draft was not easy to obtain. Off the football field, Michael ran a dogfighting business in Virginia. At the time being one of the most highly paid quarterbacks in the NFL, Michael Vick had other interests. Vick had a passion for dogs, but he did not know how to train them, feed them, or any of the things necessary to sustain their general well-being. Vick reportedly "enjoyed family pets in the ring with fighting dogs." After serving 23 months in federal prison, Michael declared to himself he would never participate in or associate himself with dogfighting again.

He recognized the need to make people aware of the issue with "dogfighting". Vick knew that the issue was much bigger than him. In his effort to expand public awareness, he arranged partnerships with Humane Society, helped get the Animal Fighting Spectator Prohibition Act passed in Congress, as well as reached many different audiences, nationally, to help spread the message that supports the well-being of pets. Throughout his career, Vick donated over 1 Million dollars to charities and other positive causes. Although Vick was putting forth his best effort to raise awareness, many people still chose to identify Vick by his mistakes, despite his efforts to fix his mistakes. Despite his commitment to spend his lifetime raising awareness, some people couldn't dismiss the thoughts of cruelty projected onto animals and because of that, all of Vick's efforts were being merely overlooked, if not forgotten.

Everyone will make mistakes because mistakes are a part of life. By avoiding mistakes, you are avoiding life itself. Mistakes are great teachers because they help create focus. In other words, Vick's mistakes gave birth to the opportunity to expand national awareness about dogfighting.

Although Michael Vick served his time and even partnered with anti–dog fighting campaigns, critics still argued: "when can a person who committed such a horrible crime be rehabilitated, did the crime fit the time, who's to say he won't do it again." No effort was enough to gain their forgiveness because they couldn't let go of the unpleasant thoughts.

Through the unfavorable momentum of being cast out, harshly criticized, and unfavorably judged, Vick made a profound discovery that attributed to freeing himself from the unfavorable momentum of people.

One of his primary points of emphasis made in his public announcements and appearances, which is well served, is to keep in mind as a part of Doing the First Job that "not everyone will cheer you on, don't pay attention to people who want you to fail." "Stand up and be an instrument for change" Vick stated. After spending years in the spotlight and having millions of fans cheering him on as he threw the game-winning pass and scored the game-winning touchdown, which was a benefit of doing the SECOND job, Vick realized that he never learned to CHEER FOR HIMSELF. It was this new shift that permitted him to see that.

Now in the position where millions of fans are cheering against him, Vick was brought to a place of lowliness in order to discover one of the fundamental keys of doing the first job, which is to BE YOUR OWN CHEERLEADER. Because even when the fans or supporters fade away, you must support you and cheer for you during adversity.

Everyone advertises the importance of forgiveness and promotes the importance of moving past our mistakes. In fact, when we make mistakes, we desire not to judged or harshly criticized or identified by our mistakes. The reasoning behind these types of occurrences is because we tend to focus more on the negative than the positive. In order to truly pass mistakes, we must choose not to stay focused on the negative. Although negativity provided Vick a new focus, some chose to focus on the negative.

"Doing the First Job" makes it a top priority to identify the thoughts that have trained you to see life the way you see it. Meaning look inside of your mind for the answer to the who, what, when, where, and why questions as it relates to your current reality. Hence the new slogan "your first job is to get to your inner-views."

In other words, love yourself enough to eliminate the person, people, places, or things out of your life that creates unfavorable thoughts in your mind. No AMOUNT OF MONEY, NO RELATIONSHIP, NO RELIGION, NO LEGAL COMMITMENT, or any earthly tie is worth more than your happiness.

"Being Loyal", "Being Committed" or "Being faithful" to causes that influence a strong distaste with yourself can only be fixed by doing the first job.

Chapter 5

Discovering your Inner Guidance

(Being In-formation)

There is a road in the hearts of all of us. This road is hidden in seldom travels and it leads to an unknown sacred place. We are taught to SEEK Outside of ourselves for the guidance and roadmap to this journey. Perhaps that is why it takes so long for the Seeker to find because the truth is that the answer is within.

The human body stores an inner presence that provides us guidance. Your ultimate responsibility is your ability to respond to this inner presence and adhere to the guidance. It speaks in a sacred whisper, uttering increments of guidance to you that can only be interpreted by the world, through you.

The inner guidance system works like this (read over and over). We all come forth from non-physical and invisible energy to live in these physical bodies. But all our being doesn't come from the physical. A large quantity of us, the God part of us, the eternal part of us, the source energy part of us remains non-physically focused. In other words, you are created from divine and eternal source energy. You're not a body, you merely live in a body. The physical body is nothing more or less than a template where your true non-physical self is expressed. Through your life experiences in your physical body, you will develop a desire for more. After asking for more, that request will then be answered by source energy because the source (God) then gives its undivided attention to what it is you are asking for. As thoughts, beliefs, and ideas are flowing through you to create the unadulterated combination of what you desire, it calls for a magnificent amount of source energy to sustain the body.

Everything you see in this physical world reflects a thought created by the mind to experience itself. The body was created as the host to experience the thoughts that are in the mind because thoughts cannot experience anything by themselves. The mind interprets everything you see, touch, smell, hear, and taste. The mind is made up of a collection of thoughts, ideas, and concepts that patiently awaits an opportunity to be communicated through the body.

Every thought you have in your mind needs a body or world to make it real because every thought in the mind needs a physical body to have that experience that the mind is creating.

People think to identify themselves by their body or when they die, that their body remains in the earth, but their spirit self is uplifted. Perhaps these mental archetypes suggest why we spend so much time searching outside of ourselves for things that we already possess inside of us. When in truth, the standard operation of all humanity, with respects to our inner connectedness with the true guidance system, is just like when one plugs their cell phone into a charger that's receiving power from an electrical socket within the wall. You don't ask the cell phone to be the charger. You are happy that the cell phone remains a cell phone, as well as the electric socket, remains an electric socket. You are delighted that the energy from the electric socket powers your appliances. You understand the difference between the source of the power and the cell phone. With all due respect, you are the charger. You are the extension of source energy (GOD), but the source will always remain non-physically flowing to and through you.

The source is always moving to and through you and as you undergo your physical experience, this connection to the source will cause you to have an overflow and expansion of personal desires.

In other words, every human is having their understanding of life and exposure to experiences in life, which gives birth to greater ideas and experiences that will improve their quality of life. Once that which one desires to improve is declared, whether written, unwritten, verbally or non-verbally, source energy (God) will channel its undivided attention towards what is being asked for, towards improving the creation that is going to reflect it, and source creation will channel the larger part of itself towards the manifestation.

Do not classify it as wrong to explore your Earth and see things that are of concern to you. That is what we are created to do. So, when we see things that concern us, we immediately ask for an improvement and immediately the overflow of improvement happens through you from source and source creation is with you on your path towards manifesting that improvement.

But when you connect to the opinions of others or overly rely on others, including all persons, places, or things outside of yourself for guidance, you experience the horrible feeling that is only the result of looking in the opposite direction of where source momentum is leading you. By looking in the opposite direction, which means keeping yourself accompanied by those who are not likeminded, not accepting yourself enough to accept that you're enough, not standing up for your truth, you hold yourself with millions of others in energetic resistance or out of formation with the progress that moves you towards what you've asked for. In other words, you didn't have to wait for anybody to help you figure it out. You can have it right now and you can tell by the way you feel whether you are experiencing this right now.

Unfavorable momentum is only a symptom of moving in the opposite direction, too far ahead or outside, of the confines of your vibraction, which is the invisible storehouse around your physical body that God communicates to you through. When you come out of formation or are not moving in harmony with the current of your vibraction, you will experience the horrible feelings that happen when you look back.

Consider the idea here to bridge any gaps of misunderstanding. If a car was driving down the freeway and you get in a collision with a car driving in the same direction, then it's not as extraneous. When you collide with a car coming from the opposite direction, it's much more damaging.

When you are flowing in-formation with the current of the non-physical presence and energy, then you have a much more comfortable and enjoyable journey. When you are operating against the current that has been summoned upon your life, that you've been asking for, it will not work out very well. And the most lucid signal that you are going against the current that the non-physical presence is when you feel negative emotions.

The preceding example should give you a thorough understanding of what's meant by flowing against the current of your Vibraction. You could just have a conversation with a well-meaning father about his child that he adores more than life itself and listens to all the gyrations about what he is going through in order to understand what is going on with his child at school. He will find himself getting frustrated with the petitions and contradictory energy of the school system in the name of gaining a proper perspective. When truth be told, all he needs to do is step away from what is bothering him and focus on something that gives him access to his vibration and from inside the vibration everything is peaceful.

The fundamental key mentioned in this chapter is "Discover Your Inner Guidance System." God source intelligence can and always will flow freely and effortlessly through the human body.

This fundamental key is the pinnacle of the knowledge offered in this book. It can be interpreted, comprehended, and applied only by "Doing the First Job" of mastering your own thoughts.

The inner guidance system is the channel of momentum that leads to direct communication with this non-physical presence within you that has been referred to as your inner being God, Source, SPIRIT, and many other name variations depending upon one's culture. It has been recognized as jumper cables from the perspective that your body is like a car. Your thoughts are referred to as being like a car battery.

If your car battery dies, in order to start your engine, it is important to make the right connection with jumper cables. As you know, it is pivotal to be sure and connect your cables properly. If you don't, you will blow the engine.

The inner guidance system transcends the common form of explanation. It cannot be effectively-known or understood by one who has not grasped, through the application, the fundamental keys of this book because such a person has no experience or understanding with which the inner guidance system may be compared.

Grasping the concept of discovering your inner guidance system comes only from attuning to your thoughts and how they are expressed through you. This inner being in you can only be discovered through you mastering your relationship with you.

For this reason, it should be encouraging to know that all the POWER, KNOWLEDGE, and WISDOM in the entire Universe is already within you. It's all a matter of becoming connected to that part of you that this great presence flows through.

At this point in reading the fundamentals described in this book, your mind should be prepared to accept, as truth, a statement that may otherwise be deemed as farfetched through the aid of Socratic questioning. You will now discover a truth of forthcoming importance to the human family and all that exist to understand.

THE TRUE IMPORTANT RELATIONSHIP

(How many relationships are you in?)

Are you in a relationship? There are seven important relationships that you have been in and will always be in. The seven relationships directly influence each other, ensuring the magnitude of one's growth, freedom, and well-being.

The human family's greatest misfortune consisted of men and women who graciously try and fail to build relationships with people and things without ever truly developing a relationship with themselves.

I have had the honor of being hired to mentor thousands of men and women in the area of relationships. There is something cheerfully wrong with a society that projects the importance of building relationships, but 85 percent of relationships end in BREAKUPS. This book was not written for the sake of subjectively claiming men or women as the cause of this reality. That would create an uproar that will remain ongoing.

My examination work showed that the primary cause for relationship failures is because it's become common to forge into relationships with others without ever establishing a relationship with yourself. As you undergo this process, you are forced to learn yourself through something or someone else. As you read through the list of relationships, notice the order and observe, point by point, how one relationship projects itself in the other relationship, which will ultimately influence the harmony you experience and your freedom.

1. First Relationship: **THOUGHTS** - relationship with thoughts.
    We are all like satellites. We emit vibrations to all Mother Earth. The nature of vibration is totally based on the nature of our thoughts. ALL THINGS BEGIN WITH A THOUGHT. The ideology is given more depth when described in chapter one. Whatever you think is what you become. People take on the nature of their thoughts. Observe with excitement, in our own life experience, ALL feelings, ALL emotions, ALL conditions are effects caused by the repetition of consistently nurturing your thoughts.

2. Second Relationship: **BODY** - relationship with the Body
    Your second relationship is your relationship with your body. All feelings and emotions that the body experience is a direct effect of momentum caused by thoughts. The way you feel (in the body) communicates the harmony or discord between the thought vibrations you have going on and the thought vibrations your inner being has going on vibrationally. Everything the body's eyes SEE is always a reflection of the thought pattern projected by the thoughts that dwell in the mind. There is no freedom for the person who makes it more of a priority to focus totally on the body and not practicing a thought pattern that is in-formation with the bodily projections. 95% of those who are not experiencing freedom make it their chief aim to put forth effort into building their bodies. Perhaps this was the primary cause of the failure.

3. Third Relationship: **THE WORLD** (anything outside of you) - relationship with the World
    Your third relationship is your relationship with the world or anything outside of you. It has become overly popular to skip relationships 1 and 2 and adopt the habits of thought patterns and habits of things outside of oneself (environment, friends, and family). Any person who is to experience freedom must discover their true eye-dentity aside from the version of themselves they've become due to the conditions the world presents. Experience has been proven to be a great educator, but freedom comes from knowing that all relationships outside of you, are far less important than the relationship you have with yourself. In fact, experience with things outside of yourself are designed as tools to discover who you truly are. BE AWARE, that if you have not fine-tuned relationships 1 and 2, then your understanding of self is based on relationship 3. FREEDOM COMES FROM BEING AWARE THAT YOU CANNOT DO ANYTHING ABOUT SOMETHING YOUR NOT AWARE OF.

4. Fourth Relationship: **THE SOURCE (GOD)** – relationship with your inner being source
    Your fourth relationship is your relationship with Inner Being (Source, God, Higher self). Thoughts are projected into the BODY from the WORLD. Some of the thoughts we think come from a component that distracts one from God. The body is always practicing the thought pattern of God while also keeping active,

the thought patterns of the world. The sorting through of these two opposing thought patterns is the key component that dictates our relationship with God. In other words, one's ability to obtain a relationship with God will only come through mastery of the previous relationship. In doing so, you will enter a state of awareness that maintains the highest vibration because of the ability to focus without being hindered by unfavorable momentum. When you are in–formation with the inner being within you, you will see things as God sees things.

5. Fifth Relationship: **TIME** – relationship with Time
   Have you ever noticed that hurrying frustrates you, frustration leads to mishaps and slows you down, when compared to moving quickly and with focus? Have you ever worried about what might happen? These situations exemplify our relationship with time. Our relationship with Time and God serves as the hidden but supernatural gateway that limits or permits the actualization of our desires at a given time and place. Time is both our limit and our opportunity. The three components that are magnified with our relationship with time is our connectedness with our past, present, and future.

6. Sixth Relationship: **EGO** – relationship with the Ego
   No one can truly experience success or freedom without mastering the egos toolbox. This means you must obtain mastery of the tactics of the ego. Understanding the relationship with the ego is one of the healthiest relationships known to humankind. You may discover, at one end, the ego is your best friend and at the other end, your greatest enemy.

7. Seventh Relationship: **MOTHER EARTH** – relationship with Mother Earth (the universe)
   There is no greater caregiver than one's mother. Mother Earth is expanded to include ALL THINGS MADE OF MATTER AND ENERGY in one basis. An enlarged circle that hosts the interconnectedness that exists within ALL THINGS. Mother Earth is represented by its people: HUMANS. Earth is our caretaker. When you are disconnected from this relationship, you have no sense, no awareness, and in-effective communication. When this occurs, it creates polluted environments. Consequently, due to the interrelationship we have with Mother Earth, if we pollute her environment, our circle of life will be marked by polluted beliefs and unfavorable momentum. While on the contrast, if we

treat Mother Earth as a "circle of care and connection", we will experience HEAVEN ON EARTH.

Remember all 7 relationships described in this book are relationships you will always be in for the remainder of your life. Truly, it has become overly common that WE only connect to and define ourselves by our BODY and relationships created through associations with The World.

Do not get discouraged if you do not fully comprehend all that has been stated. Unless one has done "the First Job" or mastered your first relationship, it is not expected that this awareness will be understood fully upon just reading this chapter.

The idea of relationships that the World projects make it normal to engage in relationships without never actually having a relationship with oneself. Unless you are from another planet, it is ideally expected in relationships that human beings "Get Engaged then get married."

This book advertises the proper God designed relationships, which is one of the keys to establishing harmonious relationships. The truth of relationships is the exact opposite, meaning instead of getting engaged and then married, MARRY YOURSELF THEN ENGAGE THE WORLD.

The fundamental key of marrying yourself then engaging the world will open the door for the discovery of the inner being within you.

HOW TO CONNECT to your Inner Being

The Truth shall set you free. Truth is the universal manifestation of intelligence. The discovery of your true self aside from the self we've become acquainted with as a result of defining ourselves by the facets of the World (relationship 3). For humans to yield towards that discovery, this section will use different illustrations with hopes that they project the specific information concerning the design by which the polluted beliefs planted into the mind by the world interferes with our freedom and our connection to our inner being.

Mother Earth and all her children, including humans, plants, and animals, are effects caused by organizing very small increments of matter in-formation. Reread this statement – it holds extraordinary significance. Mother Earth and all of her children, as well as every single one of the cells that construct their bodies and every other atomic structure, starts as a non-physical form of energy.

Mother Earth, as well as the entire universe, is constructed of ENERGY and Matter. There are two forms of thought vibrations: DESIRE and DOUBT. Thought vibrations are forms of energy. Meaning, when you begin to think a thought derived from the impulse of DESIRE, you are summoning the same "non-physical energy that the creator used in constructing all Creations, including the mind, body, and the world through which thought vibrations flow through".

As far as science, this perfect process exists due to the undeniable laws of vibration and attraction. The summons of nonphysical momentum that thought vibrations and thought impulses create emits a vibration.

As you read this book, you are welcoming this same method into your personal experience. You are genuinely and unwavering in utilizing Mother Earth's perfect laws by cultivating your desire for freedom into its physical or tangible equivalent. ALL THINGS are created this way. YOU WILL BE NEXT TO SUCCEED BY FOLLOWING THIS BLUEPRINT.

You will experience unlimited magnitudes of freedom through the aid of adopting this truth that exist due to the natural laws of the universe, "AS YOU THINK YOU VIBRATE, AS YOU VIBRATEYOU ATTRACT, AS YOU ATTRACT YOU MANIFEST, and AS YOU MANIFEST YOU FEEL EMOTIONS". In other words, emotions are indicators of thoughts practiced on the inside.

Thoughts enter the body through the mind in the form of vibrations which are interpreted through the five senses. Once they are interpreted and mixed with feelings and emotions, a non-physical magnetic force is created which ATTRACTS based on the dominating thoughts occupying the mind. In this instance, your thoughts or focus activates the momentum of a vibration that is then mixed with the law of attraction. The law of attraction responds by creating the radiant non-physical environment around you called a vibraction which radiates and permeates our human body, attracting to it experiences and manifestations of its same nature.

Examine the quotes of some famous successors, who have paved the way for new discoveries. If you read their quotes, you will see how the universal laws of vibration and attraction display themselves. As you read, give yourself permission to find security in the laws and their power. Unlike any law, rule or regulation humans created, none of these laws can be adjusted or manipulated. They are definite and all things hoped to be attained will call for the perfection of these laws.

Metaphysics of Law of Vibration and Attraction

Quote or Phrase	The Law	Nature of Thought	Message	Humanitarian
"Misery Loves Company"	The mind stores our thoughts, molds your emotions and transmits a vibration that attracts the same frequency.	Misery	If your miserable, you are having miserable thoughts, then you will be drawn into conditions and circumstances that sustain misery. You will also find happiness in knowing others are not happy.	William Shakespeare
"If you can imagine it in your mind, you can experience it in your reality"	The dominating thoughts in the mind form a vibrational point of attraction that directs one's actions based on our thought quality.	Imagination	Energy (thoughts) of a certain nature tend to attract the energy of similar nature and vibration.	Rainbow Warrior
"Thinking positive thoughts, you will attract	Positive thoughts produce positive vibrations,	Positive	Positive thoughts = Positive experience	Maya Angelou

positive outcomes"	which produce a positive point of attraction, which creates a positive experience.			
"What we think is what we become"	Thoughts become vibes which we broadcast through a series of wave patterns and draws to us similar patterns in the form of people, places, ways of life and experiences.	Neutral	We experience whatever our thought pattern attracts.	Buddha
"A man is but a product of his mind, whatever he thinks, he becomes"	I attract to my life whatever I give my attention, energy, and focus on whether positive or negative.	Neutral	If you think it, you can be it. What is IT for you?	Mahatma Gandhi
"Thoughts are things, if you see it in your mind, you can hold it in your hand"	As you think, you vibrate, as you vibrate you attract, as you attract you manifest	Vision	SELF EXPLANATORY	Bob Proctor
"Whatever you are	Thoughts are like magnets.	Nuetral	SELF EXPLANATORY	-Anonymous

going through in your life is what you are attracting"	They release a vibration that attracts to it whatever stores a similar frequency.			
"Most people spend more time thinking about what they don't want and wonders why it keeps happening"	As you think, you vibrate, as you vibrate, you attract, as you attract, you manifest	Problems	Due to the law of attraction and the law of vibration, whatever you focus on, read about, think about or talk about intensely, you will attract into your life.	-Anonymous

There is a magical reward for all who learn to consider these laws. When you possess chief understanding of this, you will possess the keys. Surely there is much more information to learn on these laws but the basis of this book is not to teach on these matters, more so stress the importance of being aware of them. Besides, it would take about 300 pages to cover each law.

The fundamentals of these laws store the keys to activating your relationship with God. Moreover, you will be drawn into putting less effort into controlling your thoughts and just identify and free yourself from the thoughts that control you.

What magical power does the law of attraction and vibration give you? How amazing does it feel to know that if you set up in your mind some form of positive mental or chemical activity, that gives access to the supernatural forms of infinite energy? How amazing does it feel to know that infinite energy is always available to those who choose to summon it at your aid, even if the entire world was on the opposing side?

These and many other similar statements that appear in the mind as I have observed men of God like Jesus, who started as "carpenter and built an entire following, as inspired by the dominating thoughts to free humans from a life marked by SIN". Harriet Tubman, who with all odds stacked against her, became one of the world's famous abolitionists and humanitarians, who summoned to her aid the momentum of the nonphysical energy and discovered the "Underground Railroad" which was conducted as the path to free people from slavery.

I have had the fortunate privilege of examing both Jesus and Harriet Tubman, day by day, over extended periods of time. Therefore I speak from a space of knowingness when I say "God" used these humans to perform Miracles through. Remotely their major source of direction came from the vibrational environment that their alike desire to FREE people created.

There are many phenomenal demonstrations of how vibration and attraction are evident in many of our everyday experiences. It takes a person who's aware of the law, to gain clarity of these unwavering occurrences and how they influence freedom in one's relationship with God.

Destiny was hired as a police officer, in a small city after getting out of an eight-year relationship. She was 27, with what appeared as a perfect life. Her "bad" experience with her ex-boyfriend gave birth to the thought pattern "bad things always happen to me." Because of that dominating thought, she continued to attract unfavorable relationships.

Ray Lewis, constantly told himself that he would be the greatest football player to ever step foot in the University of Miami. The law of attraction aligned with his belief and presented him with conditions to transmute his desire into physical reality. Ray Lewis was not only abducted into the Hall of Fame at the University of Miami but also in the NFL.

In the 1994 American animated Walt Disney feature, the Lion King, remember the scene towards the end of the movie, where Simba ascends up pride rock, roaring and taking his place as TRUE King. Upon hearing Mufasa's voice telling him to "Remember", Simba mustered up courage, assurance, and willpower, before roaring over the reclaimed Kingdom. In the moment he roared, the sound waves of his roar were interpreted by the rest of the pride and created a vibration to solidify Simba's place as

King and in turn, their surrendering to the King through roaring back their approval.

Bald Eagles have been the national emblem of the United States since 1782. In their distances, Eagles usually communicate through emitting a series of high pitched vibrations through whistles. This vibration travels through sound, unlike any other calls in nature, from over a 7-mile radius, attracting their mate to them.

Once upon a time, you woke up "feeling great" and slowly rose to your feet and said "today is going to be a great day" and later horrible things begin to happen. Shockingly you were not as emotionally phased by the horrible things. Whether you were aware of it, the law of vibration and attraction came to your aid. For holding onto the thought "today is going to be a great day", you created a world where you could only see the good in horrible, which keeps good momentum flowing into your life.

Again, each of the above situations are examples of evidence of these laws. In each scenario, vibrations traveled, whether through thoughts, spoken words, or animal sounds and created the reality that was information with the momentum projected through the vibrations.

How amazing is it to know that the instant you think about something, whether intentional or not, you create the basis for that manifestation? Because when you think about a brand new car, your mind will start to create the pathway for the manifestation. When you think about making a million dollars, these divine laws will begin to create a way for the manifestation.

Before leaving the subject of the law of vibration and law of attraction, examine yourself. Determine in what ways, if any, you can identify how these laws influence your personal experience. Examine yourself thoroughly, courageously and willingly, thought by thought and see how your thought pattern projects itself into your physical reality. The analysis of the thoughts flowing through your body holds dear to the discovery of that which will give you an advantage point when connecting to the God presence within you.

Here you will find the real factor that interferes with you and your relationship with God. Here you will find not only the factors that interfere with the holding of this relationship but also the basis of being able to inherit an active relationship with the creator. Read this section carefully and face yourself willingly, IF YOU TRULY DESIRE TO KNOW WHO YOU TRULY ARE AND WHAT YOU ARE CAPABLE OF DOING. These are the KEYS that must be mastered by all who desire to grow a relationship with God.

We were non-physical before we lived in this physical body. Now that we are in this physical body, we are both physical and non-physical. In your physical awareness, you have two vibrational thought patterns, outlooks, and perspectives. You have the vibrational thought pattern of your non-physical presence, which is God, and we have the thought pattern of the physical part of you, known as a human being.

Let us further explore the facets of the non-physical presence. The majority of people are not in tune with their non-physical presence. Most follow relatives, friends and the public at large to influence their physical awareness, at such a magnitude, that they cannot interpret the thought patterns of the nonphysical because they've been clouded by the thought patterns adopted by association with things outside of them.

Now that we are living in these physical bodies, we are both physical and non-physical. The mixing of the nonphysical and physical awareness creates what you know as DESIRES. Your experience in the physical body gives birth to desires.

HERE IS WHEN THE MAGIC HAPPENS. Whenever you have desires in our physical awareness, the non-physical part of you immediately becomes the version of you that you desire to be. And this version of yourself that your nonphysical presence has become can only manifest when you are in-formation with the thought pattern of the non-physical expanded part of you.

Those were a lot of words, which may cause confusion upon a first time reading. Allow me to simplify the keys that are pivotal points of knowingness in regards to How to Connecting to God really works as well as how ALL manifestations occur.

1. We are Non-physical than Physical
2. We become both Non-physical and Physical
3. Physical Gives Birth to DESIRE

4. The non-physical becomes the desire that the physical gave birth to.
5. In your physical awareness, practice the thought pattern of your Non-physical desire.

Let great excitement follow reading this section. Generally speaking, everyone grows up with a desire to become a millionaire, which is launched in their physical awareness. How amazing is it to know that the moment you have the thought of becoming a millionaire, your nonphysical presence, immediately becomes the version of you that is a millionaire. Now, through continually, practicing the thought pattern of your non-physical presence, in your physical awareness, your non-physical will be in-formation with your physical presence, which gives birth to the physical manifestation of that desire through the physical body.

There are many instances, where people experience extraordinary outcomes as a result of flowing with the momentum and thought pattern of their non-physical presence.

In Steve Jobs's physical awareness, he was just a college dropout who purchased food by returning soda bottles. In his non-physical awareness, meaning flowing with the thought pattern that God chose for him, he was a mastermind behind the creation of Apple.

Known as "Jenny from the block " or JLo, Jennifer Lopez, as a child, enjoyed singing and dancing even though her parents did not in favor of her desire of dancing and singing. To make her mother happy, she went to college. After a semester, she couldn't take it anymore and dropped out of college to pursue her dreams. In a year, she became a successful dancer and quickly rose to the spotlight.

In Jim Carrey's physical awareness, he was a child with dyslexia who had a struggle with learning. After sifting through his physical awareness, he discovered a comedian in him, born through his knagging desire to make people laugh. Jim Carrey introduced "Jane" and moved forward to star in "Dumb and Dumber" which cashed him millions of dollars.

In Tyler Perry's physical awareness, he was a victim of sexual abuse and someone that was kicked out of school. The thought pattern of the physical awareness even led him to two suicide attempts, at the age of

22 and as a preteen. Age 23, he began to flow with the thought pattern of this non-physical presence, moved to Atlanta and began to work on his stage career. Perry finally broke through and became a success, named the highest-paid man in entertainment in 2011.

Many more great examples, which emanate the power of the non-physical. All throughout the world, people have come to Miracles through seeking, sorting, and sifting within themselves for the discovery of their Natural Desire that we recognize as our passion. True Success, True Freedom, True Fulfillment or whatever it is that human beings deploy as a means of happiness will not be experienced without discovering your true desires. Once you discover what that desire is, while taking steps towards the manifestation of that desire, the non-physical presence, whereby God communicates to you through, will begin to align itself within your physical body. As this happens, those who mastered the art of not following their desire or passion will make it uneasy for you to conquer your desire. Unfortunately, life plays out that way. Because of the dominant presence of those who master the art of not following their desire, it has become hard for people to free themselves from the voices of doubt in their physical awareness which separates them from interpreting the flow of the non-physical thought pattern. It also makes it challenging to recognize when the thought pattern of your non-physical presence is active in your physical awareness.

There are some common human symptoms that indicate that the non-physical thought pattern is active in your physical awareness. Connecting to God, your non-physical presence, requires no great amount of intelligence, no higher level of general knowledge, just the special awareness of when it is active in your personal experience.

1. Thinking about your Dreams, as in aspirations.
2. HAVING DREAMS, non-physical presence may reveal itself when the physical awareness is silenced, which is when the physical body is in a state known as "sleep".
3. RECEIVE A VISION – non-physical presence will reveal itself to you the physical awareness in the form of a vision.
4. Wishing and Imagining - the Imagination is the storehouse of ALL thoughts of your nonphysical self.

These and many other symptoms will present themselves into one's experience as a sign of your non-physical presence communicating to you. I have experiences where I adhered to the communication of my non-physical presence and experienced a "MIRACLE" on the path of following the spirit of it. After spending two months in constant prayer and meditation, I kept having visions of BALD EAGLES and CEMETERIES.

As one may read the previous sentence it may be deemed as so far-fetched to motivate you not to continue reading. IT IS A TRUE STORY. From this story, I hope that one will be drawn to the inevitable resonance that God, the source of all non-physical and physical awareness, moves in mysterious ways, with many wonders to perform.

I, therefore, speak from experience when I say that maintaining an open mind is the key to allowing God to move in your experience in an extraordinary way. Creation is a reflection of the creator; the Universe is full of things God created, by which God will use to reflect himself to you through. Being closed-minded will blind you from seeing the mysterious ways God desires to move into your life. Maintain an open spirit, determination, and effort towards your greater cause and concentrate on how God looks at you aside from people's opinion of you.

Ego to the Eagle

It took constant prayer and meditation, for me to connect to God. I was praying and meditation, 20 minutes a day, for two months straight. In my meditation and prayer, I am constantly seeing images of BALD EAGLES and CEMETERIES.

I spent an entire summer in South Dakota working and building grounds with the Native Americans. As summer reached an entire, I asked a Medicine woman named Lula Red Cloud "will I ever be honored with Eagle feathers?" Lula Red Cloud was my spirit leader and mentor, descendent of legendary Lakota Chief Red Cloud and Crazy Horse. She said, "you will get your eagle feathers in Canada."

"I have never been to Canada before, how will that ever happen?" were my thoughts. Two days after my departure from South Dakota, my basketball trainer contacted me and said the National Basketball League of Canada was hosting a basketball combine in my hometown and asked: "Did I want to enter the draft?" As he asked, my mind immediately wandered to Lula's words, about me getting my Eagle Feathers in Canada. I entered the Canadian draft for the NBLC.

Traditionally when preparing for a basketball season I spend countless hours in the gymnasium preparing for the season. I had spent that entire summer engaged in spiritual growth, in other words, I was not physically prepared for a combine. It is now time to play basketball on a higher level, without being physically prepared.

Many people fall short of connecting to God because they fall under the influence of there physical awareness, instead of attuning to their non-physical. In my physical awareness, I was not physically fit to produce high results at the combine. Through attuning to the momentum of my non-physical awareness, I not only showed up at the combine, but I was drafted to play in the NBLC for the Moncton Miracles.

Lula stated that I would get my eagle feathers in Canada. I was unaware of how it would happen but within a month, I found myself in Canada. To the world, getting drafted to the NBLC was an opportunity to make BIG MONEY, in a surely credible manner. Americans have a tendency to conducting professional sports that way. Although it was awesome to get drafted by the NBLC, playing basketball was not my focus in Canada. I was focused on Lula's words "You will get your eagle feathers in Canada."

Once I arrived in Canada, I made it a priority to spend at least 30 minutes per day meditating and praying. Surely we all pray and practice some form of meditation, but this was different. During and following every prayer and meditation I engaged, I had CLEAR visions of Eagles and Cemeteries.

To honor the vision, I began to ask the citizens of Canada questions pertaining to the Vision. "Are there any bald Eagles around here", "How close are we to a cemetery" and further questions of that nature. "There are NO bald eagles in this part of Canada", "The nearest cemetery is 5 miles", "Why would you be looking for a cemetery", were the nature of responses.

After weeks of constant seeking and running into constant doubt, I slowly began to lose faith in the vision, but I never gave up. The knowingness that the vision did not come with clear directions was beginning to weigh on me but the vision was clear. After spending months of sustaining hope in the midst of what appeared to be a hopeless situation, my persistence began to pay off.

After losing a basketball game, I decided to walk home to release the frustration of losing. One of the fans noticed me walking, pulled over and stopped to speak with me.

Fan: Why are you walking home?

Me: I just want some relief from the game.

Fan: You played a great game. How about you hop into my car, drop me off home and keep the car for tonight. Take a ride around town. Just bring it back to me tomorrow.

I have always heard that Canadians were nice people but this moment showed me how true that statement was. I drove around for an hour, driving nowhere specific, but praying to God during the entire ride asking "God if this vision is real, show me what it means."

Upon finishing the last word of the prayer, I felt an unusual feeling come over me. I felt a strange feeling in my heart and over my body. Mother Teresa once stated, "We need to find God and he cannot be found in noise and restlessness." Many people believe that simply praying and meditating permits them the space for God to speak. Well here is a fundamental key that is important to all who desire to connect to God. Know that there is a supernatural favor shown to the one who's willing to remove themselves from the confines of their comfort zone and seek TRUTH from an open heart.

While riding in the car, I drove past a sign that said DO NOT ENTER. On the other side of the sign, it appeared to be a dirt path. While driving past the DO NOT ENTER sign, the MOST powerful thing happened to me. I was driving at 45 miles per hour when passing the do not enter sign. Although in my physical awareness, I was going 45 miles per hour, but it felt like I was driving 5 mph. At this moment, it felt like time had slowed down. As if at this moment, God was directing me from being so physically focused on being nonphysically focused. Some cultures describe this space as the STILLNESS.

In an attempt to articulate the stillness of God's presence, this brief section is written: Inside of all of us, there is a holy space, sacred place, where God dwells within us. When we entered the world, the space was open and readily available for God to flow through. Traditionally, after experiencing what we call LIFE, this still space within becomes clogged by unfavorable thought patterns and beliefs. Imagine humans being a river, whereby God flows through. ALL thoughts that are not in-formation with God's thoughts interfere with the flow of God's presence within you.

The stillness is a solitude place in our human body where God's presence dwells. This presence is activated through the sustaining of an open heart and practicing the thoughts of God. The thought pattern of this inner being, this God presence within you creates a momentum in the body, that once followed, leads to a path marked by Heaven on Earth.

After being swamped with frustration and dealing with the doubt projected by others, I finally caught my break. After walking down the dirt path with the DO NOT ENTER sign, I discovered there was a cemetery ways down that path. As I entered the cemetery, I bared witness to a bald eagle flying back and forth from tree to tree. And from this bald eagle, I received my eagle feathers in Canada.

Despite the discouragement that was felt from the opinions of others, my focus and commitment to the awareness of my conscious allowed me a miraculous experience. In fact, if you are reading this book, then you are also a part of another miraculous experience.

A Game: A Metaphor about Connecting to God

Allow me to shift the focus to a childhood game I enjoyed, which now will be used to expand on how to connect with God. How many of you remember the game "Hot Peas and Butter, Come get your Supper?"

Hot Peas and Butter is a game of Hope, Faith, organized planning, and cunning logic. Objectively you take one group of boys and one group of girls, one group will be given an object (a belt) that they have to hide from the opposing group, in an UNKNOWN area. Once the object is hidden, he or she will say the magic words: HOT PEAS AND BUTTER, COME GET YOUR SUPPER. Then each boy and girl has to try and find the hidden object. As the party searches for the objects, the group that hid the object tells them they are HOT if they are close to the belt and COLD if they are off course. Once the hidden object is discovered, those who discovered it claims the victory for that round of play.

I can remember observing my brothers, sisters, and cousins while playing this game in hopes to find the hidden object and quitting the game from the discouragement of repeatedly being told "your cold." On the other hand, I remember those same relatives in a state of relaxed ease and eagerness and once the phrase "you are HOT" is spoken, a huge rush of momentum and unadulterated burning DESIRE would flow into their bodies. And every time the phrase "your HOT" was repeated, this burning desire would grow.

I can also recall times when they were cold, as in far away from the object. After searching, they would get HOT and sometimes take the wrong turn, leading them directly back to the COLD zone. Now able to remind themselves of the supernatural feeling it creates while in the HOT zone and using that feeling as motivation to create a focus that leads to the HOT zone and the path towards the discovery of the hidden object.

Evaluate the methodology in the game. It amazes me how 99% percent of the most powerful life lessons were taught to us when we were children. If you survey this game properly, some will be shocked, a few will show happiness, others will be awakened, but ALL will have been shown the process of recognition, the path to Heaven on Earth, road to the hidden treasure on Earth that awaits all who are willing to endure the process of discovery.

"Hot Peas and Butter" is juxtaposing a Supernatural God "Truth" and a figurative game to add meaning to the concept of the figurative game. The true meaning behind the concept of games such as Hot Peas and Butter, Hide and Seek, I SPY, HIDE THE HIMBLE, Easter Egg Hunt, Scavenger Hunt, Whose got the button is this:

God hides treasures on the Earth, that awaits those who are willing to dig in the depths of their mind, sift and sort through thoughts in their mind and commit to, in action, the thought pattern that moves you towards your treasure. The God presence in you will create momentum, whereby you must follow, as it leads you on the path towards your eternal treasure. As you move towards your treasure, you will feel it. The key is to recognize that the treasure is inside of you.

How to CONNECT TO GOD

Four simple steps lead to the development of a relationship with God. They require no high level of intelligence or no advanced level of education. But they do require special awareness of oneself.

1. Discover the hidden treasure within you known as your "Burning Desire".
2. Follow the momentum of that Desire and commit to it, in continuous action.
3. Keep an open mind at ALL times: A closed mind will cause resistance against the flow of the momentum that leads you to your hidden treasure.
4. Be willing to follow that Desire and momentum through the confines of doubt, discomfort, and fear.

These are the keys to unlocking the doors to the hidden powers that determine your future.

These four steps are the keys to building relationships in all aspects of life. The key purpose of the points of emphasis is for you to apply these keys as a Practiced Lifestyle.

These are the keys that lead to FREEDOM and GENERAL WELL BEING.

These are the keys, which permit mastery over discomfort, doubt, and fear.

These are the keys that lead to wealth, abundance, and prosperity.

These are the keys to experiencing Heaven on Earth.

Throw yourself into the basis of this process and bear witness to your supernatural fate. When you begin to face negativity, REMEMBER, the triumphs you overcame to reach this point.

NO FOLLOWER OF GOD CAN EXPECT A TRUE EXPERIENCE WITHOUT PRACTICING THE HIGHEST FORM OF TRUTH. For example, UNCERTAINTY is not a true reality. People only accept uncertainty as a reality, when they are not aware of the highest truth, that UNCERTAINTY creates focus.

Remember, when uncertainty comes, it is only an opportunity to create a focus that declares certainty. If you forge in giving up before you have effectively established the focus that leads to your desired outcome, you desert your DREAMS and DESIRES. Every time you desert your DREAMS and DESIRES, you set more limitations on yourself. Before this reading, you may have followed or supported the idea that "the sky is the limit."

When you begin to apply the keys mentioned in this chapter, as well as this book, you will experience more refined thinking from the swerving understanding of this quote.

The TRUTH is the Sky is not the limit, because if it is, that implies that there is still a limit. In other words "the sky can't be the limit because if it is, that means there is still a limit."

When in TRUTH, there is NO LIMIT to your GREATNESS. REMEMBER NO FOLLOWER OF GOD CAN EXPECT A TRUE EXPERIENCE WITHOUT PRACTICING THE HIGHEST FORM OF TRUTH.

God said FREE yourself from the belief that the sky is the limit because that's what is limiting you.

Elevate this statement, write it on the ceiling over your bed so it is the first thing you see in the morning when you wake and the last thing you see every night before you go to sleep.

When you start to practice the highest form of TRUTH, which is the thought patterns of God, you will be selected as a person with whom can experience God personally.

The remainder of the chapter will be devoted to raising our awareness about the factors that interfere with developing a relationship with God and ALL other forms of relationships. The information displayed in this section will provide a practical basis to gain clarity on the factors which influence the prosperity in your relationship, but it will be the GOLDEN KEY to those who desire to build a relationship with God.

Being aware of the factors that interfere with the relationship is just as essential to know how to build the relationship. In this section will be found concise details to those who desire to begin a relationship with God.

It should be exciting to know that ALL great things were created as influenced by the blessings of God. What reason would one have for ignoring an intimate connection with the source of ALL creations?

Generally speaking, there are two types of people in the world: those who Pave the Way and those who are In the Way. Those who pave the way are willing to take the necessary steps to bring forth new creations, new ideas and new miracles to the world. In the way, it includes those who exist as hindrances to the manifestation of newness, through being a distraction, being distracted, led by fear, actionless talk, and other unfavorable expressions. Choose whether you have been called forth to pave the way or are you in the way.

The difference is God's favor is different. The one that is in the way cannot expect to experience God at the same magnitude as one that is paving the way, although people that are in the way expect the same favor as one that is paving the way. The responsibility of the way paver is greater. The greater the power, the greater the responsibility. With God being the Almighty Source of Power, it is essential for God to move in the lives of those called to Pave the way.

There is nothing wrong with being in the way. In this space, you are designed to discover the "way paver" within you. In other words, being in the way is just as important as paving the way. Most great Stewarts discovered that they were in the way of their own greatness, which is a reality reached through taking FULL accountability for one's thoughts and facing their TRUTH. At this renewed basis, people begin to think things about themselves that is in the way of this great version of themselves flowing through their experiences. Then, immediately fine-tuning themselves to a place of receiving the greater version of themselves into their personal experience.

People who practice this form of thinking are usually those who are successful, free, and more likely to develop a relationship with God. The true way paver makes it a priority to take full accountability for all their thoughts and actions.

We have reached the section, where we will bring together all of the teachings of the chapter. For we know it is just as important for us to be aware of what draws us away from God as it is to be aware of what draws us closer.

The primary cause of unfavorable outcomes in all walks of life is found in this section. It will be a huge resource if you can inspire someone who finds themselves trying and failing, feeling empty, unbalanced, or been trying to find God or have been praying for a thing for years and still have not seen a result. It may be beneficial to know that this book provides the keys to understanding why these types of things happen.

The commonly used advice "get to know yourself." If you absorb the content of this chapter profitably, you will make this profound discovery. The same discovery that serves as the key to ALL unwavering outcomes. You should know that the version of you that you are or have become, known as "self", is entirely based on the influence of things entirely outside of you. You should know that the version of self that you identify as "you" is not the version of you that you have been created to be. If you are reading this book, you are on the path to discovering your true self. You cannot discover your true self until you have professed that truth to yourself.

The unbridged ignorance in connection with the self we have been created to be is displayed by those who surrender their happiness and well being to a paycheck. As an effect, we begin to define ourselves with respects to our self-worth, by our body and the trajectory of the world, instead of by our thoughts. In other words, we get attached to the faculties of relationships 2 and 3 and they become the reason we are forced further away from discovering and practicing the thought pattern of God. Are you happy? Yes, BUT. Well when we are the version of us we have been created to be, there is no IF, ANDS or BUTS after that question. Before you can be led back to your first relationship, which is your relationship with your thoughts, you've become attached to the faculties of relationship 2 and faculties of relationship 3. Even though you are aware that you were worth much more than your current experience, even though you know you deserve better, even though you know you can do it, you become FEARFUL of detaching from the comfortable thought patterns, physical connections, and relationships you've collected throughout the process of discovering your true self.

"I want to become a doctor but "it's hard" because I have to spend time with my children and I can't afford the schooling."

Before you can truly start to connect to God, know that, by making choices to commit to things outside of you, in action, even your children, you start to readjust your life in a way where it pulls you further away from discovering the thought patterns of God or attuning with yourself enough to identify your true thoughts aside from the thought pattern you've been practicing, as an effect of identifying yourself by things outside of you; including your family, sports team, your religion, social media, your job, your children and more. Whether favorable or unfavorable, that's the version of you, that you have been tempted to be as a result of outside influence aside from who you have been created to be, as influenced by God.

It is a huge difference between the "SELF" we have been tempted to be and the version you have been created to be - "TRUE SELF." The "TRUE SELF" knows their value, values their time, turns their dreams into reality, just due to their connectedness to God. The other version of "self" is only happy when they have things outside of them (money, nice house, jewelry, children). ALL things become the CONDITIONS they begin to depend on for their natural state of happiness, well-being, and sense of freedom. Your fulfillment, well-being, and freedom have nothing to do with things outside of you. Your true fulfillment, well-being, and freedom is established entirely by your ability to be a useful service to yourself by practicing God's thoughts and providing services that induce others to follow the same path.

This misunderstanding of self is essential in the path of becoming who you have been created to be, which will happen once you have built a relationship with God. Moreover, those who deem this version of themselves developed as influenced by the world as their TRUE SELF, this decreases the likelihood of connecting to God and increases the likelihood of being separate in nature from the version of you God created you to be (TRUE SELF). One's life will become a reflection of their failures, stand still's, give up's or they will go backward in life, due to this lack of awareness. One will begin to be dishonest with themselves by force or dishonest with themselves by choice to ensure a sense of comfort in this state.

"I know I have the potential but what if I fail?" SOUNDS FAMILIAR? Whenever we avoid the path of our potential, we miss out on building a relationship with God. It's on the path of your potential that you find God and become who you've been created to be.

Your degree of honesty with yourself about whether you are who you've been created to highly influence your interconnectedness with God. If you feel incomplete, empty, or not satisfied, these are physical symptoms of not being who you've been created to be. Take this survey by answering the following questions and by permitting someone to review your answers who will not sway you from your truth.

TRUE SELF SURVEY

1. Am I working the same job, like my parents? (You should know there is a difference between who you truly are and who you've become as a result of following the path laid by your parents).
2. Am I willing to pursue a passion, even if it means leaving the job that brings me money for my responsibilities RIGHT NOW?
3. Am I putting forth my best effort to running towards my fears?
4. Am I confused about my capabilities?
5. Am I connecting to things and people that value me, as well as themselves?
6. Am I living or tiptoeing through life, to make it safely to death?
7. Am I "In the way" of my own greatness?
8. Am I afraid to be my true self, even if it means to be rejected or judged by your family?
9. Am I in receiving mode for what God has for me?
10. Am I constantly feeling sluggish, fatigued, and lack of energy?
11. Am I afraid that I will be successful?
12. Am I willing to detach from things outside of me to discover the experiences that influence my current thought pattern?
13. Am I aware that when I avoid my calling, I am teaching myself "I don't love me enough?"
14. Am I aware of the difference between making up my own mind and "letting people own your mind and then making up your mind for you?"
15. Am I ready to face the truth to be set free?
16. Am I open-minded?
17. Am I in a relationship with myself?
18. Am I willing to be my true love?
19. Am I following the path laid out for me or the path that I followed based on observing others, instead of following the hidden road God put in me called my "desire?"
20. Am I dishonoring my calling by working at my job?
21. Am I focused more on what I can do or what I have not done?
22. Am I being honest with myself?
23. Am I dishonest with others?

Upon reading and answering those questions, honestly, you will have created the basis for clarity to flow through your experience and now God will cooperate. From this point on, your feelings of worthiness, fulfillment, and empowerment will come in proportion to the degree of honesty you can sustain with yourself, knowing that every time you are honest with someone else, you are always listening. Those who chose to be dishonest with themselves and protect their comfort in misery based comfort zone, REMEMBER that true wealth, prosperity, freedom, and abundance are discovered on the path where you are being your true self, which is only activated through continually being TRUTHFUL with yourself. It is therefore essential to all who desire an experience with God to know that, continually seeking for higher truths will bring you a great advantage point.

Awareness in this section will serve as the fundamental keys to ALL who desire progress in any path. It will be specifically beneficial to those who desire chief understanding of themselves and the faculties that influence their experience.

Thoroughly comprehending the information displayed in this section will be useful in all aspects of one's personal, business, and/or spiritual life. It will be useful in creating a world where we learn to understand each other on a deeper level. This information will create a basis of truth, that will be used as a personal directory towards your destiny.

WHAT DISTRACTS US FROM THE OPPORTUNITY TO EXPERIENCE GOD

Now that we have examined the faculties by which influence many to be swayed away from experiencing a relationship with God, where many are introduced to the faculties that creates the most deterrence from building the relationship. Let's take a step further and see the listing and review what the Western Civilization offers us that innocently distracts the person seeking a personal relationship with God.

To start, let's be reminded, we live in a world, where people are aware that "the truth shall set you free." Most of us have never taken the time out to face their truth because it offends the ego. We thereby cling to our illusion and limit ourselves from our growth and freedom. We have become accustomed to this form of living in our society.

We have the privilege to experience freedom of thoughts, freedom in opinion and religion, freedom in sexual preference, freedom to vote, freedom to make money, freedom of speech and expression, freedom of occupation or profession, freedom to rent, own and lease property, freedom to eat all types of food, freedom to dwell in all states, freedom to reach your fullest potential, but equally freedom to be a failure, freedom to be limited in opinion, freedom to be confined by religion, freedom to be sexually confused, freedom not to vote, freedom to be broke, freedom to keep our thoughts to ourself, freedom to be lazy and not work, freedom to live in poverty and freedom to obtain any degree in life which we are prepared and ready for, and more. Many of the other forms of freedom exist, but this catalog gives the EAGLES point of view of the areas where the thought of freedom stores the greatest value.

Large quantities of people make mistakes in building relationships with things outside of them and unknowingly commit to them in action. Next, let us focus on some of the key factors that our widespread human family is attached to and is unintentionally pulled further away from the discovery of their freedom and a relationship with God.

- JOB. Because of the universal desire to make money, the average person has made it more of a priority to commit to a job, than their destiny. This choice seems sensible when reassuring the benefit of being able to purchase FOOD, WATER, and CLOTHING, but unknowingly limiting our ability to experience our true freedom and truly experience God.
- FAMILY. Family is a human's most reliable source of directional influence. Traditionally Mothers, being the primary caregiver, secures the most influence. However, there is more to life than your biological family (mother, father, brothers, sisters, cousins) can understand. To discover the expansion that life offers, it is important to experience life outside of the confines of the family paradigm. "A bird is always supposed to live in the nest until it learns how to spread its wings and fly on its own." Your wealth, growth, expansion and your true experience with God awaits you, but you must spread your wings and be willing to journey through Mother Earth to discover the treasure that dwells dormant waiting for you. Practicing the thought patterns of your family, by merely, following their same religious mode or beliefs, working the same job, living in the same state, etc limits one from being in the RECEIVING mode for the very thing they desire.

They receive just enough to be alive but always will feel a sense of "SOMETHING IS MISSING." And truth be told, something is missing.

- RELIGION. All humankind is naturally influenced by some form of practiced religion. Religion trains us to practice a BELIEF through a story, which gives us a vantage point during various points in our life. Among these beliefs, it doesn't emphasize the distinction between beliefs and knowingness. The average human believes in God but does not truly know God. How can you believe in someone you don't know? For example, when Robin Williams died, he left many stories. "Robin was a great father", "He was funny", "Robin was crazy", "Robin had a bad attitude" are just a few of the comments taken from those who observed him. But there is a huge difference between information (beliefs) gained through stories, versus, knowing someone personally and intimately. Mistakenly, religion has caused us to deem beliefs as knowingness. In other words, humans master the stories that project God's power and they interpret that as having a relationship with God. Religion has caused people to deem the art of mastering the stories of God to be the same as knowing God. As an effect, the average religious person has NO relationship with God, because they deem religious doctrine as a revelation. This next statement will surely, raise a lot of eyebrows, but if I did not share the truth, then I would be doing my reader a disservice, but the truth is that the TRUE relationship with God will not be discovered until one closes their Bible, Quaran, Zohar or whatever religious book they practice. Because the book, reassures beliefs through story and the more you practice comfort in beliefs, the further you are pulled from you building your relationship and knowingness.

What is the GREATEST POWER in ALL CREATION?

Without the desire to judge, no subjective outlook, and no hidden motive, I am honored to be in the position to simplify the greatest mystery in the entire universe, which is well misunderstood, but highly sought throughout Mother Earth, as God offers you complete freedom, abundance, fulfillment, and wealth for the price of the relationship between you and you.

I have the privilege to experience God intimately and walk in this non-physical power. God created ALL things, God being the creator that organized this great non-physical power and created ALL things (humans, animals, and trees) made of matter. On that note, I choose to pose an important question to all Humankind: What is the greatest power in ALL CREATION?!!

God is the greatest power, but the MIND IS the GREATEST POWER IN ALL CREATION with God being the creator and the MIND being the creation. CREATIONS ALWAYS REFLECT THE CREATOR.

If God created ALL things, since creations reflect the creators, then God will use any creation to reflect the mysterious presence through, as in my case God used an Eagle, which is something God created. Believing, alone, does not permit you a relationship, but more particularly adopting the MIND of God, the mind being the greatest doorway that reflects the power of God, will create the experience that we ALL are seeking.

The procedure for adopting the mind of God can not be taught through science, math, chemistry, physical education, social studies, drama, or Arts. Education of this nature, alone, will influence Humans in all fields to feel stripped of their freedom, whether they are a lawyer, highly paid professional athlete, doctor, teacher, or preacher if they are working from a space outside of the mind of God because it is only God that supplies the truth, freedom, awareness, wealth, and appreciation that allows human progress.

Power without education is always dangerous. Riches without first adopting the Mind of God is the recipe for disaster. Establishing a relationship with God is the most important key to freedom in all civilizations. Simple appreciation of this relationship, in action form, could create a HEAVEN ON EARTH space that finds satisfactory by merely being alive, able to breathe, being supplied with food, water, and shelter and deem everything else as a "BONUS" or "BLESSING".

Strangely we identify freedom as a space that is dependent upon "THINGS" outside of us. With the quickness that THINGS come and go, imagine how short-lived your freedom will be if it is dependent upon THINGS.

To depend on money for freedom, you would have to create a time machine and travel back to 1958 when the money machine was invented. Then, you will be presented with another issue. What would you use the money for, even if you had it?

To depend on your job, you would have to create a job where you are funded to be " not be yourself". At some point, you will run into problems, because freedom is only experienced when you can be your true self.

You would be surrendering your freedom to things you can't control but you have control over what you subject yourself to.

The true freedom which everyone seeks is readily available through "Doing the First Job", all of which allows an interconnectedness to God.

The purpose of this book - a purpose to which I have committed my life to - is to present to all who desire the knowledge and most practical steps that can be taken to experience freedom; emotionally, financially, and spiritually.

I have organized the faculties on each relationship that shifts our vantage point or distracts us from seeing when God is trying to show up in our experience, in more depth.

The BODY (Relationship 2)

NO human will truly enjoy the quality of a relationship with God without honoring their body. Good health is the key. The primary causes of bad health are due to a lack of self-control and awareness. These are the primary actions taken to dishonor the body, which ultimately interferes with one's ability to connect to God.

- No physical exercise
- Poor supply of fresh air, due to unfitting breathing.
- Unfavorable use of sex
- Using recreational drugs and harmful substances (smoking, etc)
- Overeating foods that are not sustaining to Good Health.
- Don't Drink enough WATER
- Not getting the adequate amount of REST
- Eating out instead of quality cooked meals
- Eating more sweets than fruits and veggies

- Drinking too much soda
- Not going to the doctor for necessary check-ups
- Drinking alcohol: not in moderation
- Being in unfavorable relationships

Practicing healthy habits are pivotal and often requires one to transform their mindset. But if you are willing to love yourself enough to improve your relationship with your physical body, regardless of your age, sex or physical ability, you put yourself into RECEIVING MODE for an experience with God.

The habits that you supply the body, directly affect what you project out into the world. The largest quantity of deterrents from our interconnectedness to God comes from the influence of our relationship with the world. Before thorough understanding can be grasped about what we are created to do in the world, we must examine, observe and obtain mastery over our relationship with our body, because ALL of your true relationships work hand and hand. This calls for no counselor, no therapist, no psychologist, just the willingness to be honest with yourself, which has become a FEAR for millions of men and women in the world.

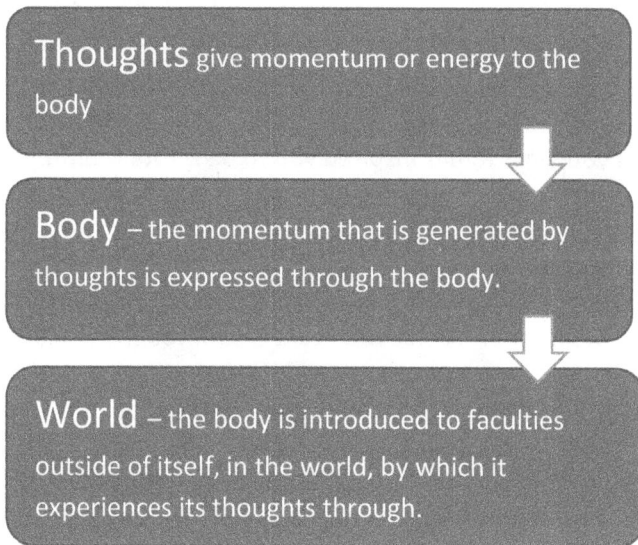

Thoughts give momentum or energy to the body

Body – the momentum that is generated by thoughts is expressed through the body.

World – the body is introduced to faculties outside of itself, in the world, by which it experiences its thoughts through.

Here are the faculties that we are introduced to in the world which serve as a deterrence from establishing a connection with God.

- FEAR OF TRUTH. All transformations through accepting the FULL truth of who you are. This means acknowledging the truth of your current state to transcend it. Before you can experience improved and honorable conditions, you must be willing, to be honest with yourself. Being honest has become one of the most difficult things to do. If you can't be honest with yourself, you will not be honest with others. You should know that "wherever there is no truth, there is NO GOD."

- "I KNOW IT ALL" attitude. There is no hope of building a relationship with God for one who knows it all. The person who repels that attitude becomes so indulged in the thought of "knowing it all", they become closed-minded to new information, new ways, and newness in general. "God can not persistently operate in someone's life if they possess a closed mind."

- LAZINESS and PROCRASTINATION. One of the primary reasons people don't build a relationship with God. Everyone says "I want to get to know God" but we get so attached to responsibilities in the world, that we become detached from our ability to respond to the directions God gives us. "I've been at work all day, I am going home and going to bed". "I am too tired to study". While we are putting our dreams to the side, you put aside the relationship with God that will be developed along the way.

- ATTACHED TO FAMILY PARADIGM. This is a hindrance that can be overcome with relative ease. ALL must be willing to accept this. The version of you, your family inspired you to be is totally different than the version of you God created you to be. It takes experience outside of the confines of the family pattern to make this discovery. Anyone who is willing to detach from the family paradigm, in action form, becomes readily available for an experience with God. Your bravery, courage, openness, and perseverance will earn you this place in God's eyes.

- INABILITY TO MAINTAIN AN OPEN MIND. Most of us are closed-minded "but" we are telling ourselves we are "open". Moreover, people are not in "RECEIVING MODE". There is no way around being open and maintaining a state of relaxed openness. God can not persistently operate in someone's life if they possess a closed mind"

- ASSUMING MENTAL ACTIVITY TO BE THINKING. People who assume mental activity to be the same as thinking tend to be able to decipher between their thought pattern and God's thought pattern in them.

People fail to make this distinction – MOSTLY ALL - will use God's name as a plan to project their pattern. Where one is found using the representation of God as a means of projecting their personal agenda, completely offsets the chances of truly experiencing God.

- WRONG CHOICE IN RELATIONSHIP PARTNER. The more time you spend with things that do not deserve you, the further you get from experiencing what you deserve. Unless your relationship is pressing, in action form, towards harmony with God.
- INSECURITIES AND DOUBT. Insecurity and doubt are expressions of fear. It is also a sign of a lack of knowledge. People who experience God bypass fear and walks in faith.
- DEFENSIVE MINDED - THE HABIT OF TALKING YOUR WAY OUT OF A SITUATION. Wordiness is used as a tool to maneuver around the TRUTH, mainly used to assure one's comfort zone. Forming the habit of systematically avoiding discomfort by maneuvering around the truth, will surely, deplete one's likelihood of intimately experiencing God.
- THE HABIT OF NOT USING TIME WISELY. Our awareness that God is always readily available to us has a passiveness about utilizing the time we have to work on our relationship with God. In other words, because we are aware that God is always there, we take our time.
- OVER-THINKING. The person who overthinks, generally, have a hard time having faith. Over-thinking is not favorable. Overthinkers see "no further than what is practical but God source awareness expands beyond practical knowledge. In fact, this book puts forth the best effort to make God practical.
- BEING SIMPLE MINDED. Being simple-minded is a closed-minded way of living and God extends beyond simplicity. Surely, nothing is wrong with going to college, getting a job, working a 9 to 5, and retiring at 65. But this lifestyle assures closed-mindedness to the expanded thought pattern, whereby our God experience will require of you.
- NEEDINESS FOR ATTENTION. In God's eyes, food, water, and shelter are our only NEEDS. Most have the privileges of having these three basic NEEDS, all the while "telling themselves they need attention", which is only an effect created by not TRULY appreciating that God "has already given you everything you need". Because you are ignorant of that, you then become more ignorant to when God is active in your personal experience.

- INABILITY TO LET GO OF THINGS THAT DO NOT SERVE OUR GREATER GOOD. There is a difference between what feels good and what serves your greater good. When you hurt someone's feelings, it doesn't feel good to apologize, but it serves the greater good of the cause. One must identify the distinction between the two and as a gesture of self-love, be willing to let go of that which does not serve your greater good, whether it is family, friends, co-workers, or even your current state of mind. If not, you limit your chances of intimately experiencing God.

- LACK OF SELF LOVE. There is a shortage of SELF LOVE and respect within the human family and as an effect, a stronger dependency on things in the world to provide a sense of self-love, self-worth, self-purpose, and self-importance, be it (social media, jobs, children, etc.) Unknowingly, the more we commit to these things in action, the further we are pulled from the relationship with God that can only be discovered through the interconnectedness with self, at the price of detaching from the things of the world.

- NEEDINESS FOR APPROVAL FROM OTHERS. No one gives you permission to be who God created you to be except you. Make up your own mind, don't let people own your mind and make up your mind for you.

This is an opinionated society. It has arisen through the action of men and women who projected their opinions into ideas and claimed their right in history through transforming ideas into blessings of freedom and abundance.

If you are one of those who believe you will experience freedom by possibility, keeping your thoughts to yourself, spending your time amongst insignificant people to feel significant, trade your time in for money at a job where the demands are more than the pay, if you are one of those who depend on government services for money without considering the fact that they are depending on the government for sustainability, if you are one of those that believe voting for a president whose political party you agree with is the key to freedom, you may hold onto your belief, but be aware that NO political party can assure your freedom because freedom in this country, is deemed as something totally different than it is in all actuality.

However, all humans should know the one truth concerning the concept of freedom which all are seeking. As wonderful as the idea of freedom is, the concept of "FREE THINGS", we assume "FREE THINGS" offers us benefits and privileges. The truth is NOTHING IS FREE, EVERYTHING COMES WITH A PRICE. The price is not always money.

Government programs create dependency on legal service and by depending on the service, subjecting ourselves to a sense of limitation. No government system has ever been produced by which it instills in people's mind, how to acquire freedom through providing tools and habits that lead to wealth without sabotaging one's integrity.

There is a fundamental in the world known as "SELF WORTH." This concept brings more than speculation to the human family. It has brainwashed our understanding in a manner that must be brought forth.

Let's make it clear, the excitement that the thought of "FREE THINGS" or "FREEDOM" has had more influence on the human family than we are aware of. It is one of the biggest polluted beliefs used by government agencies and political influences who exercises their influence of freedom to control others mind. Offering free things and freedom has been used as a tool to win over the minds of people for the sake of criminals, crooks, and government outlaws whose been illegally and legally appointed as leaders to establish control over the mind in the area of their chosen purpose. In other words, it takes REAL EYES to REALIZE the unseen mission of our world leaders who make it their responsibility to keep an up to date report on all the human progress and activity in business by offering "free" products and imply it doesn't come with a price or some form of product in exchange for their sense of self-worth.

The economy and business make "top dollars" through employing the methods of using a systematic approach of marketing THINGS as having VALUE, which in actuality, generally is much less valuable than its marketed price range. Surely, we all must respect and utilize this economic basis of goods and services but this cyclic continuation has caused many to depend on things of low value in exchange for a sense of self-worth.

Remember all things have worth, but this economy and market make it perfectly difficult to truly understand the difference between value and worth. Only a few material splendors actually have value. But remember, all things God has produced, created, and permitted to be utilized to further our careers, personal goals, and endeavors have worth, but too many men and women give chief value to things that only have mere worth, and by doing so, they freely exchange their self worth for the price of materials and luxuries.

Keep in mind that "NOTHING IS FREE" and if you deemed anything as free before reading this, then you were unaware of the intangible or tangible exchanges that occur in all human interactions. If Johnny goes to the store and purchases a candy bar, after telling himself he is going to lay off sweets. When he eats the candy bar, he will feel a sense of less high self-worth.

The church gives "FREE hot dogs" to the community, but every time the community member takes a bite out of the hot dogs, it reinforces the belief that things are "FREE", which deviates one from discovering the truth, as well as creates more dependencies on the church and state to acquire a sense of fulfillment and well being.

Kason Cheeks goes to Mount Olive College because they offer "four years of free education" and denied an opportunity to play basketball at the University of Chapel Hill for one year and potentially earning his other three years. He made this decision from a poverty-based mindset. In other words, fears of having to pay at the moment contributed to making a decision that could've guaranteed him years of freedom if he was aware that by playing at UNC alone, regardless of his performance, would've offered him a better opportunity for his talents to be furthered. In other words, although he was given FREE MONEY to go to school, in exchange for FREE MONEY, he risked the potential of tapping into a much more advanced basketball network.

These examples may be deemed as minor upon first reading, but in these types of instances, our freedom is affected.

There is NOTHING FREE in the world and ANYONE engaging in careers that utilize "free offers" are not aware that by subjecting yourself to that, strips us of the freedom of seeing that "NOTHING IS FREE, ALL THINGS COME AT A PRICE". There is nothing wrong and right about businesses engaging in the motto. If you are one whose been prosperous, built clients or expanded your business at the expense of offering "free services" or products, this is not written to judge you. At some point, we all will adopt this method of labor.

I PUBLICLY ANNOUNCE TO HUMANS

"The Truth Shall set you FREE" is a statement that will continually be uplifted in this book. It is important that we become aware of the thought that NOTHING IS FREE and by accepting that as truth, you create the freedom of a thought pattern which permits you to see what is really being exchanged when we assume it is "FREE". "Nothing is Free" because we are always exchanging our TIME, INTEGRITY, SELF WORTH, DESIRES, and RELATIONSHIPS for something. In God's eyes, those things will always hold the UPMOST value. More than any opportunity, service, or luxury any bidder can offer you.

The orderliness in the world is not set up in a way where it effectively emphasizes that truth. You can not offer this clarity from a premise where the basis of your information subjects some form of limitation. This basis limits one to know just enough information, whereby they remain in a state of neediness to a service of the bidder. This does demonstrate nor implements a pattern that leads to freedom, wealth, and abundance.

It reinforces the idea of giving value to things that don't hold sheer importance. It reinforces us to believe that just because "IT has worth, that means it is WORTH IT". It reinforces "that we have to depend on things outside of ourselves for freedom. It reinforces that "MONEY is worth more than HAPPINESS". It reinforces that spending time assuring you're well being is not as valuable as clocking in and clocking out at work.

It doesn't tell you that when you work, you are being PAID to help someone else's dreams come true. It doesn't tell you that the more you associate yourself with things that do not value you, the more you tend not to value yourself. It does not tell you that just because something has worth, it does not mean it is worth it.

Observe how this truth pertaining to value and worth is uplifted in this real-life situation. If you go to the convenience store and ask the clergyman "can you give me change for a dollar" the clergy may give you four quarters. You go to another convenience store and ask the clergyman for change for a dollar, the clergy may give you one hundred pennies. In other words, whether it's from a dollar bill to four quarters or from a dollar bill to one hundred pennies, "No matter how scattered our understanding of our self-worth is, in God's eyes our value REMAINS

THE SAME."

Blessed are we to live in a FREE society, where all humans are declared rights, privileges, and opportunities to expand, which happens as a benefit of birth.

We get absorbed in a world that has a hard time distinguishing between value and worth. Consequently, we join alliances with things that create reasons for us to ignore our own value, make money to hold the door for someone else's desires in life and sabotage our relationship with God through the thought patterns we are rendered to through forging ourselves to these experiences. Then comes a life marked by finding comfort in misery.

We have not reached a stage as humans where we are collectively accepting of the truth, but this book will move us there. The misleading distinction between value and worth has led us to a vibrational space of placing more value on things, than your relationship with God.

Unfortunately the more we continue this pattern, freedom will remain a thought and we will not discover that the most valuable things in the world are free. It does not cost any money to be nice, it does not cost any money to hold the door for someone, it does not cost any money to say "God bless you" when someone sneezes, and it does not cost any money to say "THANK YOU" when someone gives you something. Those are the useful services that God desires to see more amongst the human family. Gestures of gratitude are proverb ways of showing God that we appreciate the life we have been provided. Gratitude produces the virtue of attracting and vibrating positive energy, which keeps us in RECEIVING MODE for an experience with GOD.

"Thank you" for reading this book. The power of two words. The energetic power that's channeled through those words is worth more than money. Free to receive as well as free to give. Thankfully we have reached a point in this book where truth can be revealed that is extremely important for us to be aware of: Time is FREEDOM and Connecting to God is FREE. Take out the TIME to CONNECT TO GOD to experience freedom, because the only thing in the world free is God.

This chapter is at its closing point, I hope the CLARITY in this book is serving you. The observations come from 28 years of detailed-oriented study of the methods of those who experience God and those who are unaware that they are practicing the thought pattern instilled into them, by the world, known as the United States of America.

Chapter 6

"Be Well Structured and Precise"

(The Way from Change to Transformation)

You have discovered that all accumulation or manifestations begins in the form of thoughts, repeatedly thinking a THOUGHT creates a DESIRE, the pursuit of that DESIRE declares the beginning of the journey to freedom, in all forms, from the nonphysical to the physical, into the workroom of the mind, into a vision or dream, where ideas for its transmutation into the tangible reality are constructed and structured.

In this book, you will find many fundamentals that are necessary to move you from where you are to where you desire to be. One of the primary fundamentals is the development of a concise, well-ordered plan or strategy through which the transmutation of your plans will be made.

You will now be instructed on the pre-planning process for "The Birth of New Born." Allow yourself to see how important it is to have a well structured and precise plan.

Every parent discovers how true it is that nothing is more precious than life itself when they are preparing for a child to be born into the world. First, they have to wrap their heads around the thought that they are having a baby. Little by little, a sense of nervousness mixed with excitement, until the thought turns into an unadulterated desire to assure a comfortable delivery.

When this desire or thought grows, parents will experience a series of undesirable emotions. The thoughts of proper funding, the child's name, whether the child is a boy or girl, are they Healthy, navigates through the mind, creating this emotional state known as "scary excitement". Understand that pre-delivery planning, the baby shower, decorating the baby's room, attending hospital classes, buying new clothes, and finding a baby sitter are actions used to assure a comfortable, welcoming, and organized set up that creates the basis for a child to experience.

The parents organize their efforts to meet the demands of the child. No child should experience LIFE without structure. All humans have the natural ability and willpower within their minds. You may feel uncomfortable about this question, but can you imagine what life would be like for a child if they were born without pre-planning?

If the baby was born and there is little to no care shown towards the well being of the child if the crib was not purchased to assure the baby sleeps peacefully and safe. Imagine if the mother did not exercise to PREPARE a healthy childbirth. If the parents did not attend the doctor's visit, but only came to the doctor on the day the baby was born. Not letting go of things that may create stress on the women and ultimately effecting the child's birth.

If you fail to recognize the reason behind the illustration, you should realize now that "things will not operate sufficiently where structure and precision does not prevail". Here is the pivotal point that most lack and consequently failure prevails.

You must know that in God's eye, your vision is to God, the same as giving birth to a child is to you. You must nurture it, you must prepare for it to be brought forth into the world, you must organize plans for delivering it to the world, that is precise. Every decision you make, you must consider that your life is not just about you, it is about the thing being born through you, for the world to reap from.

The intelligent person would say, "only women can succeed in giving birth to a child." Just keep in mind, TRUTH VARIES BASED ON YOUR LEVEL OF AWARENESS. It may seem true to those who have reaped from organizing their plans and efforts, but whether male or female, everyone has a child called VISION building within them, created to be born through them for the world to see. In order to assure that your child (VISION) is successfully born through you, one must organize plans that are well constructed and precise.

As when a family is preparing for a child's birth, there are a few things you must always REMEMBER.

1. REMEMBER. God gave you this vision, idea, or purpose to be born through you. Without a well structured and precise pre-planning, it will destroy the vision. Be aware that God gave you the vision and you are automatically a Generator or Operator or Destroyer.

2. REMEMBER. Your vision brings life and light to as many people who bear witness to the creation and execution of your strategy or methods of transmuting your vision into the physical reality.

3. REMEMBER. You are involved in the commitment of a supernatural cause to you. You must put forth a qualitative effort to assure that your plan has the natural ability to gain the favor of those who behold it.

4. REMEMBER. At some point, Business Partners will replace "friends". Form a team of qualified individuals who can offer LEVERAGE through services and assets to the members of your team in return for their synergy. Do not expect someone to be a helping hand without some form of reward. No person will receive true service without giving or should expect to receive adequate service from a thing they are given nothing to. The reward may not always come in the form of currency.

5. REMEMBER. Organize meetings with your team, minimum twice a week or more if time permits until your members have total mastery about the strategy or strategies for the acquiring of your freedom.

6. REMEMBER. Maintain INTEGRITY between yourself and the members of your team. If one is passive about this specific principle, you are sure to be met with permanent failure. "Teamwork makes the dreamwork". When the team is not working together, the dream will not work.

Kaden asked one of the people at the peace march, "How much are you worth?" The person replied "one million dollars." Kaden asked, "well do I have your support?" The person said "YES." Kaden said, "well I have a million dollars." Review chapter 4 for more depth on the story but that story symbolically represents a TRUTH that is important for all to know on their path to freedom.

NO GREAT IDEA, NO VISION, NO GREAT COMPANY, NO HUMAN, NO RELIGIOUS DIETY, NO TEACHER, NO MILLIONAIRE, NO LAWYER, NO DOCTOR will possess the awareness and ability to secure their freedom or create freedom in any form without the compliance of other people. Every strategy used in your undertaken should be a reflection of the collective efforts of you and every member of your team to create a well-structured, practical, and step-by-step basis, through which you may birth your vision.

If you've forged all your effort into a strategy that does not provide the results you hoped for, implement a new strategy. If the renewed strategy is not effective, substitute it with a new strategy and so forth until you configure an effective strategy. BE FROZE. This is the point where most people accept failure and defeat as their reality because of their lack of focus and determination or inability to START OVER without thoughts of past failures damaging their effort and momentum.

The most independent person living cannot achieve true freedom, nor any endeavor is supposed to be accomplished alone. Being self-made or independent does not mean "DO IT BY YOURSELF." In fact, the only thing you do by yourself is "give yourself permission to be helped by others." To the independent person, KEEP THAT IN MIND. If you are telling yourself you accomplished SOMETHING ON YOUR OWN, it means you are not appreciating the support you have been given.

Bill Gates, the richest man in the world, "failed" in his business. He created a company called Traf-O-Data. The short term losses for Gates and his partner were critical because they gave birth to the more clarified focus which was pivotal in the creation of Microsoft.

Short term losses or setbacks exist for one reason; the reason is to yield you toward long term victories. The setback offers the opportunity to review your plans and make the necessary adjustments. If you are one who is constantly experiencing unfavorable outcomes, this means your plan is not working, which means its time to create a plan which will create a life marked by freedom.

Soichiro Honda became a multi-billionaire business. Honda began as a series of failures but he adopted the habit that most people do not adopt through failure, simplifying the plan in a way that increases its accuracy. Millions of people who acquired greater levels of education, but live inside the confines of limitation because they do not hold the most effective strategy for accumulating.

Issac Newton surely had many failures early in his career. Undoubtedly the genius was phenomenal in math. After miserably failing over and over, he decided to attend Cambridge for school, which is when the genius evolved into the educator we know today, through changing his setbacks into victory.

Vincent Van Goph experienced what felt like a lifetime of defeat as he could not sell any of his paintings. But after experiencing dissatisfaction, he created a new approach towards PAINTING. Now Vincent lives in financial freedom because his paintings now bring in hundreds of millions.

We have a tendency of observing people who have accomplished great mountains, often only focusing on their success, failing to notice the obstacles they had to overcome before the "transformation."

No true way-shower can rationally expect to acquire freedom; financially, emotionally, physically, or mentally without experiencing some degree of "DISCOMFORT." When discomfort comes, accept it as an opportunity to connect to your plans on a deeper level, through fine-tuning your plans and focus your efforts towards the desired outcome. If you give up when you face discomfort, you are not "living."

"TRUE LIFE BEGINS ON THE EDGE OF YOUR COMFORT ZONE"

Nothing within your comfort zone brings you a sense of LIFE. Staying inside of your comfort zone is like tiptoeing through LIFE with hopes to make it safely to death. Only those who are willing to face the terrorist (fear) within them, understand the full meaning of LIFE.

When you begin to choose the members for your "TEAM", select those whose LIFE displays they will never settle for Defeat. Some people foolishly define life as the space within their comfort zone. This is not true. Being in your comfort zone is equivalent to being ALIVE. Living is different than being alive. True living is giving, being alive means merely existing within the confines of our comfort zone. Living is a path that leads to freedom. It can not be obtained by being alive. Being alive is a state that declares comfort in limitation.

PRE-PLANNING THE BIRTH OF YOUR VISION

The rest of the chapter has been utilized to offer a variety of practical ways and instruments of bringing forth your vision to the world, as well as marketing services. The tools displayed here will be evidence-based to help any person or group having to elevate their products, sales, or business but it will be immeasurably valuable to those whose desire is to bring forth new ideas or leadership in their profession.

Well structured and precise planning is the key to success in any endeavor intended to lead to abundance, wealth, prosperity, or freedom. This section will provide precise direction for those who must sell products or services to acquire wealth and/or freedom.

Since ALL things begin in the form of thoughts, it is important to know that great inventions, ideas, products, etc., require a certain amount of well-structured and precise thought planning to pilot your idea from the intangible to tangible form. Most ideas remain ideas because they are not backed with well-structured planning.

Generally speaking, the thought of organizing and planning tends to create favorable momentum. Make the choice, whether you desire to surrender yourself to the structure of being well-structured and precise or chosen to scatter your efforts. The vast majority of the people in the world are simple-minded. This is not a bad thing, it just means you have to break down your vision into the simplest form for it to be interpreted by the average human mind. When a baby is born, you don't start off feeding it steaks and lobster. You give it baby milk because their body can easily process and digest that. In other words, people have a hard time understanding beyond SIMPLICITY. Most leaders make the mistake of assuming the people will be able to understand their vision because, in their mind, it is so clear. There are more concrete thinkers than abstract, so do not expect such things out of humans.

It is not expressed that way to degrade humans. On a higher note, it means nothing to harness or possess power in the form of skills, talents, great ideas, inventions, and/or millions of dollars, if one does not know how to bring them forth to the world in a form whereby the human family can reap benefits from it. Most leaders get more attached to the thought of having power, totally unaware that the world cannot follow a leader based on how powerful they are. People are more drawn to what a leader can do with the power. It is not about how much power you have, it is about what you do with the power you have. A result-driven leader utilizes structure and precision as tools to expand their knowledge, power, and influence.

Next, we are going to get to make an observation that is critical to one's freedom. Most people mistakenly associate leadership with power and authority. These presumptions are far from the truth.

All Leadership, and quite frankly, the most successful form of leadership is lead by example, and with the support of action backed by your desire. The most common is leadership by title, with the influence of commands and control as a way of swaying people away from their true desires.

Take into account all human repor, ALL effective leaders lead by example. Leadership by title or authority has been noteworthy. This form of leadership means that a hierarchy will be used to assure a sense of control between employer and employee, which creates the conditions whereby the employee is paid to make the employer's dreams come true. Those who adhere to this traditional form of leadership by title render their time for money and also creates health issues due to the disempowering pattern that comes with this. They see manual labor or their job as their only way to experience freedom.

The truth about the relationship between employer and employee, in the near future, will be made clearer. The truth is contrary to the understanding you were taught when you get employed in a business. The greatest risk factor to an employer is not the consumer or customer, it's the employee because the employer has to pay the employee. The leadership style learned through your job is only supposed to be temporary. People tend to follow the leadership by tittle modus operandi ALL of their lives, but they will not experience freedom by doing so. Leadership by action, as driven by desire, is the only style of leadership that permits freedom.

The SYSTEM

(College, 9 to 5, Retire)

We have come to a place where we deem it favorable to go to college, get a nine to five job, and then retire at 65. We come now to the major fault of following this paradigm because it is important to know what happens during this process instead what is hoped for out of this process.

People make their decisions with college being the basis of their life. Without being subjective, answer this question, what does college actually teach you? SCHOOL TEACHES YOU HOW TO GET EMPLOYED. In other words, college teaches you how to obtain a title that will gain the respect of your followers. Anyone who's actually been to college, it does not teach you how to be free from the DEBT that is built-in loans from financial aid. Schools train you to be employed not free or wealthy. Before leaving school, you feel like a degree or diploma automatically opens the doors to an office. Only to discover that businesses not only require a degree or diploma for hire but WORK EXPERIENCE outstands the piece of paper that you spend your entire college career working to earn. Even for those who get hired, instead of being content with the fruits of obtaining their degree, they become enslaved MORE DEBT, MORE DEBT, and MORE DEBT.

Unintentionally, they surrender their time for money, which they intend to use to pay for their debt. In the field of the 9 to 5, they subject themselves to leaders that lead by title, which makes you believe "Time is MONEY."

Innocently, we induce ourselves to believe that "Time is MONEY." Those who lead by title, know as long as they can induce one to believe that time is money, you can make them believe money is worth more than time. Then the employer can continually influence the employee to trade in their time for money.

Subjecting oneself to this type of system is the MAJOR REASON we do not experience freedom. Anyone who subjects themselves to a 9 to 5 life, prompts themselves to a life without freedom. Leaders who lead by example aspires for us to see "TIME IS FREEDOM" and free yourself from associations that project otherwise because in continuing the association, we subject ourselves to the thought pattern of loneliness, worthliness, poverty, and limitation.

Once the 9 to 5 mentality has completely become your standard of living, you have created the Blueprint for true happiness to never be obtained. Carefully answer this question. Which is more valuable: time or money? Time is because it can never be replaced.

Remember another thing, YOUR HEALTH IS YOUR #1 RESOURCE. Meaning time is valuable because it can not be replaced but your HEALTH is the only factor that can extend or shorten your time on Mother Earth. Therefore to commit to in action, ANYTHING or any thought pattern that makes you feel angry, disappointed, stressed, grumpy, fed up, whether it be your JOB, RELATIONSHIP, CHURCH, etc, you are disallowing yourself from experiencing freedom.

Review your life carefully and if you desire to truly experience freedom, make sure you elevate this next statement.

"You are worth more than the money you have been making."

Rewrite in first person.

Perhaps you are a reader who questions the truth of this statement. Remember the truth is not afraid to be questioned. The truth wants to be questioned. The vast majority of the beliefs you have are not true and by practicing them, they are taking you away from the truth of yourself.

The keys described here is the thought pattern practiced by many men and women who were able to obtain financial freedom by applying these concepts. Therefore, they can be deemed as valid.

- "Less is more, More is Less." It took Rosa Parks two letters "NO", to transform the world. In other words, less wordiness and complication leads to more understanding and effectiveness in communication.
- "Time is Now." One of the biggest lies you tell yourself is "I have time." You don't have time, time has you. Now it is time to utilize time, every minute, every second, every hour, in favor of manifesting your freedom; emotionally, spiritually, financially, and mentally. Do not wait because the time will never be right.
- "Time is Freedom." Time is money is what we were taught to believe. This belief causes you to be willing to trade your time for money. Time is freedom and people who plan to trade in time for money will never create definite plans to experience their freedom.
- "Chase Hard Specific." Hard work + Smart work = Results. Figure out specifically what you are working towards before you find yourself working hard but not getting any results.
- "True Leaders are Readers." On average, adults and teens are watching a minimum of five hours of television per day. While on average adults and teens are spending 6 to 21 minutes per day reading. Not reading enough leads to poor communication skills and IGNORANCE. Which will disallow one from having a rich vocabulary as well as the thought pattern of the wealthy.
- "Just because it has worth doesn't mean it is worth it." Everything the creator made has worth. But there is a difference between value

and worth. Just because it has worth does not mean it is worth the value of your time, energy, or money.

- "Health is my number one (#1) resource." The only factor on Earth that influences time is HEALTH. Meaning, the creator can contract you a life expectancy of six years, but if you are not upholding your end of the bargain, meaning sustaining Good Health, your time will be cut short.
- "No Complaints, No Excuses, No PAIN." There is no hope or freedom for the negative personality and those prone to focus more on reasons why things can't happen. Make no excuses and just make it happen. Freedom is discovered for the person who repels through complaining and excuses, on to discover the NO PAIN mindset attained through the constant effort to "keep going."
- "Sex is a tool." "Sex is a drug" is a common belief. Drugs are used to usher you into a higher state of consciousness. The sexual energy is the most dominant force of all forces that influence one's actions. Due to the domineering influence of emotions, emotions must be channeled favorably. "Sex is a drug" is a polluted belief we were taught, which trains people to depend on sex to usher them to a higher state of consciousness. In truth, sex is just a tool used to usher you to a higher state of consciousness.
- "Life begins on the edge of my comfort zone." A comfort zone may be safe and comfortable, but it's a place where NOTHING GETS DONE. Life starts on the edge of your comfort zone, meaning, if you are operating within the confines of your comfort zone, you are not living. You are tiptoeing through life, hoping to make it safely to death.
- "The public is my TRUE EMPLOYER." Every gesture of compassion, kindness, and genuinity rendered through service to the public will be transmuted into freedom. You are employed by the public with whom you are born to serve.

SEEDS THAT WILL NEED TO BE CROPPED OUT

Before leaving a life of limitation, you must be aware of the seeds (thoughts) that were planted into our mental garden (mind) that need to be cropped out (acknowledged and replaced) in order to permit a fruitful harvest (true progress and freedom).

- "Money is the root of evil." Money is not the root of ALL Evil nor is Money evil. But here is the real truth. Money earned honorably allows you to do miraculous things in the world. A lot of people behave unethically for the sake of earning money. Because of the unwavering number of people who behave unethically for money, money itself is getting a bad name. Money is a tool that can be used to create freedom.

- "I need to stay busy." It means nothing to be busy getting things done, but your health, happiness, and freedom are not reflected in the outcome. Be productive by organizing your efforts and practice the habits that will lead to your freedom.

- "I can do it ALL by myself." There is no subject of greater significance than relationships because, without others, you could not be yourself. Others with whom you share your planet with are of huge value to you when manifesting any desires. No one can transmute any belief, interest, or desire into the physical reality without the aid of others.

- "I am supposed to compromise or sacrifice." You were taught COMPROMISE or sacrifice is how you build. Compromise or sacrifice means giving up what you desire. Well giving up what you desire is the basis for Permanent Unhappiness.

- "I should not be selfish." Simply put, be selfish now, so you can be generous later.

- "I am not Perfect." You are Perfect. The only thing you can be perfect at or do perfectly is be yourself. This means that every time you say "I am not perfect", you have not fully accepted yourself. Total acceptance of who you are is pivotal in regards to freedom.

STARTING YOUR OWN BUSINESS

The knowledge shared here is the basis of many years of observation of successors who created strategies that were deemed as necessary to connect the seller with the buyer. This section assumes you are one who desires freedom, desires to make money, have an urge to be financially free, are unhappy with your job, or is craving a more secure future?

Awareness to Connect Buyer to Seller

1. Expectation And Gather List Expanded: Utilize the "who do you know?" approach. Write down anyone you know and be "without

judgment." Begin with your top 30. Include cell phone numbers, references, email addresses, etc.

2. Format-List Yourself: Sort the people in groups that are associated with one another. For instance, friends, family, school, sports, co-workers, etc.

Focus Specifically on your List

- Recognize the people with the most self-drive and the highest platforms of impact. Put a check next to these people's names.
- The first step in starting a business is not merely starting a business, but expecting the business you create to be prosperous. To do so, one must set the expectation and create a list that entails a gathered list of people with phone numbers, emails, etc. Your list will be your launching pad of the rockets of desire within you. Format the list yourself into different groups. Within each group, list every person you know. Be "Without Judgement" towards all regardless of their color, culture, profession, financial rank, or closeness of your relationship. Never allow your preconceived thoughts to replace the opportunity to discover someone's interest because truthfully, everybody yearns to be apart of something bigger than themselves. Then focus specifically on the top 6-11 most self-driven people.
- Think about how many people you interact with daily, our co-workers, people at restaurants, the bus driver or your insurer. Your interactions with people offer the opportunity to grow your list.
- You should include a minimum of 50 names, if not, you are judging and should not expect to experience freedom nor gain the support of others. Remember this list is the key to your freedom. Enjoy the process.

Surely someones going to read this and say to themselves "well I don't know anybody." This section is organized in a manner, that unless the reader is completely illiterate, they should be able to see that they know more people than they thought.

Expectation and Gathered List Expanded

Profession	Name	Email Address	Number
Automobile Body Repairer			
Barber			
Banker			
Coach			
Doctor			
Electrician			
Friends			
Guidance Counselors			
Hairstylist			
Instructor			
Journalist			
Kitchen Clerk			
Librarian			
Marketer			
Nurse			
Office Manager			
Police Officer			
Quarter Back			
Restaurant Owner			
Speaker			
Tax Agent			
Utility Operator			

Vendor			
Waitress/Waiter			
X-ray Tech			
Youth Pastor			
Zoologist			

In all fields whereby growth and expansion are insisted, the urgency of marketing is the key. Too many people have become attached to the stone age, before the emergence of technology. This advancement in technology created the basis for humans in all businesses and industries to connect with each other without being hindered by the inability to travel.

The technology is a tool that can attribute to our freedom. The collective society will continue to shift due to technology. One effect in this shift will be the lost quality of human relationships. Already people would rather look in their phone instead of conversing with their loved ones and have set in motion, the minimal level of socialization between humans.

The world is searching for up-to-date leaders. The old type leaders were driven by fear of competition and spend more time mocking the trend of their competition instead of focusing on ways to expand. The new form of leadership must deem themselves community stewards whose calling is to manage their corporation in a way that will minimize losses, maximize wins, use fundamental analysis, use organized planning, use precision, and strategy (Math) as the basis of their decision making. Oppression of employers will not serve the human family anymore. Those who desire to stake a claim in the industry: REMEMBER, BUILD AN EMPIRE, with the goal to see how many lives you can inspire before your life EXPIRES.

In the profession of religion, the stewards of the upcoming will be required to focus more on the part of us that is HUMAN in regards to the effects of the economy, poverty, and other personal issues of the modern-day and put less effort into the stories that project Gods plan.

In all fields, new leaders are important but this will be more true for education. Stewards in this profession must create practical ways of teaching people how to apply the general knowledge they learned in school. It is not about what you know, it is about what you do with what you know.

New stewards will be needed in the profession of law. In order for the community of the future to be managed efficiently, we must divorce the idea that law officials deserve the benefit of serving the community without evidence based on action, that they are devoted to serving their community.

These are some professions awaiting opportunities for new leaders to emerge. The world is transforming right now. This transformation solidifies that the means of marketing through which will be requested to solidify the transformation must be updated to match the transformation. The marketing tools described here are ones that will be useful, to set the trends for future generations.

The PITCH

The Pitch is prepared with as much precision as a building constructor would use to prepare to build a NEW Site. Regardless of what profession, the candidate is pursuing, the preparation will always dictate the outcome. Successful stewards are those who take serious, the science and psyche of marketing their services to the buyers and sellers of today. All who have services for sale should practice the same modus operandi. The following pitch will be relevant to those LAUNCHING YOUR BUSINESS, INVITING PEOPLE TO YOUR BUSINESS, USING THE TELEPHONES as a METHOD of MARKETING or ARRANGING MEETINGS.

Pitch Format

1. Hello (caller) this is _____. Did I catch you at a bad time? Awesome. The reason I am calling is, have you heard of Nimiq International Institute, yet? It is a financial education leadership program that a co-worker introduced me to. It shows people debt, how to make money, get out of inflation and pay less taxes. I am really happy about it and I am actually working with them to help grow the time program and I thought of you.

2. The Pitch for Personal (One on One meetings). I gathered some

information for you and I'd like to get together for a few minutes to sort through details and benefits for you. What time do you normally get home from work? I have some time on (day) or (day), which is more convenient for you? I could do it at (time) or (time), which is convenient for you?

3. The Pitch for an in-house Meeting. One of the most successful leaders will be in attendance at our house to go over the details at (time) on (day), I would love for you to be in attendance. Can you and your (wife, husband, co-workers) make that work?

We see people who have new ideas all the time, but often we wonder why some succeed and others triumph. The key that separates the successors from those who fail is the mastery of the pitch and the fundamentals that must be taken into consideration when presenting your pitch, which will enhance your effectiveness. The following keys are all faculties that should be taken into consideration when marketing an idea or service to anyone.

Educational background - Give a brief but precise explanation about the schooling you have had and your specific area of concentration.

Personal Experiences - If you have experiences that display, you possess the skill set necessary to obtain the position you desire, give a brief description, emphasizing all previous organizations and the name of the previous employers. Make sure you emphasize ALL special experiences which would deem you as deserving of the position.

Info through Testimony (share success stories) - I've been using the program and it has really helped me with respects to my financial freedom, growth, and expansion much faster than I thought. I know if this can happen for me, this can happen for you. This opportunity is perfect for you.

Don't ask too many questions - Hey you seem interested and appear to have a lot of questions. How about I direct you to a 5-minute video link that will give you a better idea of what I am talking about. The video will only take 5 minutes. Do you have time to watch it? "I'd love to." Awesome, I will send it over and give you a call in about 15 minutes or so. "Not now, this is not a good time." No problem, when will you have five minutes to watch it?

Set a Time and Date - I am writing this in my calendar (planner). Do you have a planner to write this in? Can I count on you being there?

Leave a voicemail - Hello, this is ____. Give me a call back at your earliest convenience. I have a very important question for you (Spend less time on the phone). This call is just a reminder of our seminar on (day) at (time). Hope to see you there.

Invite, Invite, Invite

Have you ever heard of "_____"? It will be more clear when we get together. You really don't want to miss the opportunity to see this.

ANSWER QUESTIONS

(If you are asked a question, respond to the question)

Have you ever heard of "Millionaire Success Habits"? It will make more sense when we get together. It is important that you see this. How is (day) at (time)?

Then they ask more: What is Millionaire Success Habits?

Have you ever heard of Dean Graziosi? He is a Successful Multimillionaire, entrepreneur, author, and investor. How is (day) at (time)?

Then they ask more: How does this relate to you or me?

Have you ever heard of (super leader)? It will direct you to them and things will make much more sense. How is (day) at (time)?

Get a "feel" for the person or group

Sure. What has been your experience in the work field? I am not happy about going to work. I want to spend more time with my children. I do not have a social life. This life is much more different than what I imagined. Well, you really should take a look at Nimiq International Institute. They have been successful at teaching people the tools for financial freedom. Once you have obtained financial freedom, all of those problems go away.

One who has services or merchandise to sell must master the psychology of marketing and advertising. The emergence of technology has made it fairly easy to market a service. The following information shows the approach necessary for marketing through text messages.

(Sample Text)

RECIPIENT	YOU
	Hey (name). How are you doing?
Hello, my name is ___. I hope you are having a wonderful day.	
	Hey (name). This is (your name). How have you been doing?
Pretty good, what is up?	
	Putting together this phenomenal project that is super cool. Would love your feedback? Do you have 7 minutes to watch a video right now?
Yes, I do, but now is not a good time though.	
	I want to get your input directly after you finish watching it? When do you think you will have time?
I should have time around (time).	
	Awesome I will send you the video link around that time. I want to get your input when it's fresh on your mind.

Pitch for Calling Back

(3-Way / Handoff with Mentor)

You: Hi (name). Wasn't that video awesome?

You: I am actually conversing with my mentor who has been extremely successful and is mentoring me with this and I would like to introduce you to them. Give me one sec.

Mentor: Hi (name). It is a pleasure to meet you. (Name) has said some awesome things about you. So I am excited to get to know you a little better. What do you remember most about the video? That's wonderful. Well, I am excited to share some of the details and also answer any questions you have about what we are doing. But before I do, if you are willing, I would love to hear about your story. Whatever you are willing (Guide their story) to share. I appreciate you being willing to share that. I will share some things about my story.

(What didn't I like about my life, prior to my success?)

(What I was hoping for?)

(What I desired/ and the results of my discovery?)

Arrange a Meeting

You: What did you like best? That's awesome. A co-worker introduced me to Nimiq International Institute Inc. I enjoy how it teaches people the keys to financial freedom, wealth and abundance. I am really pumped up about it and I am actually working with them to help expand the program out here and I thought about you.

Keys to a Successful Meeting

I am so happy about why we are gathered here tonight. We have proven our commitment to our future by showing up to the program. I am very excited that (speakers or co-host) could be here tonight. He or she has become a very close friend of mine. He or she is truly phenomenal in what he or she does and will be talking about (Business name), which has been extremely prosperous and has been recognized for accomplishing high levels of success in this field and we are honored to have (him or her) here tonight. Please help me welcome (speaker).

Keys to Closing a Meeting

Now you can see why we are so enthused about this. (Speaker) did an awesome job of explaining it and we appreciate him for taking the time out and coming tonight. We are totally excited and have decided to move forward and think it would be awesome working with other organizations as well. He has some flyers and brochures that we can offer you to get more information. It is really awesome. We are extremely excited about the things (Speaker) talked about. We have our tickets and would recommend you join us. We want to give a special thanks for (speaker) coming tonight. We have some refreshments here and (speaker) has agreed to stick around for a few moments to answer any questions you have, in person.

Keys to Personal (One on One Meeting)

- Dress for Success
- Feed Desires, Starve Distractions
- Keep cell phones on Silence
- Turn off TV
- Accept the offer of beverages and refreshments/Non-alcoholic
- Set up your upline to WIN by properly introducing them
- Direct a meeting at a comfortable place
- Avoid one on one meeting with the opposite sex unless their spouse is present.

Keys for a Successful House Meeting

- Dress for Success
- Have the room cooler than usual, rather than much warmer.
- No alcoholic beverages and refreshments/non-alcoholic
- Keep simple refreshments, served at the end. If not set aside a break for refreshments.
- Don't discuss those who didn't come.
- Don't interfere and always look happy and excited. Keep in mind, your supporters are watching you.
- Set up projectors, boards, etc. to enhance the speaker's effectiveness.
- Set them up in a way where the people are facing the speaker with their backs to the entry door.

- Set the speaker up to win by properly introducing them and serving them (saving a parking spot, help them carry materials, get drinks for them, get them a shoffer).

Keys to Introducing: a Personal One on One meeting / Seminar / A Meeting

- Be Enthusiastic
- Be Committed
- Speaker is your friend
- Speaker is an Expert/Master of the Craft

Keys to Closing:

- Be Enthusiastic
- Be Committed
- Promote Materials and products promoted by speakers
- Give thanks to the speaker for being there (offer surveys)
- Offer refreshments
- Keep the conversation limited with the speaker from the guest. Let your support answer their questions or schedule follow up appointments with speakers.

"Pitch Keys"

The "Pitch" keys are a fundamental basis builder plan created to produce sustainable, long term and qualitative results. It summons all the key aspects of marketing a business, that's totally based on awareness, results, simplified education and precision. By showing people a more precise and simplified way to focus their efforts on the more qualitative aspects of their business, the Pitch Keys offers to you, a well structured and precise approach towards your vision, goals, and dreams.

WHY

The Pitch keys do the organizing for you. Your only instructions are to plug your information into this marketing system. In doing so, you will discover that the system will be relevant for marketing every type of service. These keys will be of value to you unless you decide that you plan to fail.

WHO ARE YOU

The pitch keys entail of strategies utilized for more than 300 of the most successful men and women of my time. The Pitch keys are TOP NOTCH business growers and have granted many successors their accomplishments. They deserve special acknowledgment, attentiveness and should be held in high regard as they are the tools that lead to higher levels of achievement.

WHEN

The Pitch keys are readily available to all those who are in receiving mode for them.

What is your standard

The keys to success in marketing and advertising services efficiently have been simplified. Without utilizing and implementing these keys through the application, no one can promote their products and services effectively and with definance. It is your responsibility to market, advertise, and sell your own services. The standard that you set for yourself as a person, will directly influence the quality of effort and momentum put into projecting your service to the world. The standard you set for yourself, in large, influences the prices and caliber of people you can employ to further your efforts. One of the fundamental keys in effective marketing is to set a standard, that exceeds the expectations of the competition, which means don't follow the modus operandi "the sky is the limit," because that means there is still a limit. The truth is there is no limit to your greatness. The standard you set for yourself projects itself into your business, influences the quality of your products, influences the quality of people you can employ and dictate the spirit momentum that will be created when your product hits the market. Remember, your success goes no further than your standard.

Let us view the levels of standards to be clear in defining where we are on this scale:

High Quality: renders the presentation is precise and relatable in regards to connecting with the consumer, with respects to your position with the FOCUS of obtaining the highest level of success. Revenue is the focus.

Quantity: renders the pattern of putting forth your best effort all the time, with the intention of growing the number of sales or services as you "perfect your craft" through practice, trial and error. Focus on constantly giving your best EFFORT. Attention is the focus.

POSITIONING: renders the efforts are in accord and in unison with the cooperation and understanding from peers, associates, and family in order to deploy one's acceptability of High Quality and Quantity is not the key to sustaining, advertising, and creating a marketing basis for your products or services. The presentation and positioning, in which you render your service to the world is the primary influencing faculty with respects to the amount of money you make and the longevity of the service. Money is always looking for a place to go, you must put yourself in position to receive it and tell it where to go.

Dean Graziosi emphasizes this concept of his presentation, which is one of the many factors that led to his success in advertising his services. He emphasizes, the importance of practicing a pattern that will lead to success. He implemented that no matter how good the quality or quantity of service, he could not engage buyers without positioning himself in a place that is in unison with his desired outcome. Dean Graziosi stressed the point of simplifying efforts instead of putting efforts into so many places. As proven that Dean Graziosi's strategy is sufficient, he has been on television every day for two years and is a well known American entrepreneur, marketer, success coach, business owner, and real estate investor.

Numerous men and women have been successful, but what separates Dean was his character and personality. Your personality and character influence how your vision is brought forth to the world through you. If one does not have personality and character that in unison with the effort behind their service, one's effectiveness will be limited in the area of quality and quantity of services that can be rendered. Character and personality make up for the deficiency created due to a lack of quality and quantity.

BECAUSE YOU CHANGE, THAT'S WHY YOU STAY THE SAME

One of humanity's greatest downfalls is due to men and women who try and don't succeed, instead of transforming their thought pattern WHERE THEY ARE, they change locations, change jobs, and change schools. Only to discover that regardless of how much money they made, they still were left feeling the same: empty, unhappy and broke. The tragedy lies in the thought pattern that's being practiced which has caused most to experience limitation and failure, instead of success and freedom.

I have had the honor of presenting to you a fundamental key that will transform the lives of ALL who are considered "failures." The reason your outcome is staying the same is because you are trying to change it, instead of transforming the thought pattern that created it. It does not matter if you change jobs, schools, locations, friends, etc if you are taking the same thought pattern with you wherever you go. Due to our ignorance of this, we'd like to say that "because you change, that is why you stay the same."

The points highlighted here are to show the primary causes of failure for women and men abroad. All of these perspectives created thought patterns and emotions that disallow success. Review them carefully and acknowledge those that apply to you. By doing so, you are creating the basis to transmute your conditions.

Main Causes of FAILURE

- BAD UPBRINGING or BAD CHILDHOOD INFLUENCES. You cannot control where you are from. In fact, if you knew where you are truly from, (Chapter 7) then upbringing would not be a deficiency. Through the aid of negative upbringings, the focus is born which is meant to be the basis of success and freedom. Uplift this statement, Divorce the past, Engage the present possibilities, and MARRY a promising future.
- UNAWARE OF YOUR PURPOSE. As a car won't drive without the keys in the ignition, you won't activate self-drive until you know what cause to channel it towards. 99% of people do not make time to discover their purpose. Maybe that's why the wealthy is 1%. Your purpose will help you form your Mission, Vision, and Plan (MVP).
- NO STANDARDS OR VALUES BELOW AVERAGE EXPECTATIONS. Your altitude goes no further than the standard that you set to govern your life and the expectations you have out of yourself.
- LACK OF FAITH. Most of us are good at praising others and prayers. Prayers are words. What speaks louder than words? ACTIONS!!! In fact, actions give power to words. Most go through life praying and waiting for a miracle to show up. "The true prayer is action", meaning

until you apply actions towards your words, your desire won't manifest.

- GIVING POWER NOT GAINED THROUGH SELF-MASTERY. Men and women of rich families are given inheritance due to the efforts of previous generations. Power acquired without the experience that comes through the process is deemed as more dangerous than being successful and free.

- TALK MORE THAN YOU LISTEN. People who talk more than they listen are prompted to have the "know it all" syndrome. People who have the "know it all syndrome", fail to realize they know NOTHING in comparison to what life is trying to teach them. Listen more than you talk. You have two ears and one mouth for a reason.

- LACK OF MONEY. This is the most common cause of limitation and failure among those who intend to launch their business or ideas in the world. We don't know our true value. If we did, we would never practice the thought pattern "I don't have money." That belief is a reflection and is an effect of not knowing your self-worth. The truth is you are worth more than money, which means once you position yourself in a manner where your value is visible, MONEY will chase after you instead of you having to chase money.

- TOO SIMPLE-MINDED. The individual who fears making mistakes, taking risks or chances, typically surrenders their dreams to a more simplified lifestyle because the confines of being simple-minded permits one to never have to face their fears. Being simple-minded is just as unfavorable as being overly dreamy. Making mistakes is a part of LIFE. By avoiding mistakes, you avoid LIFE itself.

- TOO JUDGEMENTAL OR BIAS. Judgment or bias are forms of "fear" that exist due to a lack of awareness. People who experience success and freedom maintain a sense of relaxed openness and are FEARLESS.

- ENGAGING IN ENDEAVORS THAT DON'T ALIGN WITH YOUR CALLING. You can succeed at doing something that is not good for you. The key to pursuing any endeavor is to be assured that you are passionate about that which you feel obliged to give your best effort.

- LACK OF FOCUS. Negativity only exists to create focus. If negativity has not created a focus, then subconsciously you are focused on the negative. A negative focus will always be a crutch while in pursuit of greater endeavors.

- WORKING AGAINST THE TREND. The trend stores the momentum. Stop trying to work against the trend. If the trend is creating success for others, then adjust and follow the process. The trend is your friend, remember that.
- FOCUSED ON WHAT YOU CAN'T CONTROL. It is not your fault. How can you make a good investment if you were never taught how to invest? It is not your fault. How can you know how to be wealthy, if 1% of the world is wealthy? It is not your fault. How can you be expected to know how to acquire financial freedom if you were never shown how to do so? It is not your fault. But this book will give you the tools, so if you don't acquire freedom after reading this book, IT IS YOUR FAULT.
- TRYING TO SOLVE EVERY PROBLEM. Trying too hard to solve a problem, getting a hold of a problem or wrestling to the ground a problem, in doing so, in defining the problem, in looking for the solution, by telling yourself you have to figure out the problem, that makes you become problem conscious. Meaning, without meaning to do so, you are activating the problem even more. So the harder you tried, the worst it got. The more you wanted to solve the problem, the more you activated the problem itself, the greater the struggle seemed. The problem is not that there is a problem, the problem is that you are focused more on the problem than the solution.
- BELIEF IN THE TRADITIONAL EDUCATIONAL SYSTEM. This is a barrier that may not appear as a barrier unless you can attest experientially. Traditional Education (college, school, etc) teaches everyone how to get EMPLOYED but does not teach us to be WEALTHY or FREE. Most of us go to school only to receive a DEGREE and DEBT. Moreover, people spend their lives trading time for money in order to pay DEBT instead of enjoying the fruits of life. If you follow the principles of traditional educational systems, you are less likely to have exposure to resources and opportunities that promote wealth, abundance and FREEDOM. Keep in mind, the more you practice the mindset of your desire, the more you become disciplined to do the necessary things for them to manifest.
- TAKING CARE OF OTHERS BEFORE YOU TAKE CARE OF YOURSELF. If you are on an airplane and it crashes, do you grab the breathing mask and put it on someone else? No, you have to make sure you are breathing in order to help others. In other words, you have to take

care of yourself first so you can do what you were naturally created to do.

- PROCRASTINATION. This is one of the most common causes of failure. The root of procrastination is the belief that "We have time." Beliefs are more powerful than reality. The more you wait, the more you keep your current thought pattern active. The more that thought pattern is active, the harder it will be to reprogram. Let go of the belief that we have time. Time is now, NOW is the TIME to transform your life.

- LACK OF EFFORT. The fear of failure causes insufficient EFFORT. Most of us are good at trying no further than our comfort zone. The truth is "as long as you give your best effort, you can never fail, but if you never try, you will live in REGRET.

- LACK OF BALANCE IN DECISION MAKING. 99% of people do not know what they want. Therefore, they are not sufficient at making decisions. Evidence of this may be found in the percentage of people who seek confirmation from others in decision making. Thereby, making someone else's opinion as the basis of decision making instead of their awareness of their destiny.

- THE HABIT OF CHANGING. Change is inevitable, mainly because we live on Mother Earth and the planet is always spinning on its axis. Stop trying to change your location, change your profession, change your school and transform your mind right where you are. Change happens when one's emotional state is shifted. Meaning if you are hungry and you eat then feel FULL, your emotional state has shifted, which means you have accomplished the vibration of change. We are not aware that by merely living on Mother Earth, we always accomplish the goal of change and because we are not aware, we have a tendency to stay the same. PRACTICE TRANSFORMATION because when you transform the way you look at things, then things will change.

- POLLUTED BELIEFS ABOUT HARD WORK. There is no substitute for hard work. But what happens if you are channeling all your efforts, energy, blood, sweat and tears into something that doesn't serve your greater good. Hard work is not good for the soul if you are not doing what you truly desire to do.

- LACK OF DISCIPLINE. Discipline comes through structure and commitment to the daily practice of habits. This means you must practice a mindset that aligns with your expectations. Before you can experience freedom, you must first self practice a wealthy mindset. A set mind governs you from distractions, that pulled you away from your desires. Developing a mindset is the most important task you can accomplish. You will discover that your mindset can give you motivation and be your enemy at the same time.

- LACK OF RESPECT FOR THE HUMAN BODY – YOUR HEALTH IS THE MOST IMPORTANT FACTOR IN YOUR LIFE. Having energy for life starts in your physical body. It is much easier to live a great life when your body is right. Build a strong body and a mindset will follow. You will run out of time, but you can't continue to exchange time for money and expect the body not to run out of time.
- LACK OF SELF LOVE. Most of us are good at holding onto things that are weighing us down. When holding onto bad memories, past experiences, mistakes, failure, etc., you are telling yourself "I don't love you enough to let go."

Greater endeavors, big business or "reaching the TOP" or whatever word you use to describe elevation requires people to apply and respect, some form of adapting, adopting, and adjusting. These three AAA's are essential to freedom and transformation.

Keep in mind, the information in this book are tools that lead to freedom, once applied. Billions of humans are already aware of the tools mentioned. But remember a small percentage of billions of humans apply the well structured, precise and organized efficiently planned models that mitigate risks and maximize profits. The difference between the billions of men and women that make up the poor class (99%) and the men and women who make up the wealthy class (1%) is the application of a system that is well structured and precise.

Behind every great business, product, or service is conscious time, energy, and effort being put into creating a well structured and precise strategy. Freedom is experienced in CREATING this basis. Nothing is stopping you or anyone else from experiencing freedom. Freedom occurs within the system you've created. The feeling of limitation is experienced when you are forced to follow someone else's system. If you have a superior, boss, or manager, one may be experiencing the feeling of limitation. Anyone who desires to be free, create your own system that promises you a financial return that is in unison with your efforts. Then you will discover freedom.

Systems are a pivotal part of reaching freedom. Systems are everywhere around (Solar System, Ecosystem, Nervous System). Take the bank for an example. THINK WITH ME. NO BUSINESS goes without losses, the key is that profits must oversee losses. Why has the bank been successful for so many years?

The "system" the bank uses is based on the interest they give you in the form of profits they make off using your money. In other words, the bank takes your money for FREE and makes money off of it. The bank system is built on the premises of using other people's money for FREE, to gain LEVERAGE. But it does this with a system of good debt. The "system" the bank uses is built on MATH. The system is mathematically structured. Numbers and letters undeniably control the universe regarding all systems and hierarchies.

Math is a universal language. Humans can deny but NUMBERS DON'T LIE. Systems and plans should be well structured and precise according to NUMBERS. Meaning, if you follow the principles of MATH and NUMBERS, your success probability and sustainability will increase. The laws of Math and numbers can not be manipulated. They are like the sun and the moon, the laws look the same no matter where you are.

What is the outcome of adapting to a lifestyle outside of the laws of Math? Of course, we were given FREEDOM but we live in an insane world where being well structured and precise are not PERFECT enough. People try to find ways to work against them.

MINDSET OF THE 1%

Well 99% of failure, in large, is due to the lack of structure and precision that goes into planning. This analysis is drawn from MATH. Perhaps we shall explore the mindset of the 1%. With the intent to portray that the implementation of structure is not something to be curious about, because it's a life and death matter, it is something to be serious about.

Emotions

READ ALOUD: The Poor is a trillion-dollar industry. The poor knows no LEVERAGE, no MENTORSHIP, and no SYSTEM. The leverage is the most powerful force in the universe. By persuading people to work harder for less, the 1% gains leverage and takes away your freedom. Once a person's freedom is taken away, it becomes natural to make decisions based on emotions and fear instead of Math and accuracy. Once the people have become dumbed down to the point where they are making decisions based on emotions and fear, we sell them investments, products, and services whereby we make money whether they make money or not, which gives us the leverage to remain in the 1%.

Television (tell-lie-vision)

And once the consumer can no longer consume, they are worthless. Most don't have a Mission, Vision or Plan (MVP), so they watch television (tell –lie-vision) and the TV becomes the basis of their programming. The 99% are unaware that television won't exist without the 1%. Investors buy the media in order to program people's minds. The TV is really for people who have money. People that watch it think the exact opposite.

Government

Without a Mission, Vision, and Plan, people are bound to reach a state known as learned helplessness. The government wants you in this state, whereby you accept things as they are in order to disempower you. Once people accept things the way they are, they take legal measures to take control of your Capabilities, Actions, and Results. The most expensive part of controlling all things in the eyes of the government is PEOPLE. So the government is looking for ways to move people out of the equation. The government uses robots and machines to replace humans. Machines are mathematically structured and by using machines because it would cut out the cost of human labor, which will create more leverage. For the 1%, technology will create more unemployment.

It is not important to keep telling the same real-world experience. You can't afford to waste any more time. These observations were not founded upon short term experience. This entails of fundamental analysis of years summarizing ways men and women have obtained success and freedom. My mentor told me that "freedom will come by sharing the principles of WEALTH."

That's the purpose of writing this book. Every society is built on mentoring. Your mentor should help you cultivate your Mission, Vision, and Plan. Know that you have the Capabilities, your mentor should give you the confidence to take Action, and action will lead to Results.

Remember your body is like a **CAR**. And a car won't drive without the key in the ignition.

Chapter 7

The Greatest Nation in the World

(Developing the Power of the Imagination)

Having reached this stage of the book, my hopes are that now, you've realized that tweaking your thoughts, words, and actions will create a mindset, which will, in turn, shift your results and outcomes. As an effect, you will attract freedom in the form of wealth, abundance, and success in your life. Just by transforming your mindset. Beliefs are more powerful than reality. This is no mere sentence - it is TRUTH.

The last chapter disclosed that an unfavorable childhood upbringing is one of the many causes of failure and limitation. Nevertheless, adulthood offers the opportunity to put into action, the beliefs that begin to form during childhood.

Psychologically, millions of people who enter adulthood or move well beyond adulthood identify themselves promptly by their childhood experiences. Habitually this truth is uplifted when a person is asked the question: Where are you from?

The majority of people who answer this question responds by naming what city, state, or country they consider home. Now answer this question "Where do you come from?" The majority of people answer this question by naming a city, state or country that they consider home. There is a huge difference between your outlook on life when you practice the habit of recognizing, where you are from instead of permitting yourself to remember where you come from.

People who fail to realize where they come from have a hard time, getting to where they are trying to go. You are from the IMAGINATION. In fact, we are all from the imagination.

Keep in mind, the fact is, the majority of childbirths were not planned. If you were to talk with your parents freely about your birth, you may bear witness "I never imagined having a child", "I always imagined I would have a son", "I always imagined I would have a daughter", "I never imagined having 5 children", etc. Although the responses will vary, observe what their responses have in common. They all disclose realities that were never IMAGINED. Keep your eyes and ears wide open for when you hear this phrase used because that means that reality was created in the IMAGINATION. You come from the imagination.

It is a characteristic of people who accomplish the highest magnitude of success and freedom to never forget where they are from but never lose sight of where they are going. Such people generally have humble beginnings and by listening and applying, they attained the opportunities that led to MIGHTY ENDINGS. The majority of people fail to acknowledge they come from the Imagination and are generally easily influenced by the opinions of everyone that come from their same state, city, or country.

If you permit yourself to believe you come from the IMAGINATION, then your life becomes a reflection of accomplishing undertakings you have never IMAGINED.

The imagination is the mental storehouse of all supernatural plans made. ALL inspiration, energy, greater thoughts, and positive possibilities are transmuted into a vision and ACTION through summoning the power of the IMAGINATION.

Anything that one IMAGINES, can be created. All of the many things, meaning everything you see including cars, airplanes, clothes, cell phones, shoes and more, were developed in the minds of individuals, in their imagination. Everything you see, hear, smell, taste, and touch were created through the aid of the imagination. Using the faculty of the imagination, the human family has continued to evolve the way we communicate, our methods of travel, ways to market, ways to make money, which ultimately creates more ways for us to experience freedom. We have created so many forms of communication that a house phone is a poor match for an iPhone. We have created so many forms of travel that UBER can be relied on instead of a car. We have created payable tablets, whereby waitresses and waiters are not needed because you can order your meal and pay for it on the device. We have built and constructed means of flying, which allows a man to walk on the moon. Through the aid of our imagination, we have learned that the human mind sends and receives thoughts, in the form of vibrations and we project those thoughts into our actions, while equally attracting to us experiences that are a vibrational match to the thought patterns we store. We have created GPS systems, whereby we no longer have to depend on maps for directions in travel. We have discovered a way to make education into online courses, we may now log in to our class instead of driving to a classroom.

All of our CREATIVITY dwells within the IMAGINATION. We have strayed away from the active use of the IMAGINATION. We have accepted the idea that we are not very creative, which creates more of a reason to utilize the imagination in a limited way.

The imagination is the storehouse of power in our mind. The imagination is the greatest mental faculty that shows us the version of us God created us to be. Through the capacity of the imagination, plans, ideas or general notions to make your dreams come true are created. It stores the power and capability that is necessary to invent new ideas or position old plans and/or ideas in a manner that serves the greater good. Through the aid of the imagination, humans are given direct access to the path that will lead to the Heaven on Earth experience. It is the mental laboratory in which energy and action coincide to give birth to the feeling known as inspiration. It is through the imagination that one discovers the greatest version of themselves. The capability of the imagination offers to all who choose to follow their momentum or attune to it, FREEDOM.

The imagination works based on how persistent one adds energy in the form of desire and action to thought. Adding energy to a thought causes an exceptionally speedy level of conscious vibration in the mind. As the speed of conscious vibration increases, it builds more desire and motivation on the inside. Hence, motivation and desire building on the inside is called inspiration.

This section will provide a precise explanation about how the imagination works.

Thoughts activate your imagination. Remember thoughts enter the mind in the form of vibrations. The greater the magnitude of thought, the greater the vibration stored while in the mind. The conscious and subconscious mind are aware of the thoughts in the imagination. The imagination operates as a gift, if one chooses not to use it, it will seem non-existent through the lack of activity but can be activated and channeled through proper use. Process that for a second.

Be mindful that only 1% of our population uses the imagination. As an effect, the majority of decisions made by people are drawn from the subconscious mind, in regards to how to transmute thoughts into the physical reality. NUMBERS DON'T LIE. 1% of all people have a fully active imagination. The story remains that 99% of humans operate as driven by faculties of the subconscious mind.

The influential leaders of business, finance, and industry and the influential poets, journals, singers, become influential because they summon the power of the imagination as their vehicle to FREEDOM.

It begins with the thought of something you desire to obtain, whether tangible or non-physical. The desire itself launches a momentum that is subtle and brief. The desire is non-physical and can be of no value or worth to the world until it is transmuted into the physical world. While the thought alone is the way to build the momentum that supports the desire, merely thinking is important to sustain an active imagination, but you must keep in mind the importance of ADDING ACTION to the thoughts, whereby you will activate the inspiration which will help you sustain when conditions are created whereby life demands you to stop.

Focus on the positive thoughts and with your actions, nurture only the thoughts that were developed from the imagination. The centered focus will create a momentum that moves you closer towards your desire and bring it closer to you.

These desires that dwell in your imagination are always calling you, but most don't answer, whether intentionally or by default. Follow the impulse created by the thoughts that dwell in the imagination and create a reality that you never imagined would happen.

The keys in this book are essential to one's freedom, but the words of the book were created in the mind of an individual with their imagination. Key points for experiencing freedom have been offered in every chapter of this book. This chapter will offer some of the most powerful instructions deployed by the imagination which is best suited for all of those who desire freedom. Make your plan precise and well structured. Once you've done so, you are making your non-physical desire visible. Writing on paper is an important step in transmuting your thoughts into the physical reality. Writing down your goals, dreams, plans or vision is the first step that creates the basis to permit your imagination to keep active, the thought pattern that is necessary to manifest your desires.

The Planet Earth, where you live and share with all living things, is experiencing changes, whereby small particles of energy are working together. Be aware and uplift this statement. The Planet Earth, all cells of your body and everything constructed of matter is an extension of a non-physical form of energy.

As far as the importance of being able to determine the standard of operation for the entire universe, inspiration, drive, and determination are created by the momentum of thoughts. Thought momentum is a form of energy. When you apply with actions, thought momentum to a cause, you are using the same "source" (energy) which is used to create ALL things in the universe.

If you are reading this book, then you are involved in the process of using the same basis. You are summoning Mother Earth's perfect laws by pressing towards transmuting your thoughts or desire into the physical reality. THIS IS the BLUEPRINT FOR ALL SUCCESS. FOLLOW THE BLUEPRINT.

Days of the Mighty

When building your vision through the aid of the imagination, it is important to differentiate between Mother Earth's perfect laws and the laws made by man. The Days of the Week is a structured system created by man, which we have practiced with years of repetition and have subjected ourselves to the ideology of the Days of the Week on every level. As an author, my intention is to make visible to you, the secret through which the Days of the Week stores and how it affects FREEDOM and our imagination. Mother Earth is not a secret, but those who summon to aid her natural powers can use it as a way of leveraging humankind.

We all have been living by the days of the week. Perplexing, unusual or is it reasonable to infer, within the Days of the Week (weak) is the practicing of a thought pattern that PROCLAIMS that from Monday through Sunday, gradually we will get weaker.

In an allegoric way, the days of the week claim that you will practically get weaker and traditionally on Sunday, humans will use this day to recharge so that they will be ready for Monday. Chapter 6 mentioned the importance of systems. The Days of the Week is a system whereby man created to gain leverage over human success and freedom. In other words, the likelihood of experiencing FREEDOM, EMPOWERMENT and keeping an active imagination if one is following or practicing a system that's designed to make them weak, hence the DAYS of the WEEK (WEAK). THINK WITH ME.

This is not written to cause you to be disheartened or lose enthusiasm. It is being written to create the basis of freeing you from the systems which do not serve your greater good. Unless you have lived to experience the momentum created through harmonizing with the ideal of the days of the week, it is not expected that you fully grasp this concept upon the first read. But if you can assimilate the effects of surrendering your life to the system known as the "Days of the Mighty", you should be excited because, we are now giving to you, a system which can "FREE YOU" from the disempowering vibration of the Days of the week (weak). YOU SHOULD BE EXCITED. FREEDOM IS RIGHT HERE BEFORE YOU.

The fundamentals mentioned in this book were created through direct communication with the imagination. Read them, reread them and as you read them, JUST IMAGINE.

The purpose of this book, a purpose which I have devoted my life, is to FREE all who desire freedom from thought patterns and systems that disallow individuals from moving towards their desires.

The Days of the Week is a dependable philosophy but offers a very low vibration to those who seek to make progress or get better at a thing.

I have here a well organized and constructed system designed to give individuals the favorable momentum which will help develop and sustain the mental space whereby, the IMAGINATION stays active and a wealth and abundance mindset is much more readily available to those who partake in the blessing of FREEDOM. Here I present to you the DAYS OF THE MIGHTY.

The Seven Days of the MIGHTY/The Seven Days of the Week (weak)

Receive Day - Monday

Appreciation Day - Tuesday

Influence Day - Wednesday

Nature Day - Thursday

Be-You-Ti–FULL Day - Friday

Opportunity Day - Saturday

Wholesomeness Day - Sunday

Day 1 (Receive Day)

Keynote: Celebrate the Joy of Giving

"The true receiving is giving." When you give, you give yourself a chance to receive something out of failure that allows you to succeed.

Focus Point: On this day, make a conscious effort to GIVE. Giving does not always mean money. Acts of kindness such as holding the door for someone, saying "thank you", "How may I help you", feed the homeless, donate to a charity, give a random hug or treat your friend to lunch.

Monday: We wake up that morning dreading this week, waiting for the weekend to come so we can have fun.

IMAGINE what it would be like living in a world where on this day, everyone was FOCUSED on GIVING. Instead of worrying about how much time, energy, and money are being taken from them. JUST IMAGINE.

Day 2 (Appreciation Day)

Key Note: Acceptance, Appraisal, and Acknowledgement.

"Appreciation is the key to a healthy nation"

Focus Point: Appreciation makes humans feel good and it makes a difference that we take out conscious time to express our appreciation because appreciation strengthens all relationships. Write an appreciation letter, offer a hand of support, acknowledge the things you like about them, offer "public praise", look for opportunities to offer small compliments, give them another chance, write an appreciation letter to yourself, etc.

Tuesday: Still tired from the thought of Monday but dreading the remainder of the week, waiting for the weekend to come so you can relax or have fun.

IMAGINE what it would be like living in a world where on this day, everyone was FOCUSED on expressing appreciation and being appreciative. JUST IMAGINE.

Day 3 (Influence Day)

Key Note: Reminder through Reassurance (Remind those that you influence how important they are).

FOCUS: We often feel like once we say "I appreciate you", the job is done. The fact is we all reap from reassurance. Reassurance is definitely useful in improving the quality of human relationships. Devote the entirety of Influence Day to reassuring those of why you love them, how much you believe in them, remind them you are still there for them and how amazing they are.

Wednesday: Still tired from the thought of Tuesday, but bible study offers some momentary relief and it brings ease to know I am reaching the midpoint of the week, but still dreading the remainder of the week.

IMAGINE how it would feel to receive phone calls or gestures of reassurance from people like your mentor, college coach, father, former co-worker or boss reminding you of how amazing you are. JUST IMAGINE.

Day 4 (Nature Day)

Key Note: Embrace the Natural Beauty of Mother Earth.

"Even God had a Mother, her name is Earth. Spend time with her."

FOCUS: The Earth is our Mother. Nature stores more beauty than anything else in the Universe. Nature has been proven to offer the most natural benefits to humanity. Devote the entirety of this day, spending time with Nature.

Eat your lunch at the Park

Take pictures of the clouds

Meditate outside

Work the farm

Do a campfire

Thursday: Slightly energized by the thought of tomorrow being Friday but paying attention to the clock because it seems like time is moving slower for the weekend to arrive.

IMAGINE the joyous vibration created by the idea of going to the beach, mountain climbing, campfires, watching the sunset, watching the sunrise or having a picnic lunch with your partner accompanied by the wonderful vibration of Mother Earth. JUST IMAGINE.

Day 5 (Be-You-Ti-FULL Day)

Key Note: Make yourself happy.

"Fill your cup with Life, Love and Living for yourself"

FOCUS: This day is about you. Treat yourself, reward yourself and spoil yourself. We were made to be happy not to accept the comfort found in being drained by responsibilities. This habit won't lead to self-mastery nor will it help maintain healthy habits. It is important to take this day for yourself. The key to freedom is to love yourself more because when you do, you can love others more. Self-love is not selfish.

Friday: I have awaited this day all week only to discover that I am not only too tired to hang out but I still have responsibilities that I missed from earlier this week.

Day 6 (Opportunity Day)

Key Note: Expansion, Manifestation, Increase, and Abundance (Seize Opportunity)

"On this day, you must choose to be the opportunity that you desire to SEE"

FOCUS: Opportunities are constantly in front of our faces but if we don't recognize them, we can not seize them. It is important to take conscious time to create and discover opportunities to expand and grow yourself, your business, etc. What if I am not good enough for the opportunity, the mind may say. The key is to be the opportunity you desire to see. If you follow this philosophy, you discover that you have always had access to opportunity. Look in the mirror and you will see it.

Saturday: I am glad I am off work but I can not truly enjoy this weekend because I am dreading the fact that I have to go back to work on Monday. I'm still at work, mentally.

Day 7 (Wholesomeness Day)

Key Note: Restoration, Nourishment, and Replenishment: MIND, BODY, and SPIRIT

"To be thy Healthyself, one must learn to heal thyself"

FOCUS: TRUE healthy living is created through the stimulation of mental, physical and spiritual growth. The stimulation of one without the other does not create a healthy living. Your health is your #1 resource. Devote this day towards refueling yourself mentally, physically and spiritually (refilling your cup) and experiencing TRUE healthy living. Also, you truly have something to give on the next day of the Mighty which is RECEIVE DAY.

Mind

- Read a good book
- Refrain from TV

- Limit social media
- Limit cell phones

Body

- Stretch
- Drink water
- Eat fruits and vegetables
- Rest (go to bed early)

Spirit

- Yoga
- Prayer
- Meditation

The last day of the mighty is wholesomeness day, whereby we recharge and re-empower ourselves for RECEIVE DAY. The Days of the Mighty may appear as just a good idea. It was born in the imagination. There is no set price of the ideas created in the imagination. Inventors of ideas decide their own price, and if they are well-structured, precise, and system-based, they will get the amount they desire.

Millions of people go through their life praying and hoping for good things to occur. Perhaps the built-in thought pattern that's subjected by the days of the week (weak) does not create a high basis for happiness and freedom, which is necessary to keep them in the receiving mode for the things they desire. The importance of systems was discussed in Chapter 6. Systems make freedom and happiness happen for you. Experts say that for businesses to thrive and transform into greatness requires steady dedication to the development of effective business systems.

The Days of the Week (weak) is a system that governs and sustains a pattern of thinking and builds up the idea that gradually you get weaker from Monday – Sunday. The Days of the Mighty is a system that organizes the principles of wealth, abundance, prosperity, happiness and success into the philosophy of FREEDOM. Allow me to pose a question. If there is a 99% failure rate to a 1% success rate, is it possible that these numbers are effects caused by the Days of the Week? Nonetheless, thousands have profited through the system of the days of the week (weak), but IMAGINE how much more fortunes will be accumulated through the application of the DAYS OF THE MIGHTY.

Favorable systems create favorable outcomes. Systems are the gateway to transmuting the IMAGINATION into the physical reality. The most successful businesses do not experience success in one great effort. No single action, no good luck or no single breakthrough creates greatness. Greatness occurs through following a system with a pattern predictable enough to measure the build-up. It is like turning a wheel, it takes actions to get the wheel moving, but with consistent channeling action in the same direction over a period of time with force, the wheel builds the energy to sustain on its own axis.

All businesses begin with a simple idea that was developed in the imagination. The transformation into greatness requires a steady development of the imagination. Gradually, the imagination will give more power to the idea, take control of the actions and drive you towards your desired outcome. First, you must start, grow and fix the imagination, and then use its power to create a DESIRE to achieve that overstands all adversity.

The life of Albert Einstein and Thomas Edison are great examples of stewards who created their reality in their imagination. They used their imagination to go into the future and bring it into the present. They saw where they wanted to go and they acted like the person they wanted to become. How do you do that? Use your imagination.

Setting aside time to sustain an active imagination is a great investment. We were all born with immeasurable amounts of creative power. As a side note, a lot of us do not think we are creative. The primary reason is because most Americans who have been through educational institutes or manual labor are subjected to faculties that pull the plug on the imagination. WE ARE ALL like wealthy corporations with small creative departments. The truth is everyone is creative and no one is more creative than another, some make choices to use their creative faculties to a greater capacity than others.

Recognizing the need to work for someone else or sacrificing your happiness to please others are not realities created in the imagination. Your imagination sees you as the most successful corporation, meaning you are a non-profit organization, you are a billionaire, etc. In your imagination, you don't work for money, you make money work for you.

In your imagination, you don't practice the idea "the sky is the limit, you practice the sky can't be the limit because the truth is there are no limits." You don't just wish or pray to make a million dollars, you learn to see value in yourself which creates the basis for one to make true money, the money you are paid to be yourself.

Because of the power that's backed with the perceptions of the imagination, it is pivotal to practice these thought patterns. Let aiming for what's above the sky to be your chief aim. Make activating your imagination become a top priority. Many factors have been allowed to interfere with the creative production of the imagination. After subjecting ourselves to the influence of these factors, each of us will get pulled from extraordinary to ordinary living. Therefore, it is important to become aware of the factors that unplug the power of the imagination to activate, regulate and maintain your imagination and live your extraordinary promising future.

With starting, growing, fixing, and sustaining an active imagination being our primary focus, let's turn our attention to the factors that deactivate the powers in the imagination:

It starts in educational institutes, during early childhood years, the imagination was used very well. Reading books, creative play with toys, storytime, dolls, blocks, and cartoons, totally unaware of the difference between what is real and what is not. Often, educators, parents, and adults nurture you to think the way they want you to think (accepting their thoughts as reality), instead of nurturing your IMAGINATION (create your own reality). This is because of the fear that children do not know how to decipher between what is real and what is pretend. Whether this treatment serves the greater good of the child is debatable, but it affects children's creative thinking, cognitive development, and their imagination.

Albert Einstein once stated that the imagination is more important than knowledge. The imagination is the key to limitless possibilities. It is where creativity, extraordinary thoughts, and abstract thinking begins for child development. Educational Institutes foster us to believe that education is more important than the imagination. Perhaps you practicing this thought pattern, which is the exact opposite of what is true. Remember, beliefs are stronger than reality. When you practice beliefs that are not true, then your entire story and lifestyle become a lie, which will pull you further away from discovering the truth of yourself, which dwells in your imagination.

If you are one of those who never walked alone or lack accumulative experience, you are prone to adapt to others beliefs instead of learning to think on your own. Beliefs, when they come from the imagination, are always extraordinary. Generally speaking, the three faculties which dominantly influence human beliefs that deactivate the imagination.

Religion. This system project theories and philosophy into the human mind that may be useful in the procedural part of life. Practically religion is relied upon to give a sense of foundation, not freedom. I would like to remind you that religious books were written by humans and none of them were FREE, nor practiced the art of sustaining an active imagination.

Opinions. In this case, opinions influence your creativity. By adopting the thought pattern that others project, you give their thought pattern access to your imagination. The average individual does not use their imagination. Opinions always lead to a state of learned helplessness. Remember, it is not your job to make everybody happy.

Family. Your family influences your imagination. A common trend practiced by family is that the current generation should practice the habits of the past generation to sustain the future of the family. Following this paradigm restricts one's ability to EXPLORE. A willingness to explore is one of the keys to maintaining an active imagination.

Beliefs may be obtained from any of the listed sources. It will automatically be transmuted into a thought pattern that repeats the thought pattern of the mastermind behind the belief. In other words, a thorough examination of all your beliefs will readily reveal to you if a belief is really your belief or a belief that someone planted into your mind by someone else which you've practiced for so long and now ACCEPT IT as your belief system.

In expressing beliefs that are not from the imagination and giving them effort, energy and time, one is generally induced to cooperate with the "NORM" or "Ordinary life." Generally, their terms of actions become like a cycle whereby we repeat the habits of the previous generation because they are practicing the belief of others. Before you can activate the power in your imagination, you must identify the beliefs you practice that are truly your beliefs and the beliefs you have believed as a result of them being injected by dominant relationships or associations.

Developing the Power in the Imagination

The imagination may be defined as the most powerful mental faculty that pulls your mind from your current reality and gives you the freedom to create your own reality.

No human may obtain great success or freedom without utilizing the power in the imagination. Each chapter in this book will provide a solid basis of specific keys provided for the sake of creating plans that will lead to freedom. If you store these keys in memory, apply them with action, and maintain integrity in the process. Your imagination will reveal your destiny and purpose to you and things will begin to work out in your favor. So you must understand the imagination is the storehouse of unlimited potential, power, and possibilities (3 p's). The 3 p's are available to you through following the path the imagination leads you on. We will here explain the things you can do to develop your imagination.

The imagination is obviously powerful. All things were created by people who summoned to aid, the powerful forces of the imagination. This power must have a constructive outlet. No power is created to be harnessed. When power is harnessed, this leads to the power becoming destructive, instead of constructive. Your knowingness of this profound truth will be of huge influence when you decide whether or not you deem it necessary to utilize the power in the imagination to serve your greater good.

READ creative books and watch creative movies. Commonly reading fantasy books, fairy tales, watching SUPERHERO based movies, etc, activates the imagination. Acceptance of this form of presentation will offer initiative, enthusiasm, and ambition to the creative faculty of the mind.

WRITE your thoughts. Outside of its use for therapy, writing is a perfect tool for activating our imagination. Journalists, poets, songwriters, etc, project their imagination through writing. Write about your day. This is an important tool for developing your storytelling skills as well. Once the storytelling skills are cultivated, begin to tell the stories from other perspectives, which will require the skills of the imagination more in-depth.

- PLAY an instrument.
- Listen to instrumental
- Be willing to explore
- Draw. This form of art expression takes the thoughts in the imagination and gives them form.
- Paint. This form of art expression takes the thoughts in the imagination and gives them form.
- Dance. This form of art expression takes the thoughts in the imagination and gives them form.
- Sculpting. This form of art expression takes the thoughts in the imagination and gives them form.

Sort through this list of activities to do to sustain an active imagination. You will discover that they either have worked for you or it didn't. Many of those who acquired freedom or success, have purposely or unconsciously deployed the power of the imagination.

Remember that behind all creations and inventions, may be launched the usage of the imagination. The reality created in our imagination is inseparable from our freedom. Do not allow any to delay the plans and actions necessary to manifest the wonderful powers and ideas that dwell in the imagination because the imagination stores the version of you that's FREE. If one has the courage, integrity and will power to stay true to their imagination instead of swayed, influenced or persuaded by individuals living ordinary lives, they will gain control over their lives.

Look over your thoughts. The imagination is responsible for all the big ideas, visions, or duties. 1% have chosen to surrender their lives to the system in the imagination, which has given freedom to all who have grown, fixed, and kept active the power of the imagination. Any reality outside of the IMAGINATION is poverty. In other words, the continuation of freedom for the 1% depends upon honoring and staying true to who they truly are and never allowing anyone to influence them to deviate from the version of themselves they've been created to be in their imagination.

The imagination stores power at which constructs the energy of action into ALL things created by matter, including humans and every other form of matter, and creates results. The imagination denies no one of their rights to freedom, but it does not promise you results without making a conscious effort to give birth to its ideas. No freedom comes by ignoring the power of the imagination and following the herd in the wrong direction. Perhaps we have found comfort in the gruesome reality that exists outside the imagination. Remember WHERE YOU COME FROM. YOU COME FROM THE IMAGINATION "THE GREATEST NATION IN THE WORLD."

I NEVER IMAGINED

Understand that Beyonce Knowles and Michael Jordan had one quality in common, both knew the profound truth that people's opinions about you are not more important than your thoughts about you. If they follow their IMAGINATION, then that will create "I NEVER IMAGINED" circumstances.

Curtis Jackson "50 cent" began his career under the handling of poverty, ignorance, and limitation. He chose to follow his imagination, which in 5 years made him one of the wealthiest rap artists. Connect with the fact that Mr. Jackson was shot 9 times in the process of making these strides towards manifesting his imagination. Understand you will face challenges that will influence one's mind to give up or tell themselves "it was not meant to be." Understand and take notes to the fact that Mr. Jackson's most phenomenal accomplishments began from the time he got shot 9 times. This is evidence that negative experiences offer an opportunity to focus on the path that your imagination leads you because "Negativity is only designed to create focus." Which is only deemed as reality when one accepts that failure is meant to bring you closer to your imagination.

Steven Speilberg couldn't get into film school, but he imagined himself being a BIG TIME FILMMAKER. After following his imagination, Speilberg left marks on American History as a successful filmmaker, earning a net worth of over 3 billion dollars.

Theodor Seuss Geisel summoned the power of his Imagination and became a legendary children's author known for classic books like "Green Eggs and Ham" and "The Cat in the Hat."

Thomas Edison's teacher told him that he was too stupid to learn anything. Mr. Edison developed the power of the imagination, combining knowledge, intuition and spiritual awareness given from the imagination and went on to invent some life-changing devices. Through deploying this power, he left an impact on the world that can only be understood by interpreting the keys of this book.

President Barack Obama conducted the mindset of the imagination to the world in the form of becoming "the first African American President." During the election campaign and after the inauguration, Obama constantly delivered speeches in which he acknowledged how his victory related to US history.

"If there is anyone who still doubts that America is a place where all things are possible, who still wonders if the dreams of our founders are alive in our time, who still questions the power of democracy, tonight is your answer. It has been a long time coming but, because of what we did on this day, in this election, at this defining moment, change has come to America," Obama stated.

Obama accredited democracy for his outcome, but he was not aware that HE was already the President before he won the election. Winning the election was the moment that declared to the world that Obama was President. His imagination generated the idea that the man could be a President. By adding action, energy, and education to this idea, it became true.

Review this book, as it stores the same keys Obama used to solidify his place as President. It may be summoned in this success formula. He became the President through being in-formation with the version of him that was in his imagination, honoring the spirit of his imagination in action and reap the rewards.

Obama was able to become the first African American President which could not occur by luck or by mere chance. Only through surrendering himself to the spirit of his imagination, for an unlimited span, Obama became the first African American President. If unfavorable momentum, doubt or fear, is projected then command yourself to get jointly with the spirit of your imagination and press toward your specific goal or desire, which aligns you in the position to directly be in receiving mode for the great universal intelligence Mother Earth offers. Mother Earth is the host of phenomenal power. It is the power that fuels the IMAGINATION. It was the power which ALL those who live in freedom summoned at their aid.

Actions and results are the two major factors that attribute to the manifestations of the supernatural power that dwells in the imagination. Prayers are a powerful tool but prayers are not dependable if the necessary action is not taken to create the results.

In brief, ALL manifestations by which the imagination is readily displayed are sufficiently outlined:

In the imagination, first, we THINK and DREAM about a THING. Then you must add ENERGY and ACTION to a thought, then the desires create motivation on the inside. And motivation on the inside is called inspiration. Inspiration is the force that drives you towards results.

Lastly, these two steps are essential for freedom in all walks of life. Freedom occurs in the imagination and the purpose of these steps is to take them as a matter of habit.

1.First Love Yourself enough to give your dreams an opportunity despite the opinions of religion, family or any other thing that consciously or unconsciously stirs you to operate outside of your imagination.

2.Think about what you desire and give attention to your desires.

Chapter 8

Choice

"The Key to Freedom or Limitation"

The cemetery is one of the richest places in the world. It is full of men and women who had trillion-dollar ideas but did not make the choice of giving birth to their vision or following their desires as a top priority. Making a choice, is an important factor, as choice alone can lead to a better quality of life or a life of misery that drives you to death. "Make a choice" is not just an understatement, it is a matter of life and death.

Fear, the reason why 100% of men and women avoid making choices, is the terrorist that everyone must overcome.

My hope is that upon the completion of this book, you are prepared and ready to make the choices and commitments in action to the things that declares freedom.

Observation of thousands of people who experienced financial freedom emphasizes that by making a choice and committing to that choice in action, they will lead to freedom whether financially, emotionally, physically or spiritually. Those people who do not make a choice are more prone to habitually experience failure, change jobs and change job locations, often still carrying the same thought pattern.

One of Tawana Williams, born without arms, most marvelous traits was her choosing to never make excuses. This trait was so noticeable in Tawana Williams, that it qualified her the stature of Unarmed but Dangerous. This exact trait leads Tawana to WRITE books with her feet and pronounce the movie, Eagle Born Without Wings, based on her story, which led to her freedom.

It took Tawana a long time to leave this significant mark in history but on another note, Tawana's commitment to the choice produced qualitative levels of freedom before and after the manifestation of her film. Surely Tawana made the choice to commit to a NO EXCUSE lifestyle and this choice is credited for the persevering attitude that permitted her to rise to the spotlight.

People who are not experiencing freedom are only doing so because they have not chosen to be free. Generally, people delay decision making or never make decisions. By doing so, they permit themselves to be easily persuaded by the projections and opinions of others. They do not have a Mission, Vision, and Plan, so they watch television (tell-lie-vision) and they adopt the thinking from television instead of making the choice to think on their own. Other people's thoughts and opinions of you are none of your business. If you make other people's thoughts and opinions of you as your business, you will become less of who you have been created to be. If you consider other people's opinions when making a choice, you will not be successful in any endeavor, more specifically, not in the art of discovering true freedom.

If you are following the opinions and projections of others, you are less likely to know yourself.

Keep in mind, true opinions (open-yens) are expressed from an open mind. The majority of the people in the world are closed-minded. By default, they are using the word "opinion" as a means to exert the social pressure for you to conform to the norm. No one's opinion of you defines your greatness. Take into consideration the opinions of your TEAM, which means you must be very careful when choosing those with whom will be apart of the birth of your dreams, visions, and goals.

Often unintentionally, family and friends project resistance and doubt in their opinions and sometimes through the use of sarcasm which is intended to cover up their true thoughts. Every day, tons and tons of dreams and self esteems are demolished by someone who had good intentions but not educated enough to know the unfavorable momentum projected in their opinions.

We all were born with our own minds. Utilize it and make your own choices. If you desire the opinions and thoughts of others, be assured they are an open-minded person. You will probably want everyone to agree with you and support your purpose. You will probably have a strong urge to feel like someone AGREES with you.

It is a quality of those who experience failure to need someone to AGREE with them. When in truth, most people live agreeable lives, in a world where most people won't agree with you. If you are one who prolonged the manifestation of your greatness, know this, you were not born to agree with others or care about what others think. Most people have spent all of their lives trying to get people to agree with their ordinary lives. It makes them feel better when you agree with them. If you express some disagreement, they will make you feel like you are making a mistake or they will work hard at reasoning with the idea that your choice is WRONG because it is not in agreement with their ordinary thought pattern.

Those who look for agreement through opinions are always looking in the wrong place. By doing so they deny themselves the opportunity to discover the TRUTH, which this section will disclose. You don't NEED anybody to agree with you to get what you desire. You just have to agree with yourself which is what occurs when you make a CHOICE. Make a choice to agree with yourself.

Remember that every time you give attention to other's opinions and thoughts, it leads to things that you do not want because doubt is the most common emotion hidden behind opinions. It is not rational to focus on the doubt and desire at the same time and expect your desire to move towards you and vice versa. Opinions usually give more attention to things you don't want instead of your desire.

The fact is that every person's opinion holds influence in associations. Equally, we must learn to decipher the reason behind what you are told to agree to and what others do not want you to agree with. The more attention you give to people that do not agree with you, believe in you or support you, the more you are likely not to believe, agree with or support yourself.

Genuine and true support has nothing to do with persuading those who do not support you or agree with you. You must agree with you. If you are reading this and you are learning that most people you thought would support your goals, are not putting into action the support you assumed they would, I deem it wise to reread this next section.

Make the choice to agree with yourself and appreciate those who do not agree with or support you because by them not AGREEING with you, they are creating the basis for you to discover who you truly are.

As you discover and remember who you are, it will be easier to follow the intuition of your built-in guidance system, which will only be attuned by making the choice to agree with yourself.

In other words, by choosing not to explore life outside of the comfort of their agreeance, you are declared a life without FREEDOM.

CHOICE: A MATTER OF LIFE AND DEATH

The impact of choices varies based on how much determination, effort, and bravery is required to make them and commit to them in action. The choices which transformed the face of the world were made at the pressure and risking of one's Life, assuring the possibilities of DEATH.

Rosa Parks chose to refuse to give up her seat in the colored section, to a white passenger, gave momentum to the civil rights movement and gave birth to the mother of freedom movement. She was fully aware that her behavior could have gotten her killed for violating Alabama's state segregation laws. But she knew that ironically, sitting down was an act of standing up for a greater cause. She chose to give in to what she felt and as an effect, she contributed to the momentum to free millions of men and women. Although the day of her arrest is commemorated, Rosa was willing to pay the price for the cause of freedom amongst the human family. Making that choice took determination.

Harriet Tubman's choice to escape and rescue other family, friends and slaves put her in great danger but that was a choice that required courage. After spending years leading hundreds of slaves to freedom, she died and left women with an iconic figure of HOPE, COURAGE, and FREEDOM.

The choice made by Ray Lewis to turn his greatest pain into his greatest achievement is nothing short of a miracle. Ray would bare witness to his stepfather physically beating his mother. When one day, he made the choice to channel his anger into building his physical strength to a level where MAN couldn't stop him. Mr. Lewis would take a deck of cards and do the number of pushups equivalent to adding the numerical value of each card in the deck. When Ray Lewis got older, he realized that he turned his greatest pain into his greatest achievement because he channeled that energy to an NFL career.

Having read the story of these famous leaders, you may discover a powerful lesson, which this book will make plain. It is easy to admire the paths of these great successors, as well as others, but few of us take into consideration the choices that were made to obtain their magnitude of achievement. We remember Michael Jordan jumping from the free-throw line, but we overlook the choice he made to spend hours in the gym working on his vertical leap instead of spending time with his children.

In other words, we pay attention to the outcome but we are ignorant of the choices made behind the outcomes, which guaranteed freedom for Michael Jordan and Lebron James, as well as any other people who live in freedom.

We observe the stories of Jesus Christ and believe that we are pleasing God by modeling the actions of Jesus. The truth is that Jesus made the choice to surrender his life to a cause he was willing to die for. While doing so, Jesus knew the pain he would experience during that time was not about him. It was about a bigger purpose. Although not intended, we find glory in modeling the actions of great leaders, but we are not practicing the same thought pattern. It was their choices that led to their greater magnitude of achievement. We give attention to their actions and undermine that their outcome was an effect created by practicing the thought pattern that came with their choice.

It is a common mistake that we make to observe people who left significant marks on history. Behind the action of every way-shower of history is a choice that permitted freedom to those who chose to surrender to their destiny. Life requires us to make choices. And truth be told, LIFE starts when you make the choice to surrender your life to a cause you are willing to die for. - Kaden Lebray

The story of Malcolm X did not begin with his assassination in New York on February 21, 1962. Malcolm was incarcerated and during his incarceration, he openly surrendered to sharing African American rights. Malcolm was a Muslim Munist and human rights activist. Although he lived to experience his impact, he deployed the power of the mind by making choices that commanded his thoughts to seek a constructive outlet in action form.

The world was shocked when Lakers Point Guard, Earvin "Magic"

Johnson, announced having HIV on November 7, 1991. Johnson made the choice to give his testimony as the basis for other women and men to practice safe sex. He spoke courageously and that move made Magic available for outcomes that seemed impossible.

Always remember – a choice, which is the beginning of all realities, can be made at any moment. Make the choice. Remember too, that the choices you make are important because choices can lead to life or death.

Before Bruce Lee's passover, he was determined to keep a body fat level of 2 % body fat. To many, it seemed somewhat strange for Bruce Lee to think to maintain himself at such a low body fat level. Strange is not bad. Being labeled as strange, different or weird is something that has been faced by all who contributed to transforming American history and many regions of Mother Earth. It is also important to realize that the life-changing moments, begin in the form of a choice. It is normal for one to face triumph and pain as a result of making the choice but those who transformed civilization were those who pushed through this pain.

Dawn Wilkins is an important component in the unfolding of a miracle in her life because she communicated often with God (prayer) reassuring her commitment to the well-being of her children as her primary responsibility. From this communication, Dawn convinced herself to believe that (she) a single mother of five children can raise and train her children to go to college to get a degree. Keep in mind, Ms. Wilkins did not even have a degree. Growing up in New Jersey did not present her with the idea that her hopes for her children would manifest, but with definite cooperation in action to the choice to prioritize and maximize the well-being of her children, "the prayer she prayed to God came true", which created the basis for other lives to be transformed through her testimony.

Keep in mind, at the beginning of her children's lives, Dawn did not have it all figured out. The plan was not clear. It was clear that by making the choice to rely on the power of God to compel her towards her desired outcome, the basis will be created for freedom and miracles to be experienced.

Much power comes with making a deliberate choice. In the city of Boston, many professional athletes had very impactful careers, but none of the athletes "single-handedly", impacted a franchise and state like the legendary, Larry Bird. His mastery of skills and compassion set him apart from the pack. Aside from Michael Jordan, who Bird credits for putting his heart, mind, body, and soul into the choice to become the best basketball player, Bird put his heart on the floor every night.

The legacy of Larry Bird was marked by his accomplishments on the basketball court. Meanwhile, people remain unaware of the process of organizing his thoughts and gaining mastery of the mind, which was behind his accomplishments.

The famous forward for the Boston Celtics tokened the death of his father, after his parent's divorce, as the benefactor to his freedom. Larry made the choice to channel his frustration and pain into a work ethic, which led him to success and financial freedom. For making this choice, Bird solidified his place in NBA history.

We could never understand the passion that was behind Larry's night by night performance. Larry's freedom and success began with a choice.

Mary J Blige made a choice that transformed her life. We cannot judge a book by its cover. In other words, it has become more common to judge a person by their actions in ignorance of the thought pattern that's creating the actions. The opposition was brought to Mary J Blige's life at five years old, which affected her for years.

Mary J: "When I was five years old, I was molested. I just couldn't believe that this person would do this to me." said Mary J Blige about the incident that destroyed her childhood. "The memories followed me all my life. The shame of thinking the molestation was my fault, led me to believe I was not worth anything. Growing up believing I was worthless affected my life when I became an R & B singer. I had no respect for myself, I hated myself, and I thought I was ugly. So I used sex, drugs, and alcohol to make me feel better." said Mary in one of her interviews.

Mary J Blige later credited P Diddy for empowering her to see and realize her true worth. By making the choice to give herself a chance to be free, Mary transformed her pain into greatness by utilizing music as a tool to uplift survivors of all types of trauma and opening shelters for abused women.

You are not Mary J Blige, but many have not been able to break free from the unfavorable memories of traumatic events such as molestation, rape, and abuse, which can lead to a life marked by limitation and mental imprisonment at the discretion of not choosing to give herself permission to be free. But by giving yourself permission, you will put yourself in the receiving mode for your freedom, but you will have to make the choice first.

Gabrielle Union had two options: victim or victor. Innocently she was raped at gunpoint. Clearly, the time would come where Gabrielle would have to make a choice that would affect her life. She chose to be a victor. The majority of people would have found it difficult to make the choice. The majority would want people to rally around them. She chose to give honor to this catastrophic event by using it as fuel towards survival and independence.

Gabrielle's response was "I chose to make peace with the situation and be freed from the emotional language. No bad experience shall ever control me or influence me to the degree that I abandon the person I have been created to be. And getting my degree in sociology, becoming an actress and more are breath-taking realities that stem from that choice."

In regards to the magnitude of power that dwell in the mind, it should be obvious that the human mind is the greatest power in all creation. God is the greatest power, God being the creator and the mind is the creation. This is an important faculty that all who desire freedom must realize but even more important, understand that the power of the mind becomes activated by making a choice.

WHEN YOU DON'T MAKE A CHOICE, YOU'VE MADE A CHOICE

When you don't make a choice, you still make a choice not to make a choice. I do hereby declare, everything you acquire or desire will be accumulated based on your commitment in action to the choices you make. When you don't make a choice, instead of choosing your desired outcome, your fate will be chosen for you, by which you will accept as a result of instead of making up your own mind, you let other people own your mind and make up your mind for you. If you are one who has not made the choice to pursue the path of your dreams and breathtaking future, you are one of those living a life marked by limitation, whether you admit it or not. Either way, any denial of the truth will create the basis of prolonged poverty and limitation.

As it becomes more common to judge a book by its cover before actually reading it, it may be assumed that Steve Jobs was crazy for dropping out of college and pursuing his desires, rather than focusing on getting his degree. The choice was equally risking and rewarding. After the choice, Apple was created and launched, followed by self-mastery. Initially, when Jobs chose to launch Apple, he quit, only to return years later with a much more cultivated mindset and strategy. Jobs displayed that he possessed the keys and his story raised awareness that is imperative to all who desire freedom to be aware of. QUITTERS NEVER WIN AND WINNERS NEVER QUIT. It was not that Jobs was a quitter, but Jobs needed to make the choice to quit doing that, which did not serve his greater good to get access to his breathtaking future.

Huge momentum followed Jobs' choice. Of course, his mind was aware of the negative possibilities that came with his choices. The self-talk of these thoughts launched rockets of doubt regarding the likelihood that the choice would work favorably. Steve Jobs, Mary J Blige, Harriet Tubman, and Gabrielle Union pursued their desire until their doubt was reduced to a point of insignificance.

Remember this, behind every choice, is doubt and desire. If you focus on doubt, then you will not progress towards your desires. You must make the choice to follow your desires, no matter where it leads you. By not making a conscious choice to follow your desires, you are choosing to flow with the momentum of doubt.

Before moving forward in this book, we must draw our attention to a significant factor associated with choosing to follow your desires. Jesus, another great leader, was crucified on his journey of spreading the truth of God as a means to restore hope and freedom for future generations. He was a representative of the process of which all who chose to have a relationship with their destiny will endure. Not to make the notion that one must be scorned on the cross, but at some point, prepare yourself to be abandoned by your followers, be falsely accused of things, being rejected by other leaders, being mocked, and verbally misrepresented, as an effect of living in a country where it is more common to focus on unfavorable things than favorable.

Jesus was willing to die for the lives of future generations. Shortly after the death of Jesus, salvation was restored and many were inspired to live a better quality of life and used Jesus' story as their comparative story. What would Jesus do? If Jesus was crucified, I can do it? I should be living a better quality of life because someone died for me are some of the thought patterns that would not be solemn without the choice Jesus made.

Inspired by Jesus' actions, we boldly gain momentum by reading his story, which will forever be a classic. It was such men as Jesus who, without money, without force, without weapons, served as a conduit of God, who was crucified and sacrificed their lives for a greater purpose. The purpose being: SO PEOPLE CAN BE SET FREE.

I have here two keys that will give you the tipping advantage of the leader who chooses to follow their destiny:

Sometimes you will have to walk alone in the right direction, rather than follow the herd walking in the wrong direction.

The pain that will be present on this path is not about you. The pain is about a bigger purpose. You don't have to suffer. Suffering only happens when you make the pain about you instead of choosing to focus on the truth "that your pain is not about you." You are only experiencing the birth pains that are required for the vision to be born.

Ladies and Gentlemen let's make a conscious effort to transform our outlook of pain. If we don't reach the collective decision to transform our outlook of pain, not making the choice will surely bring you danger. No human will experience FREEDOM until they make the decision to transform their outlook of pain.

Before leaving this chapter, know that the root cause of ALL failures and limitations is the innocent choice to hold onto pain instead of embracing a lifestyle of limitless possibility. Let's keep in mind, by not making the choice to be set free from pain, we give conditions the freedom to choose your fate.

One profound discovery will be discussed briefly that must be taken into consideration. Traditionally, we have life experiences, which we tend to give more attention to problems (pain) or issues, instead of the lesson (solutions). It has become normal to follow the course of pain. Once inspired by the momentum of pain, we boldly project ourselves realities that shall cause us to remain under the influence and control of pain. Forging us to use emotions as the basis for decision making, instead of rational thinking.

It was such men as Michael Jordan, who without exception, took authority over his pain and used it as fuel to propel him towards his destiny, which began when he got cut from his high school basketball team. Years later, Michael became negotiably the best basketball player to ever play in the NBA.

Before he was able to use his pain as fuel, Jordan was required to make a choice as to whether he would settle for defeat or be willing to risk his life proving that he was the best basketball player in the world. He chose to continually practice his skills and project his emotions and efforts into his desired outcome. Jordan knew if he placed his future in the hands of his effort and determination, he could not lose. Shortly after college, Michael Jordan became the face of the NBA, decreed in physical form, by the choice he made to prove to himself and others that he was good enough to make the team in high school.

Long and hard hours were spent practicing his skills in the gym, which are actions that backed up the choice he made to transform pain into greatness. Michael Jordan unlocked the door within himself and set his champion free. Should anyone choose to be inspired by Michael Jordan, know the key was not his ability to jump from the free-throw line, shoot threes or dunk the basketball. The key to Michael Jordan's freedom was the choice that presented itself in his accomplishments.

EVERY HUMAN WHO CHOOSES NOT TO MAKE A CHOICE, you are chosen to have your reality chosen for you. Most lose sight of who they are as an effect of being who someone else chose them to be.

In the process of discovering your true self, you must allow experience to serve as a teacher. Among the many lessons that can be taken from pain, it has become more common amongst the human family to take the wrong lesson from pain and live their lives separate in nature from their imagination, confined by the memories of pain, which depletes them of their freedom.

By taking the unfavorable lesson from pain, we are prone to allow conditions to offset us from the path that leads to freedom. Let us remember, pain is a basis for us to learn through, but just as it brings us freedom and fuel if we focus on the favorable lessons taken from it, it equally brings limitation and insecurity if the unfavorable lesson is taken from experiences with pain.

Analyze the stories of successors who have transformed civilization because they were reborn through the fuel and momentum created by taking the favorable lesson from pain, which served their greater good as well as the human family for their contribution. Be sure to observe that it was a choice that was made in the hearts and minds of every SUPERSTAR who fought against ALL doubt and chose to forge their efforts into the power of the imagination.

It was the pain of being removed from a community he started that left Steve Jobs in a state of depression. Jobs chose to use that pain as fuel which drove him to become one of the wealthiest men alive.

Shortly after being cut from his high school basketball team, he locked himself in his room and cried. Through that emotional experience, the momentum was built for Michael Jordan who later retired from basketball as a six-time NBA champion, four-time NBA ALL star, and five-time NBA MVP. Michael chose to use his pain as motivation.

Throughout the process of getting his first book published, Dr. Seuus was denied by over 25 publishers. The pain of rejection weighed on Dr. Seuss, but he chose to turn his pain into power and soon became the best selling author in history.

Imagine being told "you will never be anything when you grow up" by your teacher. Surely Albert felt uncomfortable every time he stepped into a classroom, but whenever the pain arose, Albert used PAIN AS AN OPPORTUNITY to practice higher perspectives. PAIN used constructively drove Albert Einstein.

It was a choice made by a man, Lionel Messi, who was diagnosed with a growth hormone deficiency which made him have a smaller stature than most kids his age. It was the choice to use the pain of "being picked" as fuel which led him to become a three-time Fifa World player of the year.

The embarrassment he felt after being fired from the newspaper for "lacking imagination and not having original ideas," Walt Disney used that pain as motivation to create Mickey Mouse and become a winner of 22 academy awards.

Despite her undeniable work ethic and skill set, Oprah was fired from her job and her bosses reasoned that they felt "she was not fit for television." Failure gave Oprah the momentum to succeed. Oprah Winfrey became the host of a multi-award-winning talk show and one of the most influential women in the world.

The personal struggles with drugs and alcohol led Eminem to an unsuccessful suicide attempt. Eminem made the choice to find a constructive outlet for his pain and later became a 13 time Grammy Award winner who sold over 100 million albums worldwide.

Pay attention (pain into power) that the triumph allowed them to discover their state of freedom, which was an effect of being self-empowered by pain, which is a reward that can only be reaped by individuals who choose to take the favorable lessons from pain. This book stores the keys to discovering that power within yourself. In reading those failures to famous stories, recognize that no degree of difficulty is more powerful than making a CHOICE: MAKE the choice to practice the highest perspective that's organized in difficulty.

Throughout life, difficulty will present itself. But if you make the choice to take control of your life, you will learn to appreciate difficulty because it offers you the opportunity to discover your greatness. In the process of discovering your greatness, one must display these key qualities: EFFORT, DETERMINATION, DEDICATION, FAITH, and DISCIPLINE.

If you are wondering what approach should be taken in discovering the favorable lessons to be taken from pain, we will show you how to find out. You will only find the favorable lesson through knowingness of the difference between what feels good and what serves the greater good. This understanding is available to any person who has the desire and courage to apply it knowing that the difference between what feels good and what serves the greater good is pivotal to all who desire freedom or to become wealthy. The time spent learning to differentiate between the two is necessary and priceless.

Feel Good vs Serves the Greater Good

Those who make choices prompted and motivated by what feels good, generally make decisions based on emotions and what benefits self as fueled by the momentum of the moment. Leaders in every walk of life are required to make choices. Their ability to make choices is the primary based on feelings (emotions) instead of something solid and measurable (numbers and system).

It feels good to make decisions influenced by the impulse of emotions. It would be more beneficial to take SELF out of the equation when making major choices. It is still important to consider SELF when compelled to make a choice, but if your making choices that involve more than one party, train yourself to make choices in a manner that sees past the satisfaction of self on the subject and advance your focus to the bigger picture.

The habit of making choices based on what feels good "emotional impulse" has led to much deficiency in our world, as people make their relationship choices, business choices, financial decisions, and job choices based on emotions, which always feel good in the moment. Generally when people do so, upset is right around the corner. 99% of the human family base their choices off the impulse of emotions, unaware that emotions should not be used as a basis to measure defiance, considering the ever-changing nature of emotions.

People have developed the habit of using emotions as the basis of their life-changing decisions and short term choices, because at the moment, making the choice felt good. As an effect, we are left with a nation marked by personal problems, high divorce rates, racism, NO financial independence, disunity amongst cultures, segregation, WAR, and more. Examine the events that occur and you will discover that the root cause of these conditions were created by reacting based on the momentum of emotions, because whether positive or negative, at that moment, the choice "felt good."

A few common examples of people making their decisions prompted by EMOTIONS (what feels good).

- When Alexus gets LONELY, she calls her ex-boyfriend who cheated on her and spends time with him because it feels good to have someone to talk to, even if they are not worthy of her time.

- When an African American male is shot by a police officer and the community responds by rioting.
- When you and your spouse disagree, you choose to fight instead of having a civilized conversation.
- When someone offers you something and you accept it because it "feels good" to be the person something was offered to instead of considering "was the offer worth your time, energy, and effort?"
- When Christians "judge" other children of God, because their emotions are attached to the Bible doctrine.
- When a person becomes addicted to drugs, based on the reminder of how their first moment of getting high "felt good."
- When a person reacts without thinking.

Throughout the course of gaining this awareness, the thought may be present that emotions are "bad" or "it is not good to be emotional." The human mind tends to process what it wants to hear instead of receiving the exact point of emphasis. Before moving on to discuss the concept of making a choice based on what serves the greater good. I will exit this subject with this truth which is revealed in this story and all stories whereby one finds themselves hoping and praying for different results, but the outcome has stayed the same and you wonder why? EMOTIONS DO NOT TELL THE WHOLE TRUTH. They may be used as a way-shower to bring you to the truth and freedom but you will not experience true freedom through deeming emotions as the basis of choice. Emotions can be blinding. Although it is necessary to express self emotionally, it is equally necessary to understand and know the difference between following the impulse of what feels good and following the emotional impulse of "what serves the greater good" when one makes the choice to express themselves emotionally. Relative to freedom, "emotions are poverty."

Greater Good

Those who make choices guided by what serves the "greater good" generally make their choices based on their awareness of a greater purpose which overstands SELF. When leaders make choices based on "what serves the greater good" the choice is not self-oriented and does not necessarily always feel good or assures a comfort zone. These types of thought patterns require one to rise above the selfish orientation of emotions to align with the spirit of courage and selflessness which happens as a result of choosing to flow with the momentum of what serves the greater good.

Let's not forget, when Jesus was crucified, that day marked an event, whereby a human was put to death, religiously beaten, shamed and betrayed, as a part of the plan of salvation and redemption for man's sin. The event of Jesus' death is necessary for all to take this proper lesson from. God knows that it is human nature to be drawn into the momentum of the emotional state created by SELF. Therefore God used Jesus, a human, to show that we are entitled to choose a lifestyle revolving around making choices that serve the greater good, which impels a lifestyle whereby you surrender your mind, body, and spirit to a greater purpose. Large respect to Jesus for focusing on what serves the greater good of the human family instead of being deterred by the momentum of his emotions.

Jesus' actions undoubtedly displayed and made practical the art of yielding actions to the choice that served the greater good of others. He understood and used this choice basis in connection with the manifestation of what we know as Christianity. Those who follow Jesus believe that no human being could bare what Jesus endured. That was the case while he was alive. Truth is, you can have an impact far greater than Jesus, as long as you utilize the application of consciously making choices that serves a greater purpose to guide you.

ALL great leaders such as Martin Luther King, Jesus, Buddha, Krishna, Mohammad, Wakan Taken and more understood and practiced the art of basing ALL of their decisions and choices around their awareness of a greater purpose and when met with adversity instead of "doing what feels good." They continued to remind themselves through PRAYER, MEDITATION, and YOGA that the pain they felt was not their pain to bear, because the pain was about a greater purpose.

By now, you may have realized that this section of the chapter addresses a topic which most people are unaware of. The greater good choice will be of great benefit to the person who desires to acquire freedom, wealth, abundance, or riches but in a manner where your path is honorable.

The greater good choice is something one can practice daily. The ability to activate the great power birthed through the application of the concepts mentioned in this book. It takes a rare person to follow the path of the greater good. It's more often to meet those who are more readily available to walk the path of the average because they lack the understanding and become more attached to the momentary pleasures and become content with mediocre.

If you reading this book, you will have to cultivate your ability to follow the greater good choice. Some people who have gotten great riches, lost all their fortunes because of their lack of financial literacy to maintain their money. Developing the habit of taking the action which serves the greater good is important for those types of people to pay close attention to because the greater good choice can transform their lives.

Those who have developed the habit of making the greater good choice seem to enjoy discomfort and adversity. No matter how difficult, challenging, or painful things may seem, they arrive at the choice to confront adversity with the mindset to "keep going" based on their awareness that on the other side of pain is greatness. Sometimes it appears, there is no reason to keep going because their willpower will be tested through all sorts of discovery experiences. Those who choose the greater good choice tend to pick themselves up when they feel like quitting because they REMEMBER where they started. "I can do it". "I can make it". "It doesn't matter about my defeat". "It doesn't matter about my failures". Every time they are tested by failure, they always pass. Those who are driven by what feels good won't even arrive to take the test.

Those who make the greater good choice are aware that their pain is not about them. Their pain is a part of a bigger purpose. By reassuring themselves of that truth during the pursuit, it declares they will be rewarded for their actions. They realize it is not about them. They receive a greater version of themselves as a result of their perseverance. This knowledge is reflected through this quote: EVERY CHALLENGE, WITH IT, COMES THE OPPORTUNITY TO DISCOVER YOUR GREATNESS.

A few people know from the power of the greater good choice. They are those who fell forward and view defeat as an illusion. They are the ones who desire to be a part of something greater than themselves, so they surrender their actions to a cause greater than themselves. We who stand outside of this reality of life are prone to suffer overwhelmingly because we bring our pain to ourselves. These types of people are prone to learn the hard way. But what we do not see or what most of us never embrace is that PAIN is not for you but it exists because it is supposed to be shared constructively as a means of restoring HOPE for those who are losing the fight in their lives. By sharing our PAIN, pain becomes power from the observer who gains hope throught it. By keeping pain to ourselves, it becomes a destructive force. God reaps from the testimony of us growing through pain, but one does not know, by not sharing the pain, in other words, by not giving your story to the world, you will be drawn into selfishness and an emotional state which does not permit freedom to excel in any calling.

A great example of making the greater good choice is parenting. From all over the world mothers and fathers have put their dreams and goals aside for the sake of providing quality parenthood to their children. Often having to make choices and take steps to assure the child's well being. One of the most controversial issues in regards to parenting is DISCIPLINE. Although all know that discipline is not easy or fun, recognize that spanking hurts the children, as well as the parent, but the parents recognize it would pay off for the child in the long run. If the parent refused to give the child discipline, perhaps then they would be forced to learn through the disciplinary system.

The key is always to make the choice to commit your life to making the greater good choice. The greater good choice is the choice that focuses on a greater cause and considers the well being of all parties involved in an instance.

Before leaving this chapter, take an evaluation of yourself. Make the choice to improve in whatever particular areas you are lacking. Self evaluate yourself boldly, point by point, without any DENIAL of the truth. These self-evaluations may be the key to discovering this chapter in your life.

In chapter 6 on building well structured and precise plans, you will find the instructions to bring forth your "choice" to the world. You will find fundamentals and tools that will help you manifest any desire. Without choosing to put into action the tools provided, the KEYS will be of no use. MAKE A CHOICE!!! REMEMBER IF YOU DON'T MAKE A CHOICE, YOU HAVE CHOSEN NOT TO MAKE A CHOICE!!!!!

Chapter 9

Effort

(The Physical Manifestation of Energy)

Effort is an important key in the process of transmuting our thoughts into the physical reality. The root of effort is the determination to channel energy constructively and with discipline.

Determination and discipline, when mixed, create the irresistible force known as effort. People that make a choice to accept freedom, wealth, abundance, or prosperity of any magnitude are marked as WEIRD and often CRAZY. These are the phrases people use to describe an unadulterated desire that they don't have. Truth be told, they have a desire, which they are supposed to combine with determination and discipline and utilize the effort created by those two factors as the driving force to assure they accomplish their goals, objectives, or tasks.

Curtis "50 cent" Jackson was often mistaken as WEIRD or CRAZY. He was just different and if you are not different, then you can't make a difference. 50 cent's work ethic was different because he pursued every goal he set.

It has become more common to "give up" and "quit" when one faces contrast or adversity. Not many pushes past adversity until they succeed. The 1%'s often referred to in this book are those who push past adversity.

Essentially, work ethic may be one of the most distinguishing factors between one experiencing failure or success. A work ethic is just a constructive expression of EFFORT.

The creation of freedom in many regards requires the application of the keys mentioned in this book. The keys must be processed and routinely applied with effort.

The keys within this book will be of no use if not applied with effort. Upon putting the keys into practical use, you will face contrast. If you are one who has not defined your goals or created well-structured plans for the manifestation of your goals, it is extremely important that you practice these keys routinely, just as much as you take a shower and brush your teeth.

As we move forward in this book, it is important that the reader does a lot of self-evaluation and be HONEST with yourself. One of the primary causes of failure is a lack of effort. Meetings with millions of people have made it clear that effort declares failure or success. The only way that failure can be defeated is by the power of effort which matches and exceeds the force of one's doubt.

All manifestations begin in the form of a thought, keep this in mind. Bad thoughts bring bad experiences, just as good thoughts bring good experiences. If you find yourself lacking effort, this beauty mark will show itself by one not experiencing results, because the only thing that follows effort is RESULTS.

As you read this book, make a conscious effort to execute the keys given in each chapter. The momentum and enthusiasm that the keys create will be a greater way to measure "HOW BAD YOU REALLY DESIRE TO BE FREE or SUCCESSFUL."

Freedom and success are only experienced by those who obtain a mindset which is in-formation with the thought pattern necessary in the specific goal. Remember you attract to you, the conditions that are in-formation with your thought pattern. Therefore one must make it normal to practice and sustain a FREEDOM conscious or a SUCCESS conscious mindset. Just as surely as sustaining weight is important after losing it, one must make a daily effort to sustain and align their mind to the vibration that will attract their desired outcome.

If you are one that has a hard time channeling their efforts into tasks, this matter boils down to "FOCUS." Focus your attention on the thoughts which favor your desired outcome. Make sure you surround yourself with like-minded people who possess a vibration that is in-formation with that which is cooperative to your desire. You will meet adversity, but adversity creates the opportunity to discover EFFORT. Put forth the necessary EFFORT to discover your full potential that comes forth as a result of EFFORT. Follow the keys outlined in this book during those times and you will go unphased by adversity.

The mind is always active, whether you are asleep or awake. Hence, mental activity and thinking are two different things. It is essential to develop a relationship with your thoughts because thoughts that do not serve your greater good must be cropped out. Without cropping out polluted beliefs and thoughts, you can't be "success conscious" or "freedom conscious."

Understanding the next sentence is important to the reader. If you have negative or unfavorable thoughts in your mind, you are deliberately in RECEIVING MODE for poverty and limitation in your personal experience. Poverty and limitation will FREELY control your mind unless poverty and limitation thoughts are replaced with WEALTH and ABUNDANCE. The majority of humans were born poverty and limitation conscious.

Do not miss the relevance of the information in the previous paragraph as well as what is being portrayed in this entire chapter. No EFFORT, means NO RESULTS, no matter your level of success. Within effort lies a choice.

Do you have any regrets or ordeals you left unfinished in your life, "You wake up in the morning daydreaming and go back to bed at night with this feeling of incompletion." Every time you think about it, you hear this voice in your mind "I wish I would've kept playing basketball", "I should've never quit singing." You are not able to let go of this feeling of regret. You are reminded of this feeling anytime you see commercials, television shows, or experiences that remind you of it. Realize this happens to everyone which is the reason we must take control over the thoughts that occupy our minds. Through channeling your effort into practicing positive thinking, you will discover the keys to managing your mind. By continuing to channel your thoughts constructively, you will create positive vibes that will uplift you through negativity. Then you continue to reinforce positive thoughts into your mind until there is an obvious tipping point. Finally, you gain control over your thoughts and you become a mastermind. To become a mastermind, one must put conscious effort into the discipline of the mind. By acknowledging, cropping out, and replacing unfavorable thoughts, you will gain access to the power you have always had instead of depending on something or someone else to empower you.

You may reach a point where you feel the process is slow, then increase the time you spend reinforcing positive thoughts because there will be a tipping point. Put forth persistent effort, then success and freedom will follow.

The last chapter discussed the importance of choice. Make the choice to surround yourself with those who build your sense of urgency to give effort. Many people who experience success and freedom were motivated because they reached "rock bottom" which left them with nowhere to go except, to go up. They were driven to their breaking point and only EFFORT could restore their HOPE and FAITH.

NOTHING CAN REPLACE EFFORT. Effort is a character trait that cannot be overridden. It will be times where it seems like overcoming is IMPOSSIBLE.

Humans who practice putting forth their best effort have leverage over failure. Failure is always the result of not giving your best effort. No matter how much money you make, if you have not given your best effort to do so, then you have failed to BE THE BEST VERSION OF YOURSELF. Sometimes people put forth just enough effort to avoid discouragement. Those who cultivate the habit of putting forth the best effort all the time, KEEP UP THE GOOD WORK and I AM PROUD OF YOU. The key to avoiding failure is to give your best effort. Because it is easier to see failure as a lesson, when you've given your best effort instead of thinking of things, you could've done differently due to not giving your best effort.

All who put forth effort shall reap from it. They will reap the reward in whatever endeavor they choose to pursue. In addition, they will gain knowledge, experientially, which can be more powerful than any material matter. They gain the knowledge that WHEN YOU GIVE, YOU GIVE YOURSELF THE OPPORTUNITY TO GET SOMETHING OUT OF FAILURE THAT ALLOWS YOU TO SUCCEED.

It takes a very rare person to understand the effectiveness of effort. They are the ones who have discovered the keys to their freedom. They are those who understand that having a desire is just the beginning of manifestations. As a car needs fuel to drive us towards our destination, so do we need EFFORT. Those who are living ordinary lives observe many whose doing the SAME THINGS OVER AND OVER, WHILE EXPECTING DIFFERENT RESULTS. It takes a rare person to use failure as fuel to give more effort. Those who unfortunately learn to accept failure, are not likely to experience freedom. But the acceptance of failure is only the result which is created as an effect of not summoning to aid, the undeniable force which comes to the rescue of individuals who choose to never give up and keep going. One thing which can be agreed upon by scientists, philosophers, religious leaders, etc. is that NOTHING can be achieved without EFFORT and if one possesses effort, they are prone to experience success in any walk of life.

A phenomenal demonstration of effort is in business. Many people around the world travel and engage in various business endeavors in search of opportunity, gold, influence, attention, fame, or whatever desire they are pursuing. Every so often, one seeker outshines the other seeker. When their light is shining so bright, the world does not have a choice except to take notice. Obtaining a national spotlight is not an easy task, but recognize that if it could happen for them, then it could happen for you. The key is to refuse to quit, which means, always give your best EFFORT.

Will Smith, rapper, musician, actor and comedian, will not be remembered without his consistent effort.

Mr. Smith was nothing more than a Philadelphia kid with a dream, backed with the effort to transmute his desires into money. During his youth, he was inspired to be a rapper. However, along the way, Will Smith discovered this passion for acting. He became the star of the NBC television network, Fresh Prince of Bel-Air, which set Mr. Smith apart from other actors onto the path of becoming the greatest actor in the world. His acting career was successful and he began to take roles in all different movie genres.

Overwhelmed, Will reached a point where he felt he reached a ceiling point in his career as if his career was coming to an end. As a result, Will did not work for two years. He spent that time diving into himself, reading books, and reflecting on his inner self. This time created a shift in focus for Will.

Soon Will began accepting lead acting roles, but now looking at acting an entirely different way. After finding this new outlook of acting, Smith's passion for acting became stronger. He accepted more lead roles in countless films and his reputation throughout the world became FLAWLESS.

Although he has been ranked the most bankable worldwide by Forbes, there is a secret in his success that most are unaware of. Will Smith did not just rise to stardom by supporters and fame. Smith gave fans and supporters something to support, which was the effort that Will projected into his moviemaking skills.

Effort is an overlooked but major Key to success and freedom. Like all mindsets, effort is influenced by factors including:

Dreams, Goals, or Desire: In order to determine the amount of effort deemed necessary to acquire a dream depends on what that dream is.

Specify the reason "WHY": knowing why you desire a thing is an important step in developing effort. A powerful reason will summon to aid the strong force of effort. Keep in mind that your outcome goes no further than your effort.

Trust Yourself: Take a chance on yourself. Trusting your ability to execute the plan requires you to pursue your plans with effort.

Specific strategy or plans: Well structured and precise planning, even though they may appear unmanageable or exaggerated deploys EFFORT.

Proper Education: Gaining Proper Education and awareness creates the basis for sound judgment and decision making. Education gives a sense of direction as to where effort should be channeled.

DISCIPLINE: Avoid distractions, staying focused, and detaching from relationships that do not serve your greater good tends to build more effort.

SELF CONTROL: The time spent resting and recovering is just as important as time spent moving towards your dreams. Obtain a state of self-control whereby you permit yourself, recovery time, as recovery is essential to maintaining quality effort.

FOCUS: Effort is the result of energy created from FOCUSING on specific thoughts. The mind becomes obsessed with a thought which generates this power within you known as inspiration. Inspiration is effectively channeled out of the body in acts of EFFORT. Everyone who has experienced freedom knows this.

Having reached a pivotal point in this chapter, let's focus our attention on the signs of a lack of effort. Review the list and be honest with yourself. Acknowledge, courageously which of these signs relate to you. Remember, the truth shall set you free which means that by not being honest with yourself, you will remain in poverty and limitation. Always acknowledge the truth, because not acknowledging is no different than denial and denial is no different than lying to yourself.

In this section, you will discover the potential factors which interfere with your connection between you and your effort. Effort is a force that is made to self "empower." Here you will see thought patterns, as well as habits, which leaves you sitting in the seat of disempowerment and deep disconnectedness from your effort. Take this list serious if you truly desire to experience freedom. These are the thought patterns and habits that must be cropped out and replaced by all who desire freedom on any magnitude.

- Spend more time feeding your distractions than your desires.
- The habit of settling for less, in other words, not knowing your self-value.
- Taking short cuts or trying to obtain results without earning it, usually creates the basis   whereby one finds a way around an endeavor instead of summoning the effort to accomplish it.
- The fear that you will succeed.
- Unhealthy eating
- Laziness and Procrastination
- The habit of relying on it to come to you instead of you putting in the effort to make it happen.
- Abuse, drugs and/or Alcohol
- Inability to see the "BIGGER PICTURE"
- Fear of walking alone
- The fear of being defensive when given "constructive criticism."
- Compromising or sacrificing your happiness to please others
- Trying to do it, instead of just doing it. Meaning always use the phrase "trying".
- Improper dependency: Depending on things outside of you to give you a feeling of purpose instead of relying on your natural thoughts. Example: Depends on drugs to make you feel good instead of positive thoughts.

- Being passive about self-desire and more impelled to act upon other's goals.
- Practicing the thought pattern, "I have time" or "wait until the right time." NOW TIME IS THE ONLY RIGHT TIME.
- Self grief or Feeling bad for others. There is no hope when one "feels bad." Whether it is for themselves or others, feeling bad is not a good space to put in the power of effort.

Every habit or thought pattern in this list is created by fear. We innocently permit ourselves to live our lives under the influence of fear, to the degree, we are not able to see the bigger picture.

Large quantities of people spend more time feeding their distractions than their desires. As a result, they subject themselves to a life of distaste and misery. Our freedom and happiness are on the path of our desire, but we sacrifice and compromise our desires or happiness to please others (anyone who experiences this expression of freedom are more prone to make choices totally dependent upon the opinions of others, IMPROPER DEPENDENCY).

Millions of people suffer from laziness and procrastination because we tell ourselves "I have time" or " we are going to wait until the right time." Not knowing, NOW TIME IS THE ONLY RIGHT TIME.

People of all colors, cultures, and creeds do not know their self-value and because of that, they settle for less than what they truly deserve (self-value comes when you are worth more than you are being paid for your time).

Many fail in life because they lack well structured and precise plans. By failing to plan, you are planning to fail. Many people TRY to do it, instead of just doing it. We say TRY because our fear of failure outweighs our desire to win.

Lula Red Cloud told me that I would be the Rainbow Warrior and would have to devote the remainder of my life to manifesting Heaven on Earth. My initial reaction was fear of what my family, friends, and relatives might say. The possibility of her words being true was farfetched to me. Instantly, my mind began to create excuses and reasons, expressions of fear of why her words could not be true. Voices in my head said: "you can't do it", "give up", "she is lying", "Am I really worth it", "you don't deserve it", "people will treat you different", "you will lose your friends", "you will be judged", "Do you really think it is worth it", "that's not what you have been created to be."

Many questions and thoughts appeared in my mind and required acknowledgment. In that instance, it felt like I was alone and would remain alone if I accepted Lula's words as TRUTH.

This instance offered me the opportunity to gain a greater understanding of life, with respects to freedom. Millions of people are afraid to WALK ALONE. I discovered that "IT IS BETTER TO WALK ALONE IN THE RIGHT DIRECTION THAN TO FOLLOW THE HERD WALKING IN THE WRONG DIRECTION. The time is now. Every second, minute, and hour we live offers us a chance at a better quality of living. The fear of you being successful is a popular fear because it turns thoughts into words spoken without action.

Arianna Huffington's story adds to the list of success stories whereby she had to bypass negative comments and judgments to be successful. Her journalist skills were denied by 36 major publishers. She stayed true to herself and The Huffington Post was acquired by AOL for 315 million dollars.

It is unwise to think that freedom is the result of luck or mere chance. Behind every success story is a state of mind similar to this: "I am willing to risk everything it takes to be successful. I will forge my life into this cause. I will put forth my best effort. I will not return home until I succeed."

Pay close attention to the story of Les Brown, who was raised in an abandoned building in Liberty City, in a low-income section of Miami, Florida. He was declared mentally retarded.

However, he was smart enough to learn how to reach his fullest potential. As a motivational speaker, he shares the tools that teach other people to follow their dreams, as he learned to do.

Les Brown's journey requires EFFORT and FAITH. Brown battled with self-esteem issues and confidence as an effect of being labeled "mentally retarded." When all odds seemed stacked against him, when he did not have support, when his mother was not around to encourage him, when others said "you can't do it", Les Brown would respond to those thoughts saying "because I'M POSSIBLE, it's POSSIBLE."

Once he discovered the importance of putting conscious effort into replacing unfavorable thoughts with favorable thoughts, Les Brown knew that his freedom was guaranteed to come. It was not only guaranteed to come, but it had already arrived. This basis opened the window to many opportunities for Les Brown. Brown became the host of a new talk show, the Les Brown Show, received an Emmy Award and was selected as one of America's top five motivational speakers.

Despite being the father of ten children, negative opinions, going through a divorce and other forms of adversity, Les Brown wouldn't give up. He put forth effort, in the form of time, money, energy, projection, etc. into his greatest investment, which was himself. By his effort and determination, he went to financial freedom and motivated others to activate the same force in themselves, which led him to become one of the top speakers in America.

Survey the people you spend your time with. Ask them "What are your dreams?" Most will not be able to directly respond, because they do not know the answer. If you continually ask, some may give intellectual responses, meaning wordiness which no action will be put into. Some may share their dreams, many will say "I don't know, I've never thought about that". TAKE A STEP FURTHER. Ask them "What's the reason they want to be successful?" If you are one of those who desire freedom and success but do not know the reason WHY you have the desire, you will have a hard time maintaining EFFORT. Your effort goes no further than your REASON WHY. The mind only responds to situations with the amount of effort necessary to match the reason behind the desire, not the desire itself.

How to Channel Effort:

- A specific purpose and the reason you desire to manifest your goal.
- A well structured and precise strategy, which keys out everything (A-Z).
- A system that "systematically" makes success predictable.
- A mind that disallows negativity, shame, and fear to influence decisions whether it's projected by friends, family, or emotions.

- A team of qualified individuals to empower you and keep you encouraged.
- Be willing to be your biggest fan and supporter.
- Be willing to forge your life into it.

These seven steps are pivotal to your freedom in all walks of life. Practice these steps as well as the other keys in this book in order to permit you to take control over your life and freedom.

They are the keys to unlocking your inner potential.

They are the keys that lead to financial freedom.

They are the keys that lead to freedom of expression and thought.

They are the keys that allow you to take control of your life.

They are the keys that allow you to make a DIFFERENCE.

They are the keys to TRANSFORMING THE WORLD.

These keys promise freedom and prosperity for all those who are willing to apply them. How amazing is it to know, you hold the keys to your freedom? Now make the choice to use them.

Effort offers you the willpower to push through pain and adversity. Did you know that effort gives you access to the superpower that sees challenges as an opportunity to become mighty? Do you know that God honors the path of the person who puts forth EFFORT into walking alone in the right direction, while the entire world is walking in the wrong direction?

Not knowing the answer to those questions and observations have caused many to surrender their lives to FEAR. Fear is experienced by ALL who start a new endeavor and built a legacy around their contributions. Fear backed with EFFORT became the FAITH, which turned Oprah into "The Most Wealthiest woman", Albert Einstein into "a genius", Thomas Edison into "the creator of the light bulb", all by transmuting effort into RESULTS.

It has been an honor to observe Oprah, Albert, and Thomas, for seven years and be able to take notes of them regarding their habits and thought patterns.

I represent and RE-PRESENT those way-showers with high honor, knowing that by putting qualitative effort into developing and maintaining a FREEDOM mindset, then remotely success will happen as a result.

Time spent around successful people has shown me that the root of all accomplishments, is to put conscious effort into experiencing FREEDOM. As limitation and poverty are attached to all things, not obtained, freedom is attached to all realities to be achieved.

Another phenomenal example of effort is Ray Lewis, the Baltimore Ravens, linebacker. It takes a man's determination, effort and confidence to accomplish what he did.

Ray had a desire to take care of his mother, brother, sisters and his children without the burden of "financial worry." He was just a kid who would bear witness to his mother being physically abused by his stepfather. These observations caused Mr. Lewis much stress, being too young and not physically strong enough to help his mother during these times.

One day, Ray's mother was being abused. As he tried to help her, he realized the importance of being strong and if he was to get strong, he would have to put constant effort into assuring this strength. On the last altercation Ray's mother had with his stepdad, Lewis decided to pick up a deck of cards. After bearing witness to his mother being abused, he made the choice to turn his anger into strength. Ray would flip out a deck of cards and if he pulled a 9, he would do 9 push-ups, if he pulled an 8 he would do 8 push-ups. Jacks, kings, and queens were 25 push-ups and jokers were 50 push-ups. Some days doing the entire deck, reshuffling and doing it all over again.

It became Ray's obsession to put conscious effort into getting stronger. He was determined to be strong enough to bypass any challenge presented to him by man. This mindset was formed as a product of loving his mother.

The way he expressed his mindset to the world is through football. In 1996, Ray Lewis left the University of Miami (FL) and was drafted by the

NFL's Baltimore Ravens. In his years, he earned the NFL's Defensive Player of the Year, Superbowl's Most Valuable Player and was abducted into the football Hall of Fame.

Ray tokens the pain of witnessing his mother's abuse as the biggest attributor to his success. Ray made the choice to channel that pain with EFFORT in a constructive manner. His effort paid off. Ray Lewis will always be remembered for his contribution to the NFL.

As Ray became older, he decided to count the amount of cards in the deck and he discovered there were 52 cards in the deck, which he did not know when he was younger. He had discovered something amazing. There were 52 cards in the deck and ironically his NFL number was 52.

Ray was able to find financial freedom and leave an impact on people from all walks of life. Ray Lewis has become an international symbol of what it looks like to turn pain into greatness through channeling his efforts constructively and is now known as one of the NFL's most iconic players.

Now reaching the closing point in this chapter, we will leave you with this statement: If you are not effort conscious, then you will unconsciously, put more effort into making other people's dreams come true instead of your own.

Chapter 10

The Power of Words

(Controlled Language)

Language is the key to freedom and success in all walks of life.

Letters are organized to form words, which when is expressed becomes language. Letters and words carry a vibration that directly influences the growth that can be denoted from one's language. This chapter will describe the tools by which one may obtain a state of "EMPOWERMENT" through controlled language.

Language is a form of intelligence. In every language, words, symbols, and letters are arranged in an attempt to illustrate a state of consciousness. The power of words is expressed through language and the arrangement of the words indicates the potentialities of the vibration projected through language.

Controlling the power of words is essential to freedom, wealth, or abundance. Gaining clarity on the power projected through words is necessary for all individuals to sustain their freedom, once it has been acquired.

Allow me to demonstrate this power that is activated through words. If language is the key to freedom, let us explore the power of words. Language, words, and communication are synonymous. Let's shift our attention to the three major forms of language.

Understanding the Power of Words

The scripture quotes "In the beginning was the word and the word was with God and the Word was God (St. John 1:1). Therefore, God source intelligence manifests through language.

No human will have great influence without summoning to their aid, the power of words. Your body is like a car. Humans are the vehicles of conscious and unconscious language expressed through verbal and nonverbal cues. In chapter 5 (Discovering your Inner Guidance) it reads,

"We are not a body, we merely live in a body." For that reason, it is safe to say, we do not use language. God uses us as a tool to channel language through. God has programmed humans so that our brains could interpret language, through the sensitivity of the five senses. The intelligence of language is interpreted through the responses of the brain cells to the vibrations of words.

Every word has a powerful vibrational force, which is readily available to you through deploying the use of controlled language. We will describe the two foundations of which language is expressed, one of which is DESIRE, in nature. The characteristics of desire are obvious. Desire manifests in language through the words of people who surround themselves with ideas, people who follow their passions and those who are willing to focus on the positives. This form of expression, generally, has been the basis of all accomplishments, including FREEDOM. Your awareness of the language of desire will definitely influence your freedom.

Doubt is the second form of expression that language manifests through. Depending upon the nature of the person, this may be difficult to understand. Doubt, generally, expresses itself through those who are negative, those who cooperate with the opinions of others, and those who do not know their Mission, Vision, and Plan. This form of expression is generally the basis for all experiencing poverty and limitation.

The ability to distinguish between the expression of DOUBT and DESIRE is very important because they directly influence the spirit momentum with which the human mind will harness as a result of using specific words. You may understand this concept better from this statement. "I believe I can be successful, but sometimes I second guess myself because my family does not support me." I believe I can be successful (6 words) projects the emotion of desire, BUT sometimes I second guess myself because my family does not support me (12 words) projects the emotion of DOUBT. Upon first reading, you may not catch the significance suggested from the statement: DOUBT or DESIRE are two emotional states hidden behind words that create a force of energy and action or laziness and passivity.

Keep in mind that all things in the universe are constructed of energy. Energy is constructed of electrons, atoms, and molecules. Let's isolate atoms for a second. Atoms are made of a positive and negative charge.

Likewise, all words enter the brain in the form of energy, which is transmuted into words and language that is communicated through expressions of doubt or desire.

The human body is a molecular structure. The human mind interprets energy and transmutes it into thoughts. When the minds of people are in-formation, they experience spiritual harmony, which is the result of being like-minded, which constitutes the mind expressing itself in harmonious language.

Types of Language

Non-verbal Language - this form of communication uses wordless cues and visual cues such as body language, facial expressions, eye contact, posture, gestures, etc. An example is nodding your head up and down instead of saying "YES" when someone asks you to do something.

Verbal Language - this form of communication by humankind uses sounds and words to express self. An example of non-verbal communication is saying "YES" when someone asks you to do something.

Written Language - This is the most common form of communication. An example is writing on a piece of paper "YES" I will do what you ask of me instead of responding verbally or non-verbally.

Awareness of those different forms of language is key for anyone who desires to understand the power of words, which is organized in language. This power is necessary as one goes from merely dreaming into turning their dreams into reality.

Analyzing these three primary expressions of language will assure you of the many ways this power is expressed. If we are to master the art of controlling language, we must understand that language and communication uses words to manifest its power, but a picture can be worth a thousand words because non-verbal communication stills speak.

The mastery of controlled language in the expression of DESIRE was summoned by Eric Thomas. The discovery of this key is credited for the pursuit of my life endeavors.

Eric Thomas's mind was filled with doubt injected into it by hundreds of people who use the element of power within words to reduce the likelihood of him pursuing his desires. This doubt was able to dwell in his mind as influenced by the people he surrounded himself with who did not make the choice to follow their true desires or goals. Through attuning with people who attributed doubt to his life, he discovered the power of words which led to the mastery skill of controlled language.

Pay close attention to the lives of all who acquired freedom because they all had to, whether consciously or unconsciously employ the power that comes through controlled language.

All manifestations begin as energy which the human brain interprets in the form of thoughts. Thoughts are expressed from humankind through words, which stores the power to compel us towards the actions which lead to manifestations. REREAD

Energy is readily available to us that actually take time out and THINK. The brain acts as a satellite. It interprets and reads the vibration of energy from the universe, which provides life to all living things.

By continually reinforcing or repeating a thought, more energy is being added to that thought. The brain will transmute these thoughts into words, the words will carry a spirit of power (DOUBT or DESIRE), totally dependent upon what type of people we surround ourselves around. The power created through words will build a DESIRE to take action, which will propel us towards actions.

Through this process, it becomes immediately clear that controlled language (the power of words) is the key to the power summoned by all those who have acquired fortunes on all levels.

There follows now an illustration which will simplify the process for those who may have misinterpreted the reading. Transforming your thoughts will transform your words and transforming your words will transform your actions. Understand that thoughts, words, and actions have an alliance with energy, power, and manifestations.

Thoughts-------Words--------Actions

Energy-------Power--------Manifestations

Ralph Lauren began his story as a college dropout from the Bronx, New York. The thought popped into his head in the form of a question "I wonder are men prepared for a broader and more colorful design of ties?" With a few years of following the momentum of that thought, Lauren sold half of million dollars worth of ties and went on to create POLO. Pay attention to this truth, that from the time he chose to drop out of school, he became deemed as a failure by his family members, friends, and peers. If you are reading this book, you have seen or are beginning to see what type of reactions you get from people who choose to pursue extraordinary living. Summon to your aid, the power of words and remember the fact that Ralph Lauren's accomplishments began with making a choice to deploy the power of words to persevere through the doubt he was subjected to through other's minds and opinions.

There was doubt, whether minor or major, that Ralph Lauren faced in his pursuit of establishing his net worth of 6.3 billion. Breaking down his money is not the focus. Realize, Mr. Lauren's personal relationship with himself overstood the doubt of all who did not have faith in him. Understand that your feelings and emotions are based on the nature of thoughts which one is practicing in their mind. Actions become a reflection of thoughts manifested and the spirit behind actions is based on whether thoughts are reinforced by the vibration of DOUBT or DESIRE.

Ralph Lauren overstood adversity, poverty, doubt, and negativity by telling himself he would achieve and adding power to his thoughts through controlled language. Through his relationship with his thoughts, Lauren was able to add more power to his choice through controlled language and attracted more vitality, willpower, and spiritual force to his experience. Moreover, he discovered the key which many used, which is described in this book.

The keys are readily available to you.

Jan Koum brought the power of words to the United States when he created Whatsapp. Born in the UK and moved to California to live with his mother, Koum found himself in poverty and needing government assistance to survive. "I will learn computer skills" stated Jan Koum. Backed by the power which came from those words, the increased energy created a skill set that made him the co-founder of the world's largest mobile messaging service app, which sustained him a net worth of 9.2 billion dollars.

We have already discussed Martin Luther King. Maybe you are not aware of the magnitude of power an African American male had to have to influence people of all colors, cultures, and creeds to unify.

In truth, Martin Luther King was no different than you, but he generated the support of large quantities of people through his words and actions. His words drew followers, who removed mountains, which left a mark on history, making Martin Luther King one of the most powerful men of all time. He did it without MONEY.

Concentrate on the way he acquired huge power and influence. I will give you a brief. It came through adding persistent action to words, to the degree it influenced an entire generation of people to operate in-formation, with the focal point being the purpose of unity amongst the human family.

Martin Luther King was able to inspire, not persuade, others to operate in-formation and in unison. Realistically, think about how many doubted that King would be able to accomplish this task. Every person who accomplishes extraordinary endeavors knows it is not easy gaining the support and approval of others without having to extend some form of financial service.

Many attained extraordinary levels of success as headed by self-talk and reassuring themselves that they will overstand any adversity along the way. When you choose to speak power over your circumstances, it automatically creates a spirit of doubt or desire, which directly channels itself into actions in the form of effort and inspiration. Words are one of the greatest keys to success. It's the key that unlocks the door to our fullest potential. It is the key which all leaders use, whether intentionally or by default.

In this section, the methods which summons the power of words will be simplified in a manner that will prepare you to take immediate action. This is not a literature course. This concept is not written to teach you how to write a sentence. This book is written to offer qualitative keys to freedom. Therefore, this section will teach the reader to recognize the language of success and freedom and correct themselves when they are using disempowering words, so they can gain access to the power which will move the reader to their desired outcome.

Disempowering Phrases that Project Doubt

(Beside each one is an empowering phrase that projects desire)

- It is going to be risky (DOUBT) - Being myself involves no truth. It is my duty to be myself. It is wonderful to know it isn't my job to please anyone (DESIRE).
- It will be hard ------- I have the power. It is too hard is an excuse used by those who do not know how powerful they are.
- I won't have support from my family ---- It's better to walk alone in the right direction than to follow the herd walking in the wrong direction.
- I can't do it --- It is my nature to overcome any obstacles. I can do anything I put my mind to.
- No one will help me --- My help is always here and the right people will show up when I put forth the effort.
- It is not possible --- I am willing to believe in myself and my desire, beginning here and now. It is possible because I AM POSSIBLE.
- I am too old (or young) ---- I am limitless in my capabilities. My age has nothing to do with my greatness.
- I am not strong enough — I have access to unlimited strength. My strength comes from my connection to the God of life.
- I am too tired --- I am never tired. I am compassionate about my life and this passion fills me with energy.
- It will take too long --- I have patience when it comes to fulfilling my desires.
- I'm too busy ----- I am not busy. I am productive, on time, and on purpose.
- I am scared ---- Sometimes I get nervous, but I learned to use my fear as fuel.
- The sky is the limit ---- The sky can't be the limit because the TRUTH is, there is no limit.
- Nothing like this has been done like this before, no one will like it ---- It is up to me to be different because you cannot be the same and make a difference.
- It might be possible but it is difficult --- It may be difficult but it is possible.
- I am not smart enough --- I have access to a divine source that provides me limitless intelligence.

There are other words, but these are the most powerful and the ones most commonly used in people's language which project doubt. Become a master and recognize these words (they can be mastered by recognizing, acknowledging, and replacing) and use other powerful words that will be empowering and give you the desire to persevere. Remember in this section, that you are studying a book to help you develop a "freedom consciousness" by filling your mind with powerful thoughts (desire-based). You do not experience freedom conscious by filling your mind with doubt and limitation.

Language of Doubt/DESIRE

- I can't --------- I desire to be
- I won't --------- I will
- I don't think so ------- It is possible
- I might ------- I did
- Maybe I can be -------- I am successful
- I believe I can BUT no one supports me--------NO IF'S, AND'S or BUT'S

(the words IF, AND or BUT are usually doubt. The words before these phrases usually project desire but the words after are usually doubt)

Doubt and desire cannot occupy the mind at the same time. One or the other must dominate. It is your responsibility to make sure that desire influences your mind. Here is where the ability to identify the language of doubt will come to your aid. Make it a habit of applying and using the language of desire. Eventually, they will dominate your mind completely that doubt loses its power.

Only by applying these keys literally and habitually, can you activate the power of controlled language. The presence of a single thought of doubt in your mind is enough to decrease the chances of success and freedom.

Read, reread, and self evaluate yourself as you read. Now, the truth will unfold and you will see it in your daily language. You are now seeing the breakdown of language from the perspective of desire (success and freedom) and doubt (failure and limitation).

If you are an intuitive person, you must have realized that most humans resort to prayer only after everything goes wrong. Otherwise, they pray meaningless prayers because doubt and fear are the hidden emotions behind their words. If you are a praying person, it is important that you take heed to this key. YOU CANNOT DOUBT AND DESIRE A THING and expect what you desire to be moving towards you or for you to be moving towards it.

If you pray for a thing, but the mind is dominated by doubt as you pray, you will not receive it. In fact, your prayer will have been pointless.

Prayer is a powerful tool when one prays as inspired by pure unadulterated desire. Think back to a time where you prayed for something and actually envisioned it manifesting while you were praying and you will understand the concept behind this philosophy.

It is time that we break down the concept of prayer. Prayer acts as an electric battery. It is supposed to provide energy in proportion to the magnitude of emotions projected into the words the prayer contains. To all humankind that's ready to see the truth, this chapter will greatly be appreciated.

Power

Recharger

And

Your

Energy

Recharger

Lack of awareness, ignorance, and comfort in dishonesty are the primary reasons why this truth may not be spoken to you in this formation by religious leaders, philosophers, gurus, and teachers from all walks of life. PRAYER is not the solution to all problems nor does it declare freedom or success. One must be aware of the emotions that are behind the words to really interpret the effectiveness of the prayer. In more instances than less, we pray in a state of fear and doubt and expect our desire to manifest. Is this happening to you?

If you deem this concept as false, do a survey of your life and the lives of the collective human family. More than 250 years, it is believed that people of all colors, cultures, and creeds will come together and we will experience HEAVEN ON EARTH, but what is the reason that, despite years of praying, this reality has not manifested? Equally, a man prayed that one day he would walk on the moon, but is not alive to tell the story, followed the momentum of this desire-based prayer, and achieved something that was known as IMPOSSIBLE to ALL MANKIND.

Perhaps the vibration of doubt based thoughts creates the energy to pulsate you towards failure. Equally, the vibration of desire-based thoughts creates the momentum that pulsates you towards freedom in every career, occupation, and action which requires the human mind to express itself to achieve a thing.

What are the other solutions that can provide the same energy prayer does, just in case one is not a praying person?

There is no difference between meditating, prayer, self-talk, listening to affirmations, motivational speaking, or reading positive and inspiring stories. These are tools used to replace thoughts of doubt and replace them with desire. Moreover, the approach you take to claim dominion over doubt may vary based on your demographic. But either way, without replacing the thoughts or words, which project doubt, your method is not effective.

Millions of humans spend their entire lives flowing and rotating between the stream of doubt and desire and finally surrender to the stream of doubt because they find comfort in being ordinary. When the great depression came, the recession came, or the stock market crashes again, millions will be in alignment with the stream of doubt and poverty. If you desire to align or be in-formation with the stream of desire, this book was written for you.

Poverty, fear, and limitation are realities inspired by doubt. Poverty, fear, and limitation do not permit one to experience freedom. When freedom occurs, the transformation usually occurs through following the stream of desire (pursue your dreams) and making well constructed and precise plans for desires to manifest through. Doubt is the most common emotion on the planet. It needs no one to give it permission because doubt is fearless and reckless. Freedom comes through having the courage to follow your desire and most do not have that courage. But the few that do are names like Bill Gates, Warren Buffett, Mark Zuckerberg, Oprah Winfrey, Kaden Lebray, and more.

These people do not just pray, hope, wish, or dream for their freedom, but they created a system and a well-organized strategy for their desire to manifest through.

Prayer can transform your life. If you are reading this book, within it is the answers to your prayers. Faith without work is dead. Faith is only a phrase to declare DESIRE in terms of spiritual nature or spiritual expression. As you read this book, my prayer is that the keys carry the vibration to transform your doubt into desire. And when this occurs, it puts you in receiving mode for the "steps" that will propel you towards manifesting your desire.

FAITH and DESIRE are interchangeable. Equally, FEAR and DOUBT are interchangeable. Fear and faith do not operate well together, neither does doubt and desire. Where one exists, the other does not feel safe.

Chapter 11

Power of the Mind

(The Greatest Power in ALL CREATION)

Before you can benefit from the keys in this book, your mind must be open, alert, and in the receiving mode. Being in RECEIVING MODE is not hard. It begins with gaining awareness and understanding the greatest power in all creation. What is the greatest power in all creation?

The common answer to this question is usually God, money, or anything that humans tend to value more than themselves. The truth of this matter is associated with neither. The mind is the greatest power in ALL creation.

The creation is a reflection of the creator. God is the greatest power. The mind is the great power in all creation, God being the creator, the mind being the creation. Remember this as you read. The mind is the reflection of God's power on Earth. This is the reason why the power of the mind must be understood, disciplined, and utilized favorably. This chapter describes the faculties of the mind, as a whole and shows practical ways to use the power of the mind in your favor.

The purpose of this chapter is to HIGHLIGHT the causes and cures of limitation and poverty. Before we can gain a thorough understanding, we must fully grasp the mind's functions, how our mind relates to our reality, and carefully analyze yourself to gain the advantage point of your mind.

Do not undermine the power of the mind. Sometimes the power does not seem REAL, because the power will appear in subtle ways, establish itself in the form of habits, habits will form your values and standards, and your values and standards will reflect the actions you take towards your DESTINY. Commonly we practice unfavorable habits, which must be located, understood, and replaced to assure the productive usage of the mind.

The mind is the greatest power in all creation. The mind is like a garden that is full of seeds (thoughts) that must be watered with awareness in order to get a fruitful harvest (freedom and success).

The mind acts as a satellite by deploying the power of the five senses to interpret and store thoughts, which enters the mind in the form of energy. Every thought that is stored in the mind becomes words that are translated into the physical world in the form of actions. Your actions voluntarily plant habits in your mind, which acts as the basis of your value system. The maintaining of discipline and commitment to the values which are necessary to manifest your desires is the key to fulfilling your destiny.

Consider this chapter as the bridge between all sections outlined in this book. In reading, you will discover the significance of the information displayed.

THE MIND WORKS LIKE THIS:

The mind draws upon thoughts for power which it uncontrollably transmutes into the physical equal.

The mind stores thoughts, but thoughts are not just randomly arranged. They are stored in the subconscious mind. Whatever we observe in our FOCUS or ATTENTION becomes programming in our subconscious mind and creates a pattern of habits. The subconscious mind consists of a multitude of habits which is classified as a paradigm. From the paradigm, habits will flow as actions that may be done with or without conscious thoughts.

It is not possible to fully control the subconscious mind, but you can make the choice to reprogram it to align with the thought patterns that harmonize with the plan, goal, or purpose you desire to bring forth.

The subconscious mind interprets impressions or thoughts voluntarily drawn from genetic factors and environmental factors. When the two have been mixed with feelings, emotions, or impulses, they shape your reality.

The power of the subconscious mind is evident enough to aid the belief that the subconscious mind is the bridge between limitation and freedom. It is the magnetic barrier of consciousness that one may rely on for a sense of SELF-worth. The subconscious mind stores the power, which when modified and favorably channeled will serve as the KEY source of capabilities which lead to a limitless future.

The uncontrollable power of your subconscious mind is connected to ALL conditions and circumstances in our life. It inspires our thoughts. To aid those who desire to gain an understanding of the subconscious mind, the following WHY questions will prepare you. Read the questions and put a check next to all that apply to you. This will make it easier to understand the subconscious mind. Explaining it in a way a child can understand it, without insulting anyone's intelligence.

WHY - Analysis Test Questions

_____ Have you ever wondered why you have the habits of your mom or dad?

_____ Have you ever wondered why you keep getting the same results over and over?

_____ Have you ever wondered why individuals who get their degree's are not likely to become wealthy?

_____ Have you ever wondered why individuals who do not have a degree are making millions of dollars?

_____ Have you ever wondered why HISTORY REPEATS ITSELF?

_____ Have you ever wondered why you don't seem to be able to make more money?

_____ Have you ever wondered why people believe I CAN'T as true?

The uncontrollable power of the subconscious mind becomes activated when we first open our eyes as babies. As babies, our brain was in a "soaking in" phase (receiving mode) without the ability or little ability to distinguish between FAVORABLE or UNFAVORABLE thoughts, because babies cannot naturally differentiate. Whatever we observed through our eyes becomes programming to our subconscious mind and creates a pattern of habits known as a paradigm.

All observations you observe will become the basis of what you call reality. Genetic factors and environmental factors are the basis in which the subconscious minds draw its observations.

After giving yourself permission to accept this as truth, you will gain the leverage which will permit you to use the power of the subconscious mind in favor of creating your freedom. Without accepting that truth, you will not understand the efficient significance of the keys given in this chapter. You will also understand why you have been repeatedly experiencing the realities taken from your WHY ANALYSIS TEST.

The 3 primary factors which program the subconscious mind are family, religion, and environmental factors. Do not fault yourself if you find it difficult in setting yourself free from the beliefs in the paradigm that you do not agree with. Remember, the subconscious mind took shape when we were not in a state to direct our own thoughts. If you are reading this book, I am assuming you are, then this applies to you.

Whether you make an effort to do so or not, the subconscious is always observing the outside world. This means that by watching television shows that are negative and drama-based, your subconscious mind will be negative and drama-based. Imagine the subconscious mind being your child. If you fail to give it attention, it will feed upon negative thoughts for a sense of attention. Equally, if you feed the subconscious mind with good mental food (positive thoughts), the subconscious mind will respond to these impulses in a much more favorable way.

It is important to know that all living beings in the world have a subconscious mind. And that your behaviors and actions are a result of practicing thoughts in the subconscious mind with or without conscious awareness.

The subconscious mind will remain the most domineering aspect of the mind. If conscious effort is not put into programming the subconscious mind, it will respond to the thought patterns it is already programmed to practice. WE HAVE TO BE HONEST WITH OURSELVES AND express that thoughts express themselves through two emotions, being DOUBT or DESIRE. For the present world we live in, is it accurate to declare that you are living in a world where there are more negativity (DOUBT) than positive (DESIRE) impulses that are practiced?

There is some positivity in the world but more negativity active. We are involved in the process of replacing negative thoughts and consciously shifting the momentum of the subconscious mind through deploying the vibrations which reinforce positivity.

All things are constructed of energy. When energy enters the human body, it becomes a thought which is communicated through the language. The subconscious mind is the most influential factor in the mind, in regards to prosperity and creations. Due to its magnitude of influence, it must be put under administration, in order for one's desires to manifest.

Although there is another aspect of the mind that plays a vital part in determining the likelihood of one transforming their thoughts into reality, ALL things must pass through the subconscious mind before they can be transmuted into the physical reality.

From the awareness provided, you should be in receiving mode for more specific instances that demonstrate the subconscious mind and its qualities.

A famous minister of the protestant church showed evidence of being aware of the power of the subconscious mind when he was diagnosed with lung cancer.

Two or three times a day, he would put his body and soul in a state of ease, repeating these words. "God's perfect spirit dwells within me. My subconscious mind is filled with thoughts of that nature. I have perfect health. My image is pure before God. I am perfectly healthy".

The minister managed to heal himself because he was aware of this truth. Thoughts spoken out of one's mouth are captured in one's subconscious mind, which it acts as a GENIE, granting you ability to think whatever you request, while directly expressing those thoughts in the form of emotions, stories, beliefs, and ideas. Thoughts are truly expressions of energy, for that reason, thoughts offer the momentum to experience freedom or limitation.

The subconscious mind is more responsive to thought impulses influenced by emotions or feelings rather than thoughts deriving from the rational thinker within you. In fact, deem it ignorant to expect an experience from the subconscious mind if the thoughts being filled in it are emotionless. Most people are easily influenced by the impulse of emotions and feelings. Truth be told, what the subconscious mind REACTS to, is more susceptible to and is easily influenced by thoughts mixed with feelings and emotions. Therefore, I deem it necessary to raise our awareness about the ways emotions project themselves.

All emotions are expressed through words, in the form of doubt or desire as mentioned in Chapter 10 on Controlled Language. For this chapter, we will look into emotions. It is important to understand that there are seven unfavorable and seven favorable thought patterns that emotions project themselves through. Practicing the unfavorable beliefs created by emotions will permit direct access to the subconscious mind. The favorable thoughts must be given permission through affirmations, prayer, etc. in order to occupy the space in the subconscious mind (tools have been provided in Chapter 4 - Doing the First Job).

The feelings, thoughts, or emotional momentum, first may be like the root of a flower, because they are the best indicator of the action phase of plant growth, which ultimately decides the magnitude of production the flower will provide. In other words, the beliefs, ideas, and stories that dwell in your mind are a reflection of thoughts and once these thoughts are compressed into the subconscious mind, they gain influence over your emotions, vibration, and willingness to take action towards your desires.

Thus one may understand this demonstration which displays the basis of all realities acted upon or merely thought from the origination of thought to "manifestation."

THOUGHTS, they lead to BELIEFS and IDEAS

BELIEFS and IDEAS, they lead to STORIES

STORIES, they lead to EMOTIONS.

We are reaching a pivotal point in this book, in regards to understanding the faculties which disallow freedom, permit, control, and influence the voices of doubt to dwell within the subconscious mind. ALL manifestations are anchored through FREEDOM. The desire for money, which most people have, can be acquired through being FREED from the thought impulses of Poverty and Limitations. The desire for better relationships, which ALL people have, can be acquired through being FREED from the thought impulses and inner voices of doubt "saying you have relationship problems." In other words, FREEDOM IS ESSENTIAL TO ALL MANIFESTATIONS. Therefore, we must understand the design in which these "inner voices" enter the mind. We must understand its methods or you will not be able to be freed from it. It interprets the impulses of feeling or emotions. Let us take a look at the seven favorable thought patterns and seven unfavorable thought patterns being projected through emotions, so that you may be aware of the unfavorable (bad) thoughts and discover the freedom to choose to compress favorable (good) thought patterns upon the subconscious mind.

The SEVEN GOOD beliefs projected through EMOTIONS

RESPECT - based

ALTRUISM - based

INTEGRITY - based

NEUTRALITY - based

BLISS - based

OBEDIENCE - based

WORTHINESS - based

There are other favorable beliefs projected through emotions, but these are the most influential abroad and the beliefs most commonly pressed toward sustaining as you gain mastery over yourself. Keep in mind, the information in this book is key in bridging the gap between you and your desired outcome. To do so, we must occupy our minds with good thoughts, good beliefs, good ideas, and good stories, which will give us the good emotional state to propel us to take action. You are not prone to take action towards your desire if your mind is filled with bad beliefs or inner voices that project doubt.

The SEVEN BAD Beliefs behind emotions

RESENTMENT - based

AGONY - based

INTIMIDATION - based

NEEDINESS - based

BOASTFULNESS - based

OMISSION - based

WORTHLESSNESS - based

You can not have doubt and desire in your mind at the same time and expect your desire to move towards you or you to move towards it. One must have more leverage over the other. Equally, you cannot keep active, BAD beliefs and GOOD beliefs and expect GOOD THINGS to happen. It is your job to make sure you feed your GOOD beliefs and starve your BAD beliefs.

Only by applying these keys will one gain access to the subconscious mind and utilize its power to propel you to freedom. If you are reading this book, then you were the one cell out of millions to make it through the egg, which led to your birth. Remember this in connection, that it only takes one negative thought in your mind to sabotage the favorable usage of the subconscious mind.

After spending time with more than 300 wealthy men and women of my time, I have made an observation that all must take into consideration if you desire to transform your life or the lives of others. It is that most people think they can store thoughts in their mind and as long as they are not spoken or written, they do not affect your actions.

And this polluted belief has been active in humanity for so long, that it has been accepted as truth. So instead of transforming the thoughts which fill our minds, we are more prone to ignore the subconscious mind and live our lives based on the fear that comes with the thoughts of facing our own thoughts. Meaning, fear becomes the emotion that stands between you and your freedom.

WHO ARE YOU?

If you are in a relationship but have not spent conscious time facing your thoughts, your relationship is more of a comfort zone for you to hide behind instead of a channel for unconditional love to flow. If you are going to college because your parents said "you have to go" instead of "do you truly desire to go," you are ignoring your true self. Some of my readers are not in TRUE RELATIONSHIPS because it is impossible to be in a relationship with someone else if you have never been in one with yourself. You are supposed to give yourself permission to be yourself first. Most people never take time to discover themselves, so instead of mastering themselves, they master the art of hiding themselves behind someone or something else, who they are able to identify themselves by.

If you have any experiences in your life which you engage and do not find fulfillment, go back and reflect on the reason why you are doing it. In other words, the time has come to discover that beliefs absorbed through religion, family paradigm, and other ideas in the subconscious mind that you identify yourself by, are actually not you. In the subconscious mind are beliefs you've been persuaded to believe as true. The beliefs of yourself in the conscious mind gives a more accurate indication of who you truly are.

If you believe you are who your parents, religion, educational institutes, etc. told you that you are, take a look at yourself from God's perspective. The method by which to communicate this awareness in a sound manner is through understanding the life of a bald eagle. If you understand the bald eagle, you know that no other bird can fly at the altitude of the eagle. Because this is true, the eagle can also see things from a higher perspective. KEY EMPHASIS, know that the eagle can always fly down and communicate with the crows, pigeons, ducks, and any other bird species. But the other bird species can not fly at the same altitude as the Eagle.

In other words, there is an eagle inside of you. The eagle is always sending you messages and ideas which offer glimpses of who you truly are. Only by taking action or taking steps based on the intuition that's been pronounced, can one become eligible for step 2 and so forth. In the metaphor, God is the eagle. As you take steps towards becoming the eagle within, your life will begin to transform, only for you to discover this truth: The version of you, from the perspective of religion, family, and government, is much different than that from the outlook of the eagle.

If that's misunderstood, I wish to use another common metaphor which demonstrates that you are so much more than the paradigm, the subconscious mind, religion, and environmental factors tell you that you are.

If you have never flown on an airplane, then you won't understand the message this constitutes. A person can stand beside a building and the human mind will naturally deem that building as "big." An individual could be flying in an airplane looking out the window at that same building and it will appear "small." This metaphor demonstrates how the human mind functions and coordinates with the subconscious mind.

When the majority of people give their perspectives (religion, family, environmental factors) of your future, the perspectives are in harmony with ground-level thinking (poverty and limitation). Only a select few have created their reality through the aid of seeing the bigger picture (freedom and success), which is readily available to those who use the power of the subconscious mind favorably.

We must begin to bypass the fear of being your true self. The subconscious mind will subject you to thought patterns that attributed to your life, such as RELIGION can be given credit as a huge attributor to our subconscious mind.

If you communicate with God source intelligence, you will discover that we have been created to be extended far beyond the beliefs in the subconscious mind or habits of the paradigm. Imagine you have been created to be a "BIG TIME" actor. You receive an offer to play the lead role in a film paying you $100,000. You get excited but become discouraged by the opportunity because RELIGION would not approve of the profanity that you would be required to use in the film. Imagine, if you have been created to be a millionaire by God but made the choice to take the inheritance of the family company. Your family tells you "this company has been in this family for years and it is up to you to keep the tradition alive." You know that by making the choice to commit to family tradition, you are equally committing to a purpose someone else chose for you instead of the destiny given to you by God. And by doing so, you have taken on generations of debt. Imagine growing up in the ghetto and being told "you will never go to college" and you actually make it to college. Only to realize, while at college, there is a voice in your head saying "you will never make it to college", which overrides your judgment of yourself to the degree you find yourself back in the ghetto because you did not perform well in college as followed by the influence of this voice.

What reason do these occurrences happen? All of the outcomes are created through surrendering in action to the version of themselves, religion, family, or environmental faculties, which are the basis of programming in the subconscious mind, instead of recognizing that higher mental faculty, which recognizes they have a purpose much greater than the faculties of the subconscious mind can recognize. Understand the concept of the subconscious mind and you will understand why history repeats itself, why prayers alone do not fix things, why you keep having the same outcome over and over because the subconscious mind stores the keys to transforming your reality.

Before we move to the next chapter, it is a perfect time to make a statement. Be mindful to spend more time READING books than watching television (tell-lie-vision). The vast majority of the things you see on TV are not true and by subjecting our mind to it, giving it your focus and attention, you make yourself believe something false is true. Where there is a lie, there is no truth. And since "the truth shall set you free", it is safe to say, "where there is no truth, there is no freedom."

Chapter 12

Conscious Mind

(The ultimate Storehouse of Supply)

The human brain acts as a satellite, sending and receiving vibrations that once they enter the human brain are known as thoughts.

Through deploying the power of the human brain, the satellite nature of our brains is always causing us to interpret and send out vibrations. In other words, we are always having constant mental activity.

In relation to this chapter, it is important to grasp the above statement because this chapter will explore the conscious mind which is the mental storehouse in the brain of thoughts with a high rate of vibration. It is also the mental agency whereby perception, perspective, reasoning, imagination and other sources of greater awareness interprets the vibration of thoughts.

When a thought enters the mind, the mind responds to that thought based on the speed of the vibration when it enters. The speed of the vibration is influenced by the magnitude of negative or positive emotions. Based on this information, the vibration of thoughts may be increased or decreased.

Once aspired by the impulse of emotions, thoughts begin to extend outside of the confines of the physical body and communicates with the non-physical intelligence. Non-physical intelligence then stores and carries these rapid vibrations to Mother Earth, to be released into the Earth. Once released into the Earth, the vibration then travels from one mind to another. Vibrations travel in the form of energy and energy enters the mind in the form of a thought vibration. Thoughts which are backed by major magnitudes of emotional impulse, vibrate at a speed much faster than those not backed by emotions. Hence extraordinary thoughts are prone to vibrate at a higher rate than ordinary. The type of thoughts backed by emotions are those which the human brain are more prone to recognize or be conscious of.

Emotions are an important faculty to take into consideration in regard to measuring the force we will put into accomplishing a task. It does not mean emotions are a bad thing or a good thing. It means whatever you put your emotions into or whatever draws the most emotional impulses out of you, the emotional impulses of these activities are more prone to draw more energy and force from your body.

As far as emotional force, the vast majority of humans channel this energy into pleasing others by doing activities whereby you are paid to make someone else's dreams come true. Sex, by far, is the most dominant activity that humans channel their emotions through. During this activity, the mind experiences a higher speed of vibration due to the enhanced impulse created by emotions.

When thoughts are backed with emotions, the basis is created for the mind to be in "RECEIVING MODE" for God source intelligence and non-physical awareness. The moments when the mind is vibrating at a speedy rate and when thoughts are backed with emotions, not only is the basis created for the thoughts to be interpreted and compressed in the subconscious mind, but these are the moments when the mind is ready to receive thoughts and ideas and releases them for other minds to attract them at their leisure.

Hence, you will understand that the mind is the key to FREEDOM, which is created when combining emotions and feelings with thought energy and compresses them into the subconscious mind.

The conscious mind is the "receiving" channel of the mind that interprets energy and vibrations from the earth and sends them to the subconscious mind. The subconscious mind is the mental garden of the mind which thought vibrations are planted.

Alongside the importance of the conscious mind and subconscious, we will take into consideration the principle of Doing the First Job and making your thoughts a priority.

In chapter 4, you were given the keys to transmute the thoughts of freedom into the physical reality.

Summoning to your aid, the power of the conscious mind is a practical process. To do so, it is pivotal to be in tune with your thoughts by Doing the First Job and apply the power of the conscious and subconscious mind. The intensity and power created when all three are stimulated is described in this book but regardless, the process always will involve thoughts.

The Conscious Mind "The Eagle within you"

In 1996, songwriter and producer, R Kelly performed the song titled "I believe I can fly" which became the soundtrack of the popular film starring Michael Jordan who was well known for his electrifying, magnetic, HIGH FLYING aerial skills on the basketball court. R Kelly was a popular artist of his generation, known for exceeding limitations and writing "I believe I can fly" which was his most successful song.

We are going to use these icons as metaphors to unfold the conscious mind which will teach us something about ourselves. Perhaps we shall lean on the power of the conscious mind when we answer this question, "Do humans have wings?"

The conditioned human mind will respond to that question with the biggest NO response. Anyone who operates within the limitless nature of the conscious mind would respond with a big YES.

To all who desire freedom, know this, the path towards your freedom comes through the conscious mind, which is created entirely through the experiences created in the subconscious mind. We must take the favorable lessons from the experiences and they will propel us towards NEW HEIGHTS.

Surely the awareness in this chapter is something most are ignorant of. As long as we remain ignorant, we will remain silent. We will not be ignorant because, in truth, we were created to know. In fact, nothing is meant to be unknown.

The Aspects of the Conscious Mind

By default, education and culture have come to know little or nothing about the layers of the mind. We are aware that we have a brain and it is the storehouse of our thoughts. But, we are entering a generation of consciousness, therefore we will articulate further on the subject. Already we have learned that we have a subconscious mind that is programmed to practice all the beliefs you were taught as a child. While those beliefs served us well during that time, know that they are not updated enough to be used as the basis of which you are destined to be. The truth is, you were created to be so much more than the version of you, which is connected to the subconscious mind, which 99% of humankind identifies themselves by.

This metaphor is useful in the unfolding significance of the conscious mind. When a child is young, they are nurtured by their parents. While going through their stages of education, the parent-child relationship is established. It is unlikely that such a relationship will exist as the child gets older, as it is when the child was young. It is likely that one day, the child will experience growth in their mind and physical body and their growth will launch the desire to carry on and explore life. Hence, leave the nest. It is not likely that parents will adjust to their new role in a child's life, as well as the changes in their identity as a parent. While parents are encouraging children to become independent adults, leaving the nest, the thought of sending their children into the world amplifies sadness within them. The most constructive way for a parent to communicate this hostility within themselves is to induce you to practice the beliefs, hobbies, careers, educational opportunities, etc. that assures the child's attachment to their outlook of your life. Although not meant to cause harm, these expressions are deemed as constructive ways to maintain their sense of parenthood once their nest is empty.

Psychologists have developed a study that discusses parental behavior patterns that indicate the symptoms of "The Empty Nest Syndrome." It has been determined that there is an eagle inside all humans, whether child or adult and we know the eagle becomes just as equally afraid to leave the nest, as the parents are by thoughts of the eagle (you) leaving the nest.

The comparison briefly describes the system in which humans base their lives on. The same system which creates an ordinary living. The same system which provides comfort but disallows freedom. For thousands of years, we have put our lives in the hands of religion, government, family, and systems. We have looked upon them as our "parents" and had faith that they would look after us, support us, and give us what we NEED to live abundantly and free.

The service they bestowed upon humanity was well served and now the time has come for us to face the discomfort of flying out of the nest, doing something different than the previous generation, leading an extraordinary life, and be more in-formation with who you were created to be. When you are in the nest, you are more who your parents want you to be, but when you leave the nest, the basis is created to discover who you have been created to be.

WHAT is the Conscious MIND?

As kids, we read books of our favorite heroes, play video games, card games and other activities where we could imagine ourselves being someone else. These patterns are supposed to continue into adulthood as a way to excite and engage the mind for the purpose of "keeping active" the creative faculty of the mind.

Later I discovered, through observations and notations from scientists, as a result of wondering, why this creative faculty is not utilized. Educational systems do not promote the usage of the creative mind. The actual existence of art or music courses stimulates the creative faculty of the brain enormously, but the art and music projects are determined beforehand and students are taught to follow the lesson about the women and men who become regular explorers of the creative faculty of the mind. Student's willingness to keep their creative mind active becomes repressed by millions of criticisms and judgments from those who have not done their part by correctly staying true to their conscious mind.

But what is the conscious mind? This is the creative faculty of the mind, whereby reasoning, imagination, perception, and perspective exist. The power of the conscious mind is known through understanding a magnifying glass. Experiments worked with a magnifying glass revealed that a very small object can be placed under it and it will appear much BIGGER. That fact reflects the power of the conscious mind in an attempt to explain through metaphors. All known thoughts in the conscious mind are BIGGER than what one can imagine in their physical awareness. Dreams and visions do not just appear but through summoning the power of the conscious mind, it causes mental power to deploy the imagination, which vibrates and communicates and expresses itself in the form of visions, dreams, or inspirations. Most do not know, but the power of the conscious mind remains active whether you are awake or asleep, it is called "having a dream" or "daydreaming." As noted with the subconscious mind, the more emotions we add to the dreams or visions in the conscious mind, the higher the speed of vibration, which will increase our desire to transmute the thoughts into reality. The most powerful creator known to man is in the confines of the conscious mind, where ALL creativity occurs at its best.

One observation that we must draw with assurance is that the conscious mind is really powerful. That is because it is the faculty of the mind that "sees" a thought and seems to make it BIGGER than a thought residing only in the subconscious mind. There are many demonstrations of this. If you are reading this, for example, there is a dream or desire which you store in your conscious mind that brings you joy by the mere thought of it. In every attempt so far to manifest this conscious desire, you have been equally having to face the contrast energy (doubt, criticisms, hopelessness) from the faculties which influenced your subconscious mind (religion, family, environment). The conscious mind will express itself to humans as a dream, goal, desire, like no other, may also feel IMPOSSIBLE to manifest only because it is so BIG. The subconscious mind will observe an experience and accept the conclusion "it is impossible" but the conscious mind views that same experience and pulls from it "I'm Possible."

Take note of Howard Schultz, chairman of Starbucks, interviews in connection with the conscious mind which interprets everything from a much bigger, higher and greater perspective. I am honored to share this story.

"Growing up, I always felt like I was living on the other side of the tracks. I knew people on the other side had more resources, more money, and happier families. And for some reason, I don't know why or how but I wanted to climb over that fence and achieve something beyond what people were saying was possible." Soon after, Howard discovered the billionaire within himself which was revealed through adverse conditions so that the conscious mind can be made to operate in its fullest capacity.

The condition that Howard Schultz undergoes was used as the basis to align him and his destiny. Through making mistakes, messing up, experimenting, and practicing, we are stimulating our minds with the invisible force, which helps us discover our true desires. In other words, just as what you don't want helps you discover what you do want, as bad helps you appreciate good, being poor launches the desires to be wealthy, being limited gives birth to the desire to be free, so does the bad experiences in the subconscious mind leads to activating the conscious mind. All must experience the subconscious mind and become conscious of who they have been created to be, through the trajectory of the subconscious mind.

The process is not difficult. Organize time to build relationships with your thoughts, in doing so, you will know what thoughts are creating the occurrences in your life, as all occurrences stem from thoughts you carry.

Each thought was either born in your conscious or subconscious mind. Sift and sort through your thoughts and be able to identify the place that each thought came from. If it comes from your conscious mind, if it is so BIG that it SCARES YOU, follow the path of that thought pattern accompanied by God and you are guaranteed a life marked by prosperity and freedom.

If you have a thorough understanding of the concept in Chapter 10 on Controlled Language, be sure to recognize how the conscious mind expresses itself through the language of desire described in that chapter.

By deploying and using this strategy, any human, regarding your walk of life, will possess the keys which accomplished the task that motivated me to write this book. If you do not find this information familiar, read it over and over until it makes sense. If you are reading this and your mind is saying "I already know this stuff", be mindful, it's not about what you know, it's about what you do with what you know.

Chapter 13

Disarm the Terrorist

(Keep yourself in the Receiving Mode)

Before you put any of the awareness into practice, your mind must be prepared to receive it. Hence, you must be in the RECEIVING MODE. Being in the receiving mode is not hard. It is important to take note of and understand the true enemy which stands in between you and whatever it is you desire to receive. This enemy is called the "terrorist."

True freedom or success will never manifest while the terrorist remains active in your mind. The terrorist expresses itself through a series of closely related, negative emotions such as resentment, agony, and worthlessness.

Doubt is a common emotion projected by the terrorist. Remember this as you read. In order to identify anything outside of us, it must exist inside, because ALL life starts from within. Hence, doubt, insecurity, indecisiveness, and other emotional states that we feel, what part of us blends us with these emotions and finds a sense of comfort? This is the terrorist. The connotation around enemies labeled as a terrorist is very dangerous and lethal. They put forth the best effort to plant thoughts of fear and uncertainty into other's minds. This terrorist is the same.

This chapter explains the terrorist must be disarmed before you can be in receiving mode, as well as become wealthy or free. It will also expand on the conditions that people are reduced to live under if they do not make the choice to move past the terms of the terrorist and discover their freedom, regardless of whether it is financially, emotionally, physically or spiritually.

The focal point of this chapter is to make the language, tools, and habits of the terrorist visible. Before we can defeat our enemy (inner-me), we must know its thought pattern and where it dwells. As you continue to read, evaluate yourself in honesty and discover the terrorist which lives within. Do not be in FEAR of the enemy. Often the enemy will dwell in subtle places with hopes to make itself hard to find and even more challenging to destroy.

WHO is the TERRORIST

After the 9/11 terrorist attack was committed, Americans became more aware that they were targets for high levels of crime against international terrorists. Inspired by the desire to gain power, Osama Bin Laden, courageously expressed involvement with the attack, concluding his comments and opinions were a statement that shall always be remembered. "How is it right for you to occupy our countries and kill our women and children and expect to live in peace and security? The equation is clear. You are killed as you kill and abducted as you abduct".

It was such men as these who used WORDS, money, and military force, as a means of leaving us in a state of FEAR and continuing to startle us with actions made to motion our minds not to move past this FEAR.

Take note of the events in history that were led by a terrorist or leader that was convinced that violence solves problems. Observe well that it was their goal to ensure a state of fear within you because the spirit of fear will decrease the likelihood of freedom and will rob you of the spiritual power which is necessary to bypass a thing as failure.

Analyze also that the terrorist that strips Americans of their freedom is the same terrorist that must be overcome and disarmed of its power for every individual to become FREE. This terrorist is the root of the opposition you are experiencing in your life. In the story of the 99%, it will not be difficult to discover the works of the terrorist. The terrorist described in this book is FEAR and it expresses itself through DOUBT, UNCERTAINTY, INSECURITY, and FAILURE.

Fear is the roadblock between you and your destiny. It can be understood and conquered by mastering the keys in this book.

Experience is surely a part of life. Experiences are the instances that the terrorist has used to inject itself into the subconscious mind. It had a habit of engaging the momentum of fear into all ideas, plans, and thoughts that come from the "creative imagination."

The terrorist does not require much detail. It will not be understood by a person who has not had any LIFE EXPERIENCES or experienced failure because only such a person has the awareness which the terrorist can accurately be expressed. Understanding the terrorist comes by self-evaluation and looking at your life from the inside out. The terrorist is the bridge between who you are and who you desire to be. Case in point, the terrorist is very powerful because it influences the mental, physical, and spiritual planes. It is known that the bypassing of the terrorist marks the point that the mind goes from a state of limitation to FREEDOM.

Once you have gained mastery of the keys in this book, you will be ready and prepared to disarm the terrorist of the power and influence it has, otherwise, live in poverty and limitation. Accept as truth a statement that must be taken into consideration when disarming the terrorist, you will feel discomfort, face discomfort, and embrace the freedom that comes with facing it. By developing the habit of disarming the terrorist of its powers and facing your fears, you will discover a power within you that will be available to you at all times.

Your life begins outside of your comfort zone. Following the keys in this book will propel you towards discovering the truth of that statement on a personal level.

I am not a steward or representative of "luck." I have awareness of Mother Earth's perfect laws which are unchangeable. Some of the laws manmade are so easily changed and exceptions can be made for them. Mother Earth's laws are so precise and accurate that we can measure that $E=MC^2$, stating energy equals mass times the speed of light squared. All things on Mother Earth stores a VIBRATION. The terrorist comes to emit the vibration of fear, which most are not aware of how to get rid of because they do not understand the method in which the terrorist operates.

Through many experiences as a human, I have learned that all things are constructed of energy, which permeates a vibration and the vibration will solicit a point of attraction, which causes experiences and things to flow to it, in response to the law of attraction, attracting to it experiences and things which maintain a similar or alike vibration. Deploying the keys mentioned in this book will be summoned to aid in manifesting any goal or desire into its tangible form. I gained this awareness through years of experience with it and it's never been wrong.

In an orderly manner, the keys to freedom have been systematically revealed to lead up to this key. As every color is important to make the rainbow, a thorough understanding of each key is essential to your promising future. If you choose to leave out one color, then it affects the rainbow. Hence, you must gain a certain degree of mastery over each key to unlocking your destiny.

Through the process of trying to "change the world" and "solve problems", I noticed myself following the footsteps of those who I admired from previous generations. In doing so, I learned that the fact is we don't have PROBLEMS, we tend to give a greater capacity of ATTENTION to problems than solutions and that creates PROBLEMS.

I have never understood how a person could do the same thing over and over but expect different results. My experience has shown me that the reason is that people are not aware of what is actually happening when they give their attention to problems.

The process happens like this: We are a part of a universe that is vibration and attraction based. We all have been called forth by God to sift and sort through life and discover our freedom. There is a DESIRE built in us that seeks outward expression. While holding onto that desire, dream, or goal, we also hold onto thoughts or include thoughts that serve as resistance to the manifestation. In other words, the thoughts are not in vibrational harmony with your desires.

Here is the flawed premise because while we speak our desires with our WORDS, our attention is focused on or mixed with thoughts or reasons why it won't happen. Here is when we have to realize that whatever we focus our attention on, it becomes a part of our vibration and we naturally set up a point of attraction that sees our focus as reality.

Meaning, when we say, "I really want people to come together, but more of our attention is focused on the ignorance and superstitions projected in the newspaper. When we say "I really want to be rich, but our focus is on the handicaps of the environment we are in. When we say, "I really want to make more money, but our focus is on reasons why we are broke." When we say, "I really want to be in a relationship, but a part of our attention is more focused on how bad we were treated in our previous relationships, I EARNESTLY ANNOUNCE, you will attract to you the reality that is in harmony with your most dominant focal point of attention, not based on the notion of words.

I had a strong desire for being a millionaire. I envisioned it in my imagination. My peers would reinforce doubt so it would mix with my desire. I began to realize, as I shared with people that I would become a millionaire, I would say it but did not feel like it would come true. I realized that my sense of purpose and value began to spiral downward, and this is all due to this principle described here.

HOW TO DISARM THE TERRORIST

Being a wordsmith, I know the importance of words and how they can add momentum to your thoughts when the necessary amount of emotions are added to them. I know that language is a universal form of expression. I know that language is expressed through words and symbols, which become the building basis, through which all knowledge and awareness are built.

With this knowledge of how the terrorist operates, it should be fairly simple to know what is needed to disarm the terrorist of its power and influence over your life. In the story of how America found Osama Bin

Laden, the knowledge will be drawn, addressing how to disarm the terrorist.

Mission

President Obama: "I desire to bring victory to America and inebriate the fear which is drawn from the thought of your lives being taken at the discretion of Osama Bin Laden's leadership. I decided to send a Navy seal team inside of Pakistan to capture Bin Laden, being the ideal inspiration behind the September 11, 2001 terrorist attacks."

Citizens: Do you think the ability of the terrorist to launch major attacks on the US is the same, less than or greater than it was at the time of the September attack? I am scared to open my meal, scared to board a plane, scared every time I see a Muslim at the airport, etc. I request to know what our country will do in response to this attack. This matter has left me emotionally scarred.

US Navy Seals: I desire to complete the mission as a service and honor to my country. I know it will take courage, selflessness, and teamwork to summon the necessary spirit of action. To our family members, we love you and we do this for you and then to ensure the safety of every family in the United States of America.

Osama Bin Laden: I desire war with Americans, Jews, and Christians. Every Muslim, once they learn to differentiate, dislike Jews, Americans, and Christians. This is part of our culture. Our enemy is the crusader Alliance led by America, Britain, and Israel.

All involved parties in the instance are listed but take note of the outcome of these desires which I paid close attention to. I wish to highlight to you, the spirit of courage that dwells within us all must be accessed to gain your freedom.

Outcome

President Obama: I am honored to be seated as the president of our country during this operation. I credit our US Navy seal for their efforts and phenomenal teamwork. Allow me to say Osama Bin Laden is dead and justice has been served.

Citizens: Although we think that it is likely that a terrorist will act against the US in the next few weeks, it is safe to say, "the death of Osama Bin Laden makes us feel safer from terrorism."

US NAVY SEALS: There was a lot of fear going into the operation. We feared that we would never see our mothers/fathers, feared to never see our wives/husbands, feared that we would never see our children, and we feared that we may actually achieve our outcome. We had the opportunity to restore faith in the United States of America, so we took advantage of the opportunity.

Osama Bin Laden

Even with the death of Osama Bin Laden, we are left with a feeling of "fear" which will open to you at times when we remember Osama Bin Laden.

You may never know the truth of this statement, except by examining the lessons you've observed from your life-changing experience.

I am not a steward of sharing misleading information, nor an advocate of dishonesty. As an author, I have come to understand the nature of FEAR and how it leads people to deviate from their established state of freedom and well-being. Fear often seems so easily misunderstood because we are not aware of the true nature of fear. Fear comes as a vibration, momentum, or feelings that are associated with discomforting thoughts. Fear appears only so it can disempower action.

There is much power gained through the momentum of thoughts, which all living beings can permeate and embrace; that is through channeling and reinforcing the mind with thoughts that align with the corresponding thought. The terrorist causes the constructive channel of thoughts, momentum, and energy to STOP. Imagine a river is flowing downhill and a landslide blocks the flow, causing the river to flow backward, causing disharmony between nature and water. In other words, through grasping the concept of this information, be aware that the vibration of fear (the terrorist) blocks you or moves you in a direction working against the natural current which propels you towards your breathtaking future. Anyone who has acquired any form of freedom or success can attest because they have felt this experientially and must have transcended it.

Each chapter plays a vital role in mastering this chapter. Once you accept this awareness as truth, you are in receiving mode for the remaining truths of this book. Keep in mind, we are not writing this to imply or indicate you are a terrorist. But definitely, whether you claim it or not, somewhere within you lies the vibration of fear which imitates a terrorist, leaving you in a state of fear, feeling passive and lazy in regards to taking the necessary actions to unleash your breathtaking future.

Through experiencing the "terrorist", I discovered the importance of being aware of it. Commonly for those who are unaware of the terrorist, I discovered that their life generally emulates habits that display common outcomes. Allow me to demonstrate the common outcomes or realities experienced by those who are unaware of the presence of the terrorist.

Osama Bin Laden injected the spirit of fear into the minds of Americans through the painstaking 911 attack. Because of this experience, even in Osama Bin Laden's death, Americans still carry the vibration of fear that remains alive. We call it memories. Remember your thoughts act like magnets that attract it to a life force of alike nature. When you hold onto bad memories, observe that vibrations will attract bad memories. The information conducted in this chapter is vital to your future. I deem it important to know that the vibration behind ALL bad experiences is FEAR.

Osama was still alive when 911 happened. It was so impactful that despite Osama's death being publicly announced, some BELIEVED Osama Bin Laden was not dead. "Beliefs are more powerful than reality." Their reactions further the understanding of this statement.

Their beliefs evolving around Osama Bin Laden's name became so realistic that we were so sad, an entire nation remained fearful and that fear stayed with them for several years. "The experience was so sad, I was scared of going to the airport, without worrying that I would lose my life," says US citizens.

The more we follow the influence of the terrorist, the more we lose sight of who we are. Even after I became aware of Osama Bin Laden's death, I was awakened by bad dreams many nights and saw Osama standing by my bedside. The following morning, I was unable to tell whether it was a dream or if it was real. It took me a long time to learn what it was but I knew I had never felt a feeling like I felt when I was awakened from my sleep by the thoughts of Osama Bin Laden.

Go ahead and examine your life and remember an experience which left you awakened from your sleep in a state of fear, whether it was caused by a bad dream, seeing a scary movie, the sight of clowns, that was so scary that it left a thought of FEAR in the mind so strong, that it represented itself that night when you went to sleep. Observe this moment, instead of erasing the moments in your life that are of similar nature. If you neglect it, for whatever reason you choose, you will be reduced to a fear-based vibrational state and be minimized to live a life that is poverty and limitation based.

Moments like this mark the first time we have our encounters with the terrorist (FEAR). Proving the terrorist have been able to remain quiet in connection to such matters, that would be deemed as misunderstood or controversy if they were described in ignorance of knowing the terrorist. I have discovered that the terrorist will reduce you to a state of FEAR that disallows you to obtain your freedom. As I've obtained mastery in this knowledge, I have become less fearful of the terrorist and concerned about following my heart's desire. One of the beauties of growth through awareness is that it takes more discipline, willpower, and strength to be TRUE to your desires, despite the criticisms and opinions of those who do not understand.

Fear seems to be misunderstood by most. My objective here is to make the ways of the terrorist "more clear", but also make it known that bypassing the thought patterns of the terrorist led me to paths of adventure, greatness, and freedom in endeavors.

The terrorist enters the mind through thoughts, which keep us in a low vibration called ordinary thoughts (O-type thoughts). Religion, philosophers, nor science has been able to discover where the terrorist is located, but this is so important. The fact is that human beings will not accurately interpret information through their five senses if it's interpreted with FEAR as the basis. All knowledge is received when the mind is in receiving mode. Any knowledge that enters the mind maintains its place based on the amount of storing space in the mind. Imagine trying to store 50 pounds of furniture in a room that can only hold 30 pounds. The room is not in the receiving mode for the furniture. The mind works the same way. Keep in mind, that when emotions are added to thoughts, it makes the vibration more rapid and sets up a point of attraction based on the nature of the thoughts. Hence, the mind is always in receiving mode, but the type of knowledge it brings forth is based on whether the nature of thoughts already stored is favorable or unfavorable.

These truths mentioned are the basis of understanding FEAR (the terrorist) and identifying how it surfaces in our daily lives. Fear is so smooth and subtle in its ways, but while you could have good thoughts, FEAR will influence you not to make decisions that allow your good thoughts to manifest. I find it true that FEAR will permit you to acquire knowledge and understanding about ideas, but keep you in a state where "NO ACTION" is taken towards your desire. I can truly say that the FEAR injected by the terrorist is accountable for you not being in the receiving mode for the manifestation of your inspiration.

At the occasion of not facing fear - one is inclined to, instead of living at their fullest potential, live a life marked by finding a safe way to die. I have miraculously ushered myself past the confines created through the influence of FEAR.

FEAR may not be a physical being. In most cases, it is a vibration that has been impressed by one's subconscious mind, which surfaces when one is moving towards their desires. In my latest years, I have noticed the trend of FEAR shift. Because we have become accustomed to FEAR being associated with a physical being, we find it difficult to acknowledge or confront the vibration it leaves in us. Our outcomes, sense of happiness and fulfillment begins to decline the moment FEAR in its vibration form wraps itself around our lives.

You, of course, have remembered a moment where you practiced the thought "I will forgive but I won't forget", which the majority of people practice. The terrorist benefits greatly to those it can persuade to acquire a mindset of FORGIVING, but unknowingly holding onto the FEAR associated with the moment they claim their attention was not on, but that could not be true, because they won't forget.

Steve Jobs, unquestionably, gained chief understanding of FEAR and used it as the launching pad to his freedom-based future. The scale which he operated on required him to gain mastery over these principles and use it. Jobs deemed it necessary to develop an obsessive focus, especially pertaining to situations that involved details. He had the mindset of the "PERFECTIONIST." In relation to moments like this, the terrorist may develop, especially in moments involving decisions that guide you towards freedom. Hidden behind the "perfectionist" outlook, was the FEAR of making mistakes.

Bill Gates understood the tactics of FEAR because in connection to his desire to break the barrier of change, equally came the FEAR of FAILURE. Mark Zuckerberg understood the tactics of the terrorist because in connection to his desire to take big chances at Building Global Communities, instead of being crippled by FEAR projected by the popular saying "if it goes wrong, you will be broke." Hence, the fear of criticisms and opinions. Richard Branson sat amongst those who experience FEAR from the terrorist, which most are unfamiliar to because while Branson emphasized the importance of dreaming, equally, FEAR reminds us of the perceived risk which will prevent us from taking the necessary action to achieve the dream. These cases describe the path of successors on the path of discovering their freedom.

All stewards of success and freedom – such as Bill Gates, Warren Buffet, Martin Luther King, Mohammad, Jesus, and more understood FEAR and chose to use it as an ASSET. The majority of their breathtaking futures were created through the application of this concept.

Fear, backed by the terrorist, is not something one can overcome without making a conscious choice and taking the necessary actions. There is a great power that comes with moving through the discomfort of fear, which is outlined through the application of the keys mentioned in this book. It takes a rare person to have obtainable knowledge about the great power gained through moving through discomfort created by FEAR. In fact, this great power is not something that can be discovered without summoning the force of the champion in you, by disarming the terrorist vibration in you that is FEAR based.

In view of the terrorist (fear) and the great power discovered in connection to conditions where we have made the choice to move past the FEAR that is practiced in the terrorist mode of perception, I now have the privilege to share the story of David and Goliath. My peers and I deem that story as an accurate story that figuratively and symbolically demonstrates the concept in this chapter in a much more spiritual way.

It offers a more story-based view on the subject of this chapter. This story infuses the terrorist (fear) and initials the great power discovered through overcoming FEAR.

The story may be depicted in many different ways, but the CONCEPT of it is always the same. Conclude from it, those who desire freedom and prosperity, the keys which granted David his outcome, if you desire the same, the keys are in this reading.

David and Goliath – Lesson of FEAR

David is human just like you. The only difference between him and you is that David applied the keys to freedom. One of the keys to facing FEAR is to move past the point of discomfort. Pay attention to this story as you read and put yourself in David's position and configure the points which led to David achieving his desired outcome. If you can apply the same keys, if you can muster up the same COURAGE that David deployed, you will be granted access to the supernatural power inside of you, which can drive you towards the particular area of accomplishment suitable for you and your calling.

During the time of the birth of this story, the Philistines were at war with the Israelites. The Philistines had a warrior by the name of Goliath, known as a GIANT, that was nine feet tall. For forty days, every morning, Goliath would fight against the Israelites to determine who would win the war against the Philistines and the Israelites.

When the Israelites heard of Goliath and began to hear more of his impact, this resulted in the terrorist becoming activated and the Israelites being swamped by FEAR. Not only were the Israelites scared, but their King Saul was also scared. When David became aware of Goliath and that the victory for the Israelites was dependent upon defeating the GIANT, he went unto God in prayer and at the conclusion, David told King Saul that he would fight with Goliath.

David's mind was absorbed in thoughts of the failures of the Israelites who fought against Goliath and failed, which left David in a state of FEAR. There was something different about David. Unlike the previous Israelites who fought against Goliath, David had an active relationship with God. He knew how to interpret the moment where fear unfolds itself, as an opportunity to discover the power God put into you, which is activated by certain individuals who choose to follow this, which leads to the power known as FAITH, that is key to help us overcome our fears.

Perhaps Goliath was not aware of who David was, because when he saw David, he laughed at the sight of the young boy, Goliath being nine feet tall and David being the height of the average teenager. David told the Philistines that God is with him and NO GIANT is any match for God.

David and Goliath went to fight each other. David grabbed a stone, as guided by the knowingness of God that the STONE would move him through fear and a way would be created that would grant the Israelites freedom and victory.

Having trusted in God, David continued to defeat Goliath with the Sling of a stone and eventually became the King of Israel, known for being the ONE who faced the GIANT and the ONE who God used amazingly to show people that exact same source of power is readily available to them at all times.

In all dealings with men and women, who have the experience, know that every experience offers a lesson that demonstrates power or weakness, faith or fear, negative or positive, etc. Tellers of this story sometimes make the mistake of interpreting the story literally but do not grasp the practical knowledge. It has been a great honor to expand on this subject matter. Perhaps it was important that David was small, the Israelites doubted that David would have the power to accomplish the task on his own. Surely these odds are examples of what thought patterns that will create more FEAR. Surely by choosing David as the one to perform those miracles through, the soundness of the power will be felt in a more profound manner. Supernatural and unmatchable is the power created when God blends with your desire. When God blends with your desire, it is logical that humankind can accomplish any desire. We are not aware of how FEAR expresses itself through the human mind and how it attaches itself to every thought, every decision, and every physical thing within its reach as a means of converting FEAR into the physical reality. Perhaps pastors, scientists, and philosophers will cherish this key. Once FEAR is planted into one's mind, it builds the desire to have ordinary lives.

The quality of life which is created as inspired to move past the discomfort created by fear is not hard to explain. First, we must understand that "life begins outside of your comfort zone", which means if you are living a life within the confines of your comfort zone, you are not living. Instead, you are tiptoeing through life, hoping to find a safe way to death. Second, make the choice to move past discomfort in a mighty way, made available through making the choice and relying on God's guidance for strength and direction. Lastly, be who you were created to be.

I remember years ago, my best friend got into a car accident. He became physically impaired, doctors put him on bed rest for six months and told him that he would never be able to play sports again. Keep in mind, becoming a pro basketball player was his dream. But that was the doctor's thoughts, it was not my best friends. Just before he left the hospital, he said to the doctor, "Man believes in the possible, God believes in the impossible."

The doctor looked at him through the eyes of FEAR. But my best friend looked at the doctor through the eyes of FAITH. When it was all over, my best friend played professional basketball for three years after this occurrence.

He would have never felt freedom had he accepted the limitation-based lifestyle the doctor suggested. I believe this is a pivotal time to say TRUE FREEDOM is discovered on the path which is led by FAITH. FREEDOM offers the opportunity for victims to experience victory. I have observed FREEDOM as the basis in which millions of people come together and put aside their different ways. I have observed my own life go from rags to riches, despite the echoes of the naysayers. Be willing to face discomfort created by FEAR and you will find yourself in possession of a power which is the key to enable your FREEDOM and creates the basis for happy living.

Fear will not be able to sustain its influence and power once we become aware of the way it functions. In chapter five we discussed how thoughts created beliefs and ideas, which create stories, which create emotions, in that order. What is the outcome when fear is wrapped around our thoughts? We are prone to feel disempowering emotions. Doubt is an expression of FEAR. Keep in mind, emotional states such as indecisiveness and doubt are created as an effect of blending our thoughts with FEAR.

The final quarter of this chapter analyzes and describes points that are pivotal to the philosophy of this book. It explains FEAR and emotional states people feel when influenced by the vibration of FEAR. These truths must be understood to acquire freedom, in all walks of life, whether financially, physically, emotionally, or spiritually.

The primary purpose of this chapter is to raise awareness of the terrorist (fear) inside of you and showcases the ways to cure yourself of the limitation consciousness created by the fears.

Members of the human family have become accustomed to denying that these FEARS exist. If that is your mission, feel free to neglect this chapter. In order to master the terrorist, we must know its habits, strategies, language and be able to configure how FEAR is active in our personal lives. Make it a priority to monitor the habits of the terrorist (fear). Often, we are not aware of FEAR and we allow it to dwell in subtle places which makes it difficult to destroy.

Common Expressions of FEAR

In chapter 10 on Controlled Language, the spotlight was put on the language of DOUBT. Well, fear has a language and common emotional expressions that indicate the terrorist is active. All humankind experiences these emotions, whether together or one at a time. This section showcases the most common expressions of FEAR.

The fear of PAIN

The fear of FAILURE

The fear of POVERTY

The fear of LOSING SOMEONE

The fear of BECOMING SUCCESSFUL

The fear of REJECTION

The fear of DEATH

No fear is to be taken lightly. The evidence of these fears will surface depending upon the period of life you are in. From the moment we were kids and fell off our first bicycle, touched the stove when it was HOT, slipped and fell when we got out of the bathtub, we discovered the fear of PAIN. During the moments we faced with life-changing decisions, we were faced with the fear of FAILURE. Even when we are making money, we are always susceptible to the fear of POVERTY. Abroad we witness men and women in relationships where their partners treat them "bad", but they stay with them because of the fear of LOSING SOMEONE.

Fear is nothing more than a vibration. Once this vibration wraps itself around one's thoughts, one's mind is prone to be controlled and under the authority of fear. Millionaires, as well as other successors, know that in the process of applying the keys to success, we are subject to the fear of BECOMING SUCCESSFUL. Equally, in the process of pressing forward to create the basis to be successful, there is the absolute fear of REJECTION.

Remember ALL manifestations and creations begin in the form of a thought. By adding emotions to thoughts, it builds a momentum which inspires action towards transmuting thoughts into the physical reality.

It is important to remember the basis for all manifestations and understand why so little people experience freedom, while others live a life marked by limitations. This next statement may bring clarity to those who have not found the answer to this WHY question. With the account of the law of vibration and law of attraction, we attract things and experiences to ourselves that are in-formation with our nature of thoughts. Hence, if we have fear active in the mind, the brain will release thought vibrations, that attract to you, FEAR-based experiences and keep you in receiving mode for FEAR.

We have been given by God, the power to control our minds. We must make controlling our thoughts a priority, considering that all manifestations begin in the form of a thought, which we may forever be subjected to the vibration of FEAR if the principle of fear is not understood.

Fear tries to disguise itself in our lives (it reveals itself in the form of polluted beliefs and unfavorable emotions) and it is safe to say that the thought momentum of fear and limitation can only be overcome through deploying courage and willpower. Following the momentum of courage and willpower will lead to FREEDOM.

Following experiences that shake the emotions of people comes the opportunity for fear to attach itself to your life. Slowly but surely, fear will cause you to deviate from your greatness, but equally, FEAR offers the opportunity to discover the true meaning of FREEDOM, which is understood in this book.

The FEAR of PAIN

There is no shortcut to freedom. The primary emotion that leads to limitation is the fear of PAIN. If you desire freedom, you must make the choice to never accept pain as a reality (the word pain is expressed in words such as discomfort, doubt, insecure, anxious, procrastinate). The primary quality one must possess to move past the fear of pain is COURAGE. In this chapter, we gave you the complete story of David and Goliath as a story that makes it easier to understand what is necessary to overcome your GIANT known as FEAR.

This is a pivotal moment in your life that can give birth to your breathtaking future. Here is the reason why it is important to have FAITH instead of living under the vibration of FEAR. You are always in receiving mode: Meaning you are always attracting things to yourself based on the nature of your most dominant thoughts. Innocently, by never making the choice to muster up the courage to give birth to our faith-based future, we keep ourselves in receiving mode for more fear-based outcomes.

If you desire freedom, make the choice to do the necessities to create that reality. Courage is one of the key characteristics that lead to freedom. We all have been given different paths, which all lead to the same place, HEAVEN ON EARTH. Here is a point that we all need to remember "There is no place in the world where there is one route you can take to get there."

Regardless of the road you take, COURAGE must be with you for you to assure your arrival to your destiny. No shortcuts or excuses will free you. Making it your personal desire to refuse to settle. FEAR and LIMITATION is the only thing that can lead to discovering the COURAGE within you. COURAGE is not something that can be purchased or taught, it must be created through the will to overcome adversity and discomfort.

Fear of pain is a state of mind that emits a vibration that is programmed to disallow one's chances of experiencing any degree of freedom and true progress, in any endeavor. This fear makes you feel powerless and causes the mind to create reasons why you are powerless, destroys your self-esteem, discourage decision making, lead to doubt which makes you second guess initiative, creates curiosity which makes you deviate from your purpose, attracts low-energy which promotes procrastination and destroys the self-control which makes it difficult to sustain the necessary discipline to accomplish. It takes away one's ambitions, clouds their judgment, keeps you focused on problems more than solutions, disempowers your emotions, encourages dependency on material things or destructive activities, provokes laziness and fatigue which leads to misery and distaste for life and remember MISERY LOVES COMPANY. We live in a society where people desire freedom, but equally, expect to have their desire manifest while they harness misery.

The fear of PAIN, unquestionably, is the most common of all fears. It has been labeled the most common because collectively, we seem to have a hard time moving past it. It takes courage to move beyond the confines of fear and there is a champion, hero or warrior within you that accepts fear as an opportunity to discover FAITH.

The fear of PAIN, for some, tends to be a roadblock to your freedom-based future. But some discovered the champion, within them that is born, when one turns pain into fuel, but not many mastered that skill. Humans that do make that choice to turn pain into fuel, develop the capacity to experience success in any endeavor, spiritually, financially, and/or emotionally.

The generation that is current fears pain at a magnitude that individuals orchestrate shortcuts and ways around facing that fear. People are prone to consider drugs and alcohol to ease the pain, but only to discover that the pain does not go away. They begin to depend on things for a sense of ease and instead of bringing ease, these things begin to dominate their lives to the degree, it emotionally, financially, and spiritually effects a person, with respects to their well-being.

Avoiding pain brings forth more pain. Only those who avoid pain will comprehend that statement. Equally, those who are willing to face pain, understand that freedom comes forth through facing it. It is clear, the reason why the fear of pain is still common. Because through a long line of habits of finding substitutes, we have learned to avoid facing it to the degree, we make ourselves naïve to the pain. Thus, giving pain even more power when it decides to come forth.

Many relationships are based on the amount of pain one party has experienced or both endured. It is clear why relationship problems are ongoing and divorce rates are peeking. People are so excited about being in a relationship, that they never deal with the pain that disallows them to maintain their relationship.

Being honest, looking in the mirror, self-evaluation, self-analysis, etc. will bring forth the awareness which most choose to deny. Denial is one of the key qualities which declares a life marked by poverty and limitation. Keep in mind, as you are being honest with yourself, you are the coach and the team, you are the parent and the child, you are the president and vice president, treasurer, and secretary of yourself. Be honest with yourself. Ask yourself questions and make it a priority to not move forward without definite answers. Once you've gained definite answers, you will possess the awareness which is KEY to unlocking your breathtaking future. If you find it challenging to be honest with yourself, find someone close to you that can give you an accurate examination of you. It is your responsibility to discover the truth of yourself. Press forward, discover yourself, by any means necessary, no matter what temporary PAIN you experience.

Taking a survey of people, I asked six hundred people, what is your biggest fear? The majority would reply "I fear being hurt." People would not fear pain so much if they realize that pain is a sign of growth. We have conditionally become grounded in the discomfort aspect of the emotion of fear that we go through life, never discovering the growth that occurs when one moves past pain. This is when courage must be summoned to move past the disallowing vibration of the terrorist. In doing your self-evaluation, discover your personality and character.

Fear of pain expresses itself in many different emotions, which all can be disallowing. Here are some common emotional states that are created by the fear of pain which you should be aware of.

SIGNS OF FEAR OF PAIN

Indecisiveness - As a result of the fear of hurting other people's feelings, in our doings, we permit ourselves to have others to think for us. This nature leaves us in a stagnant space when it comes to decision making.

Being Negative - A person develops the habit of focusing on the negative perspective of every experience, discussing, justifying, and rationalizing reasons why their desire won't manifest. Recognizing the reasons why there is a failure, it is impossible, this is not the right time, if my family does not support me, I can't do it, as the reason why the necessary actions are taken. These thoughts cause delays and delays until passiveness and laziness become a habit. Spending time with others who failed and gave up on their goals and becoming a critic of those who are successful and dared to take big risks to reap big rewards.

Lack of Faith - Usually expressed through rationalizing, justifying, and excuses created to hide a lack of assurance that others tend to disguise through the use of projecting a self-esteem or image that is contrary to their TRUE FEELINGS.

Denial (not being honest with yourself) - Generally expressed when one is not honest with themselves. They develop a tendency to neglect their well-being, hiding, and settling the discomfort that arises through the feeling created by the thoughts which align with their truth. Habitually they can avoid facing their true thoughts, through the use of drugs and alcohol, which reveals itself through conditions such as anxiety, depression, and suicide.

OVERTHINKING or JUDGING - Judging happens when someone sees something in someone else and denies or doesn't take into consideration that whatever you identify and recognize outside of you is inside of you. Remember man can walk past an ounce of gold and if their mind cannot identify what gold is, they have not discovered the golden treasure within themselves, they will walk past it, presuming it is just a "rock." This is closely related to overthinking, procrastination, etc. which are created by spending a lifetime making mental judgments of something rather than being willing to discover the truth of something, staying on the outside and judging instead of having the courage to take the steps to elevation, listening to others thoughts and opinions instead of thinking for yourself, planning what you can do based on when others think it's the right time instead of flowing with the current of your desire. This also creates emotions such as worry, distrust, insecurity, and confusion, which depletes you of the energy, enthusiasm, and momentum that will move you towards your freedom, in any area of your life.

The Fear of Failure

Most people are not able to bear the discomfort associated with the thoughts of failure. In most instances, they live their lives making choices and decisions that assure a comfort zone when challenges present themselves. The fear of failure disallows people from moving towards their destiny, smuggles the voice of God active in your mind, cripples the ability to make life-changing decisions, draws you into ordinary living and severs your self-esteem, sense of purpose, and WILLPOWER. We are often mentally impaired more by listening to the opinions of others. Although opinions are supposed to be used as an "open" expression of thought, often hidden behind that is the fear of failing to influence someone to agree with them. You will end up under the influence of the vibration of fear, which will make you a prisoner to the terrorist.

Failure, as a possibility, is one expression of fear which we give too much attention. Everyone has an MVP (Mission Vision Plan) whether they know it or not. One of the primary factors that disconnect us from this knowingness of ourselves is the fear of failure. This is when the terrorist covers us with the vibration of fear which makes us feel inferior in the mind. While having thoughts of becoming a millionaire, we are more focused on the thoughts of what would happen if something goes wrong in the process, so it does not happen.

Failure is only an indicator that you should have done something different, meaning better planning, being more organized, less talking and more action, etc. If you discover what you could have done to improve the conditions, then failure is not a reality. Failure equals the opportunity to discover a lesson that propels growth but it is a failure if one chooses not to discover the lesson.

The Fear of Poverty

This basis of fear requires through articulation. Innocently, it is easy to associate poverty with the lack of money and the feeling of being poor.

The fear of poverty is common amongst the various expressions of fear. As a human culture, this fear dictates our growth and develops in a more personable way than others. Poverty is a state of mind based on limitation. One of the most common expressions of poverty is limitation being restricted or limited without a constructive outlet displays poverty. Everyone has a desire with which they have not given birth to. Commonly, unexpressed desires plants restriction and limitation in the heart and mind which will disallow one to build or move towards their

Freedom.

Fear of Death

The mere possibility of DEATH is one of the most dominant forms of fear. The wonder about what occurs after DEATH is the basis of this fear, aside from the pain associated with death.

The fear of death is prone to all. The magnitude it is felt will vary based on demographics and upbringing. Here is the truth regarding the fear of death, which universities, colleges, scientists, and philosophers must enforce to free people from the fear of DEATH.

Once you find a reason to live, the fear of death will be no more. Think about it Upon the world, many do not know their mission, vision, or destiny which conceals their life purpose. It is necessary to know your life purpose in order to enjoy life.

Most humans can tell you what they don't want, not knowing what they don't want (bad experiences) are meant to help you discover what you do want (good experiences). It works the same with LIFE and DEATH.

Life is something only experienced when we discover something, we are willing to die for. If you go through life never finding something or someone you are willing to die for, surely you may live but you won't experience the quality of life which you have been promised. Death is not meant to keep you in a state of fear. Death is meant to remind us of the reasons to press on to discover peace, Heaven on Earth, and your natural state of well–being which will eliminate the fear of death.

The Fear of Rejection

The possibility of rejection, which is popular as people pursue the life which declares their freedom, is a very common expression of fear. Doubt and second-guessing also enter the mind to shape the fear of rejection, as it becomes natural to focus more on the reasons why "it can't happen."

The fear of rejection is a powerful fear that gains more influence as we age. Although not everyone experiences the impact, the fear of rejection tends to affect us in a broad range of professional and personal situations.

These are common situations in which this fear is prone to destroy our lives: MARRIAGE, meeting new people, dating, business dealings, and even peer pressure. The truth is that rejection requires us to have certain characteristics and qualities to overstand it. Commonly, men and women, as an effect of the fear of rejection, become people-pleasers, non-assertive, insecure, overwhelmed, passive-aggressive and worry-prone. This feeling will deter them from believing in themselves and using their great characteristics.

The Fear of Losing Someone

This fear is traced to emotional attachments and social influence. It is common for humans to build relationships in the world because relationships lead one to establish stability. But in the process of moving towards our breathtaking future, we engage people in business and personally that are only meant to be in our lives "seasonally" but we have built emotional attachments through a social exchange, which begins to influence the decision making process towards keeping your breathtaking future alive.

At the core, the fear of losing someone is because of the potential pain associated with losing someone with whom you are emotionally attached to. While delaying the process of letting go, there is also a delay in the manifestation of the very desire you are moving towards.

A refined therapist shared that 95 percent of all people who visit the clinic for therapy are suffering from stress. It has been shown that the vast majority of stress stems from thoughts, which cause dis-ease or tension in the body, merely by the nature of the vibration the thoughts produce. Remember the mind is the greatest power in all of creation.

Through holding onto old thoughts, memories, past relationships, as an effect of the fear of letting things go, years of experience suggest what outcomes are made by this fear: We learned that holding onto fears causes you not to be in receiving mode for your desires. Let me remind you of the process of getting on an airplane. Before one can take the flight and fly high, all baggage must be claimed (baggage claim). Nothing can be carried aboard which will hold you down. Imagine baggage as weight. In other words, past experiences and unpleasant memories that you hold onto have different effects that usually provoke you to stay grounded in ordinary instead of lifting you up to your breath-taking future.

The first quote one must remember is "if you hold onto the past, the past will hold onto you". Cultivating the habit of holding onto things that do not serve your greater good, will assure comfort, but equally will bring the primitive thought vibration that brings tension and dis-ease, in the form of sickness as we get older.

There is a huge quantity of knowledge supporting the idea that mental states such as regret and stress lead to death. The vibration or impulse created by these thoughts becomes much more challenging for the human body to manage without proper awareness.

Psychologists, therapists, and doctors have experimented with different exercises and activities meant to implement the importance of transforming the mind. The fear of losing someone or something, leaves the human mind holding onto the thoughts that do not serve the greater good. Stress, anxiety, nervousness and even heart attacks are conditions created by holding onto unfavorable thoughts.

The Fear of Becoming Successful

The possibility of success, which is common, amongst those who have experienced some degree of success. Slowly but surely, as people move towards their desired outcome, this fear speaks in subtle ways. Each step you take towards your desire, it cripples one's reasoning faculty and destroys self-confidence and action. The fear of success is caused by focusing on the cons of success instead of the pros. Equally, it is caused by focusing our attention on the things you cannot control instead of focusing on things you can.

A fear-based mind accepts failure. Fear never allows the mind to settle. An unsettled mind will find it difficult to make decisions. Most people lack the will to reach sound decisions and agree with their own decisions during a sustained period of time.

These expressions of fear become the basis for a state of indecision which prompts one to experience limitation forever. You have the courage to over stand the fear of death. You are equipped with the power far greater than any pain you can endure. Prepare yourself for rejection by reminding yourself that if they say "No", that means "No you cannot do it with them", or "NO I cannot do it with you." Eliminate the fear of failure by accepting failure as an opportunity to become successful, not as a reason to quit. Spend less time worrying about DEATH and commit our actions to the habits and thought patterns that will manifest a higher quality of life. Fear not the thought of losing someone but be willing to position yourself to gain a greater version of yourself. Fear not becoming successful but understand that our dreams are supposed to be so big that they scare you towards action.

Master fear by reaching a state of faith. Release the habit of indecision by making the choice not to live in fear. With this decision, you will put yourself in receiving mode for your greatness.

Receiving Mode

Even a battery must be positioned properly, moreover in receiving mode, for a toy car to pick up the vibrations of the battery and use them accordingly. For humans, we must find this vibrational positioning that gives us the capacity to emit vibrations to the Earth which attracts the experiences that align with our desired outcome. In other words, if you desire to be a billionaire, then practice the thoughts and habits of a billionaire and by doing so, you become in receiving mode for that experience.

Receiving mode is a mental basis of allowing thoughts to pass from one mind to another, voluntarily, whether each person is aware of this exchange of thoughts. The mind is always in receiving mode for thoughts. The person who gives more of their attention to negative or unfavorable thoughts is in receiving mode for experiences that will tend to be negative and unfavorable. The acknowledging of favorable thought impulses creates favorable outcomes, also, putting you in receiving mode for positive or favorable thoughts. Keep in mind, we are all attractors of our own reality based on the most dominant thoughts in our minds. Second, it's important to focus on thoughts that repel negative thoughts and often deflates them of their power. The presence of a single negative thought in the mind is enough to trigger destructive emotions which lead to a negative personality that takes one out of receiving mode for their desired outcome. Third, cultivate the art of holding onto positive thoughts which allows you to move towards your desired outcome. Positive thought impulses launch you towards the manifestation because they fill the mind of the person storing them and creates the inspiration that leads to action.

As we conclude this chapter, allow me to remind you: We are always in receiving mode. If fear is wrapped around our thoughts, then we are in receiving mode for more fear-based experiences. Do not neglect the importance of facing fear. There is great power to be discovered on the other side of fear. Make up your mind to retrieve the power you have been rightfully granted.

Chapter 14

Channeling the Sexual Energy

(How to Discover your Destiny)

The phrase channeling implies, constructively, directing and influencing energy or thoughts into that which serves the greater good.

The sexual energy is the most commonly misguided energy known to humankind.

Lack of awareness has led to humans traditionally associating the sexual energy with the physical perspective. This ignorance has led to a collective unawareness abroad Mother Earth.

The channeling of the sexual energy is the mastermind skill which lies at the root of many human capabilities:

1. The longevity and vitality of life.
2. The sustaining of well-being (mentally, physically, emotionally, spiritually).
3. Transformation of ordinary to extraordinary through channeling energy.

Channeling the sexual energy is not hard to understand when it is explained in a straightforward way. This entails on shifting our attention from the physical expression of energy to focusing on the intangible nature of energy.

The sexual energy is the basis of our existence. Meaning, we all were born as an effect of summoning the sexual energy. The emotion of sex is the most influential of all impulses. When we flow with the momentum of this impulse, we discover the keys to activating the vital force, supernatural power, creativity, willpower, and action orientation that does not always seem available. The impulse of sex, in the physical expression, has become so powerful and influential that men and women readily jeopardize their lives, careers and well-being to experience it. When disciplined and channeled into a greater purpose or cause, the constructive qualities of this vital force will be used as the momentum basis which fuels inspiration and creative action in any calling, profession, or endeavor, including the desire to be free.

Channeling the sexual energy requires discipline and patience, inevitably, but the outcome is worth the time and energy put into the focus. The desire for sexual expression is normal and completely natural. The desire should not and cannot be removed. We must discipline the desire and learn to give the desire a constructive expression which improves the functionality of the mind, body, and spirit. If this energy is not given this form of expression, through channeling, it is prone to desire a way out through physical outlets.

Imagine putting a big dog on a small leash. Certainly, the leash will control the dog momentarily but eventually, the force of the dog will lead to it breaking free. This example is parallel to your sexual desires. The emotional impulse may be harnessed and held back for a specific period, but its nature will lead to it seeking an expression which launches the vibration of freedom. If this vital force is not channeled toward a greater cause it will seek creative outlets which lure one into less significant experiences.

Blessed and prosperous, describes the life of those who learned to channel the emotion of sex into a form of expression, that serves the greater good instead of moments that "feels good." In doing so, they will awaken the Eagles within them.

Years of study and observations of the stories of the most successful men and women abroad who have achieved extraordinary levels of success have these things in common.

1. They were inspired to accomplish, as influenced by their partners, who they have cultivated sexual emotions with and learned to channel this energy favorably.
2. They achieved phenomenal outcomes because the emotion of sex made them feel like they were a part of something greater than themselves, which launched their desire to act.
3. Their partners were highly involved with their endeavors which assured them a place of assurance, comfort, and true acceptance.

The stories that these amazing observations were drawn from remained accurate for millions. In other words, connected to the path which lead all men and women to their freedom is the cultivating of the sexual energy.

The sexual energy is the vital force, which over stands any vibration that can be interpreted in the physical body. When this energy is deployed and the emotion of this is added to a cause, it automatically expresses itself through creativity, ideas, and inspired action. Gain chief awareness of this truth, because within it lies the underlying ideal of what is meant by learning to channel the sexual energy that will help you discover the eagle within you.

The momentum of the sexual energy holds the key that unlocks the imagination. Misusing the emotion of sex, humankind is more prone to become actionless. Observe scientific research on men who experience andropause or women who experience menopause. From another perspective, pay attention to the behavior of a dog once it has been sterilized. The dog will be as unassertive as a cat once it has been unsexed. Sex sterilization draws the testosterone that produces the energy which propels one to move forward. Sex sterilization has the same impact on the female.

Certain thoughts are more prone to speed up the rate of vibration in the human mind than others such as excitement, happiness, joy, sex, intense emotions, and more. The thoughts that are prone to flow through humans freely are listed below in a systematic order.

1. The thought of sex
2. The thought of falling in love or being loved
3. The thought of making MONEY and being wealthy
4. Listening to music
5. The thoughts of having companionship with someone else.
6. The thought of connecting to God.
7. The thought of pain, negative things, or bad news.
8. The thought of the unknown.
9. The excitement that comes with the euphoric feeling of drugs and alcohol.

Being aware of those thought patterns are important. More importantly, notice the order that they are organized. This knowledge has been acquired and put in "cause and effect order." Meaning the reasons why people overindulge drugs and alcohol is because they have not made the choice to flow with the momentum behind the desire of making money etc., as an effect, attracting a lot of more unfavorable thought patterns including drugs and alcohol. Learn that the more you move towards favorable expressions, good thoughts, constructive outlets of desire, the less prone we are to be affected by the unfavorable expressions, bad thoughts, and destructive outlets that are created by not moving towards your destiny.

This knowingness is essential to channel the sexual energy which may launch you towards your destiny. Now let's focus our attention on what forms our destiny.

The soundest commentary of destiny is "the hidden power discussed when one chooses to flow with the vibration of thoughts that align with God, only accessible through the rapid vibration created by extraordinary thoughts of who God created you to be."

The human who knows their destiny should be able to answer these questions, how amazing do you dare to be? The second is are you willing to risk your life to assure the birth of your dreams? Third, what are some things you are willing to die for and exactly how does the thought of these things make you feel? If your life was a scripture, what would it say?

The answers to these questions will provide the awareness that is necessary to discover the calling, mission, or destiny which lies dormant within you waiting for you to secure the plans which solidify its arrival. In other words, the answers to these questions are KEY to your freedom. Therefore, be honest in your answers.

"Destiny" the Treasure within you

The influence of "DESTINY" benefits every person in the world, who put forth the effort to make the discovery. Destiny is like precious gold that has sunk to the bottom of the sea. Gold at the bottom of the sea may be challenging to discover and retrieve, but for those who have been fortunate enough to find it, they discover the KEY that is essential to the continued momentum of freedom.

Most people spend their entire lifetime, ignorant of their destiny. A small population of people abroad knows their destiny and, as an effect, are unable to use the creative power, understanding, knowledge, and focus that comes with it. One's destiny is the only thing that makes them different from every other child of God.

Visions, daydreaming, and imagination are mental faculties that offer glimpses of the destiny that has been chosen for you. When daydreaming, dreaming, having visions, receiving revelations, etc. occur, these indicators are signs that one's destiny is calling for an opportunity to be expressed outwardly.

God is the source that stores your destiny, which inspires your sense of life and purpose. The human mind is more in receiving mode for their destiny when it's practicing the thoughts which align with the vibration of God. That is when, you will feel your destiny moving towards you, and yourself moving towards it.

The thoughts in the mind associated with your destiny vibrate at a higher rate than ordinary thoughts. When inspired to flow with the momentum of thoughts that vibrate at a higher rate, your mind will be elevated to a higher vibration, putting you in receiving mode for a higher level of thought, perspective, and experience, aptly activating the eagle within you. While practicing ordinary, surface level, normal thoughts, one is not able to see further than the reality of limitation. Remember, when practicing this higher perspective, the eagle, one's capabilities and vision is not restricted or limited by the thought patterns or vibrations that cripple their ability to manifest their destiny.

REMEMBER THIS: a bald eagle can fly at a higher altitude than ordinary birds. Meaning the eagle can always descend and fly with the penguins, vultures, crows, ducks, etc. But they can never rise to the same place as the eagle.

We are in a world in which the truth, is easier to understand when expressed symbolically, metaphorically, rather than literally, which is the reason the eagle is used. For those who prefer the truth, literally, the next few sentences are for you. We live in a world where it has become more common to operate with the ordinary plane of mind, which is limitation based. The plane of mind that aligns with your destiny is a much higher plane than ordinary. The way towards this higher plane of mind is on the path of your destiny which can be discovered through the practice of following the momentum or vibration created by thoughts that are cultivated through experiences on Mother Earth. Once one discovers their destiny, they become more receptive to their desire. The eagle within you represents this higher vibration, higher thought pattern, a higher perspective, and a higher understanding of self that is key to your freedom.

The more we practice the eagle thought pattern, the more we are in receiving mode for our destiny and the more we move towards our destiny, the more we must rely on and develop an active relationship with God.

In fact, our relationship with God is cultivated and developed by following the path of our destiny. The path which the eagle thought pattern aligns with is discovered through pursuing your destiny. Leaders abroad in all walks of life, lawyers, professional athletes, artists and more earned their place through cultivating the habit of attuning to the "voice" or "thought pattern" within that favors their desired outcome, through the eagle faculty of the mind. Let it be known to all who are experiencing poverty and limitation, that the greatest way to discover our destiny or what you want is through contrast or experiencing what you don't want.

Greater, higher, and impactful levels of freedom and influence are experienced by attuning to the eagle faculty of the mind which is always readily available. It is inside of you. There are many who spend their lives SEEKING and never discover their destiny. Well, now you know the reason WHY. When seeking, we search in all the wrong places. The key is within you and all the experiences we face through seeking will lead us to the TREASURE that lives within, called your DESTINY.

One of the important skills to cultivate is channeling the sexual energy towards your destiny. When you make the choice to do so, God will summon the creative force and power within you to transmute your thoughts into reality. In other words, this faculty of the mind stores the creative force and power that is vital to your freedom in all walks of life. In a later and previous points of this chapter, it is referred to as "the vital force".

Every person who has used the eagle creative faculty, which is activated through channeling energy, constructively, left profound marks on history. Surely, this is where "discipline "comes to existence. This power (that every person has access to) allows access to the keys within you that this book will direct you towards.

Let us enlighten you on the power that may be acquired if one chooses to constructively, channel the "vital force". Let us examine the benefits.

- Greater sense of self-value

- Greater self of strength in the body
- Learn how to love yourself
- Less prone to experience problems
- Decreased sense of worry
- Heightened sense of appreciation
- Greater mental processing, power, efficiency, and FOCUS.
- The 5 senses are heightened, and one is made more intuitive which permits one to understand the difference between thoughts that come from others and thoughts coming from God.
- A heightened sense of creativity.

Power and influence can be gained through forging your efforts into any of these sources. It will be transmuted into supernatural power by channeling the inspiration that these feelings create into actions that serve the greater good. Constructively channeling the momentum gained from these sources of awareness will be difficult for all those who lack the ability to FOCUS. If there is no focus, then there are no results. The focus will be the threshold of all the elements of power which are necessary to transmute your thoughts into reality.

All of America's most successful and nationally known icons made it a habit of acquiring a FOCUS, that followed a decision. When adversity presented itself, the focus would not allow one to take their eyes off the prize.

Jeff Bezos, Chief Executive officer of Amazon, worked on wall street in a variety of fields, in the process of creating and expanding Amazon. This process was the same as if for anyone who desires to be an expert, master, or leader of their field, which was trial and error, but after trial, limit errors.

In his mind, he was not expecting to become the world's wealthiest person. It was not on his agenda, more so, he was proficient and knowledgeable in the areas of science and technology. His knowingness that he was equipped with these skills kept him moving forward. In his constant focus on "his skills", birthed the momentum to continually desire improvement.

"I know if I was not making mistakes, I was not innovating," says Bezos. He was prepared to make mistakes but kept in mind: "His job is to empower others and himself to behold." When Bezos described his Amazon success, "I have made billions of dollars off failures at Amazon." But after his mistakes, he would analyze the moment precisely, draw upon the force taken from the lesson and continue to experiment, eventually getting in the position where success is the only option. Through all his hardship, Bezos remained honest with himself. As an effect, he was in a position to draw power and force instead of losing growth and ideas which happened in connection with not facing failure head-on or pretending it did not happen.

Jeff Bezos earned his freedom by saturating his brain with quality ideas and beliefs. Saturating his mind with quality thoughts paid off in the form of a billion-dollar industry.

Humans have a tendency of drawing upon the negative force from experience. Experience is the best teacher. When we draw from experience, the lesson that stores the force propels us towards our desired outcome. Take a minute and examine your life and consider the lesson drawn from the influence of what's known as your "world." Furthermore, all things and realities begin in the form of a thought. Note that all thoughts carry a force, which based on the nature of thoughts, forms beliefs and ideas.

For example, Jim Carrey, laugh–out loud comedian, grew up in a low-income home and his family was so poor that he dropped out of school at 15 to work and help his family. Through combining these experiences with the idea that by making his dream come true, he acquired the willpower to become one of the most iconic comedians in American history.

Equally, Ellen DeGeneres, television presenter, film producer and comedian, who has solidified her legacy in history, was sexually assaulted at the age of 15. She drew from this experience, "MEN ARE NOT GOOD FOR HER" and began to find more comfort in being in same-sex relationships.

The major difference between "Jim Carrey" and "Ellen DeGeneres", can only be revealed through the works of the FOCUS faculty of the mind. Meaning whatever you focus on, creates a momentum (energy) within, known as inspiration. The nature of that momentum, positive or negative, is based upon what part of an experience we choose to give our focal point of attention. The philosopher says, "what you think is what you become", this is what's meant by that popular quote.

Both had to focus on a certain aspect of their experiences. If they focus on the more favorable perspectives made available through experience, their experiences will produce the momentum to launch more favorable outcomes. This method is not biased. If one chooses to focus on the more "negative" or "unfavorable" perspectives made available through experiences, their experiences will produce the thought patterns and vibrations that disallows progress and results.

These are some important points to draw from this section, regarding FOCUS.

1. The thoughts we focus (traumas, negative thoughts, emotional connections) creates a vibration, which sets up a point of attraction, that expands and creates the experiences in our physical reality that we store in our mind.
2. Focus on thoughts that allow growth through accountability. All are not aware of the thoughts that dwell in their mind. We hold onto negative thoughts and give them our FOCUS, while equally DENYING that we are holding onto the negative thoughts or being ignorant to the thoughts in our subconscious mind because we are more in tune with everyone else and naïve to ourselves.

Focus is a direct influence on the ability to activate the eagle faculty of the mind.

FAILURES THAT INSPIRE YOU TO ACHIEVE

One of the most common causes of failure is the habit of drawing upon, focusing on, being overtaken by or giving too much attention to the negative lessons from an experience. Every human has done this at some point. Many become FREE by rewarding themselves with the lessons that permit them to claim their promising future because they knew this key "Failure offers the opportunity to discover the focus that permits success."

Jeff Bezos is a success through the focus obtained through huge mistakes: such as "selling a negative quantity of books to customers." Later went on to be known as the founders of the world's largest online retailer.

Paul Allen, co-founder of Microsoft with Bill Gates, made the mistake of selling AOL stocks and missing out on over $4 Billion. Only later to become more system based in his decision making and eventually rise to a net worth of 15 billion dollars.

The name Sheldon Adelson became popular for being an investment advisor and mortgage, with a net worth of $5 Million. After being mentally, physically and emotionally crippled by unwise business decisions, he began to focus more on RISK and REWARDS instead of making business decisions as influenced by emotions. The renewed focus led Adelson to discover his passion for computers. Needless to say, Sheldon created the Computer Dealers Expo, which became one of the largest computer trade homes in the world. This new focus took Adelson from a net worth of $5 million to $30 Billion.

Another man who exemplifies the art of drawing a focus from failure that permits success is Larry Page, the co-founder of Google. Through persevering efforts, Google has become one of the most dominant internet sources and product services abroad. Page wondered "why google was not initially having the impact predicted." From the failure, Page concluded that "Google was not relatable enough to people." Once Page fixed that mistake, he never made it again.

Mark Zuckerberg, CEO of Facebook, and his team were focused on building a successful online network. In the process of building this network, Mark became distracted by ideas that seemed like "good ideas" but did not move him towards his desired outcome. Mark made the mistake of putting time, energy and effort into his distractions and by default, delayed the process of manifesting his destiny. Mark Zuckerberg, at just 30 years old, has a net worth more than $28 billion.

Like Zuckerberg, Michael Dell, founder of Dell Computers, made the mistake of channeling his focus into distractions that presented themselves in the form of ideas that "sounded good." He made attempts to involve himself in tablets, iPods, and other electronic markets. Dell became one of the youngest CEO's to be on the Forbes list of the top 500 Corporations. Later, Dell's company became one of the largest sellers of personal computers in the world.

Warren Buffett became one of the greats due to the focus gained through his failures. He failed innumerable times before he gained access to the billionaire within him. The tragedy of purchasing gas stations and not making a profit, purchasing company shares and not making a profit, and more, were the billion-dollar mistakes that launched a necessary focus.

These discoveries placed people from ordinary to extraordinary living and their reality was developed through a FOCUS. By drawing the proper focus, their outlook was backed, with the burning inspiration to transmute their desires into the physical reality.

Having read these stories, immediately, allow yourself to see the importance of drawing upon the greater good lesson from an experience. I soon discovered that the lesson you take from stories, news, media, observations, are designed to launch you towards your destiny. There was one thing all these stories have in common, which is highlighted each time, in each of the stories told. It was designed to assure that failure is not a problem, but an asset of great value because "failure offers the opportunity to be successful."

In fact, all contrast, bad, or negative experiences, equally offers the opportunity to discover freedom, positive outcomes, and the good life. We must make it top priority to continually wrap our mind, stories, beliefs, and ideas that favor the ideas of "HOPE" and "IT'S POSSIBLE" instead of thoughts that handicap us and are useless with respects to our destiny.

To make plain the underlying idea of this chapter, "Destiny requires one to channel their energy into a focus which prompts their desired outcome."

As we reach the closing point of this chapter, I can draw your attention to a phenomenal activity that has produced powerful results. Analyze your life experiences and draw from them, what they all have in common and you will gain an advantage over the next man or woman, regarding understanding your destiny. For example, Samir Wilkins was a leading gang member who did not have a college education or millions of dollars but possessed a strong desire for helping his MOTHER and would put himself in unfavorable positions to channel this desire. He was told to get a job, instead, he sold drugs and eventually made enough money to gain an advantage over his sub-society. Samir was just a boy with a desire to take care of his mother.

Notice the reason WHY George Washington was inspired to become the first President of the United States, was his mother, who taught him all the intellectual physical and moral education that he knew. When George was young, he showed evidence that he would grow to be a leader and put himself in favorable positions to create the basis for not only his mother but for one of the greatest nations to be formed on this Earth. After several years of cultivating his leadership skills, he gained recognition as a prominent leader. He was not afraid to step outside of his comfort zone and later became the first President of the United States of America. George Washington was just a boy with a desire to take care of his mother.

Well, the differences between the stories of Samir Wilkins and George

Washington are obvious. But if you dismiss the differences, the truth may come that, Samir and George were two boys with a strong desire to secure the well-being of their mothers. Here is the interpretation of these stories that lift out the perspective that leads one to the commonplace known as DESTINY, which is Chosen by God.

Many find it useful to focus more on experiences that show evidence of the doubt, which leads to a state of mindless beneficial to the one necessary to pursue destiny. All experiences are beneficial, except the one who focuses on the unfavorable lesson from an experience.

Focus on the lesson that draws accountability and represents a desire. These lessons will only be misunderstood by those who do not know the difference between going through it and growing through it. The major difference is that going through it becomes your reality when one is focused on the negative aspect of experiences. All experiences that the human mind draws the necessary lesson, are necessary and justified as steppingstones that pave the way to destiny as inspired by the momentum of DESIRE.

Experience is Life's greatest teacher

Experience brings us into communion with our destiny. When we channel our energy into a focus that aligns with desire, it may lead us far up the success ladder. Knowing the desire behind every experience serves as the roadmap of DESTINY.

Experience fashions all of life's greatest lessons, which are beautiful and inspirational. It is the interpretation that is taken from experience, when properly interpreted, aligned, and harmonized, that unites us with the DESTINY THAT EXISTS WITHIN that our souls are connected to. Being offset from the path of destiny will express itself in the form of lack of energy, laziness, and distaste for life. When the sexual energy is constructively channeled towards the focus which aligns with DESTINY that exist between you and God, you will discover the HEAVEN ON EARTH VIBRATION where freedom dwells.

It is crucial to draw from experience the understanding that aligns with your destiny. This is something you can do on your own, but it requires you to be TRUE. You may or may not be familiar with the exercise but take the exercise seriously. First, you start by writing down your three passions and professions, things you love to do, something you can do to make money and draw a circle around each activity. Example of ALANA Gilbert:

Then proceed and get the question started. Remember, you're going to have to ask yourself the questions, "what common desire is hidden in these experiences?" or "what do these experiences have in common?" For example,

Why did Alana work at the bank? Alana says, "I work there to learn the system the bank uses to store more money." Why does Alana like Personal training?" Alana says, "Because I enjoy exercise and helping others feel good." Why does it feel amazing to be a Motivational Speaker?" Alana says, "It allows me to express myself and educate others."

When you reach this point, draw from the answers the KEY principles, which relate to your core values. In the case of Alana Gilbert, her core values are system, structure, order, good health and education. When you are finished pulling your core values, you will attach each value to a bubble.

Financial Fitness

Now you are a step away from unlocking your destiny. Now you have reached the point where you must create a career or path that allows you to utilize all three core values, which will be placed in the Question mark space (?).

Years later, Alana Gilbert started an institution called "Financial Fitness" where they used a combination of exercise and education to transform lives. Well great news, I have spent the last years of my life crafting this book to provide you with the roadmap to your destiny.

There is a reward in discovering your destiny. The KEY is using the awareness of this book. There is a sense of life that comes to all who discover the purpose given to them by God. The reward is worth the effort. Will you give yourself a chance?

We are in a relationship with our destiny. You will always be in a relationship with your destiny. To conclude this chapter, it is safe to say, "if we are in a relationship with our destiny; we have to marry our work ethic and engage our soul."

Chapter 15

Questions and Quotes

Before you can truly experience freedom, your mind must be prepared or in receiving mode for it. Preparing the mind for freedom is the key. This process begins with understanding, studying and grasping the concepts of this book. Freedom is the root of all manifestations.

People who suffer must learn the KEYS to free themselves from suffering. Equally, people who desire to be wealthy must learn the keys to free themselves from poverty. Protect yourself with the concepts and principles that conduct freedom. Poverty does not permit success. For anyone to succeed in any calling, they must recognize and replace poverty-driven thoughts. If you are reading this book with hopes to discover your freedom, study this book and examine relationships and associations that bring you negative energy. Poverty and negative energy indicate you've surrendered your focus to attain a poverty-based outcome.

This chapter will include questions and quotes. Upon reading the questions, hold yourself accountable to be honest in your answers. Answer the questions with precision and know that "the truth shall set you free." In other words, your honest answers store the keys to your freedom.

Poverty and negativity served their time in your life because negative experiences offer the focus that inspires you to harmonize with poverty. Equally, poverty produces the focus that inspires you to harmonize with FREEDOM, whether spiritually, financially, physically, or mentally. Poverty and negative energy are expressions of the terrorist. They subtly present themselves, with hopes that you are not aware of their presence. More poverty keeps you in a state of mind that permits limitations. This book is not written to imply or connotate that poverty and negative energy are bad or evil. Sometimes the experiences in negativity and poverty launch desires for freedom, that desire transmutes into inspiration, and that inspiration inspires actions. At other times, poverty and negative energy create a destructive mental attitude when one tends to focus on NEGATIVITY instead of drawing the focus from negative experiences that promote the mental attitude for freedom.

NEGATIVE ENERGY AND POVERTY

Negative energy is the vibration of poverty and limitation. This energy does not condone the idea of you manifesting your destiny and reaching your fullest potential. Commonly, negative energy has influenced people to operate against their desires and surrender their minds to ORDINARY. Be aware that every human, including you, are by nature, living in poverty.

Be aware that poverty, by nature, builds the habits of building relationships and associations based on problems and shared weaknesses. Be aware that negative energy zaps you of the inspiration which makes it challenging to take the necessary actions to encourage your promising future. Freedom is the only solution.

Negative energy and poverty distract people away from their dreams. Once under the influence of poverty or negativity, people will seek for others that harmonize with them.

Allow trouble and negativity to summon the desire for happiness and freedom. Negative energy and poverty have damaged human beings for a long time because we don't acknowledge the ways it's active and tend to DENY, neglect, or refuse to correct the poverty-driven thought patterns until they become so integrated into one's habits that they accept it as is.

As a practical way to usher the minds of those who desire the freedom to become a greater version of themselves, these questions and quotes have been organized for you. Read the questions and answer them aloud. Be honest with yourself. Remember where there is no truth, there is no freedom. Feel free to share your response with a spouse, friend, associate or someone who will hold you accountable for telling the truth.

- Do you find it hard to make decisions because you don't want to let someone down or disappoint others?
- Do you like your job? If not, why?
- Are you ever fatigued? If so, why?
- Do you ever want to quit or give up? If so, why?
- Do you constantly make mistakes in your life? If so, why?
- How do you feel when others complain?
- Do you get jealous when you see others who are successful?
- Do you hold yourself accountable or do you blame others? If so, why?
- How many "distractions" do you give your time and attention to? Why do you tolerate them?
- What inspires you to get out of your bed in the morning?
- Have you ever felt like you are losing your confidence? Why?
- Do you spend more time focusing on future possibilities or past failures?
- How many friends do you have that gives you negative energy, but you tolerate it because "you love them?"
- What did you learn from your past failures?

Surrender your honesty to these questions, knowing that the understanding drawn from these questions permits you to know more about yourself. Review the questions and answers thoroughly. Revisit these questions and answers daily.

Amazingly, you will gain chief access to yourself. For all questions left unanswered, find a mentor, someone who is willing to be honest with you and desires the best for you.

You have the power to influence your thoughts. This is the most powerful fact about humans. This capability reflects the creator. Meaning, God is the only presence, that can create, by mere thought. Meaning when God thinks it, so does it become. Humans can have a thought and they must add strategy, organization and create precise plans to their thoughts to assure its manifestation. All creations reflect the creator. In other words, as creations of God, our ability to transmute our thoughts into the physical reality reflects the same power the creator (GOD) used to create us. You have access to the same power.

We must know the power that we possess to use it constructively. Your mind is the storehouse where all creations and visions are birthed. There is a divine connection that exists between you and your mind. Therefore, make it a priority to protect your thoughts, as well as, be conscious that you don't store thoughts in your mind that create unfavorable outcomes or projects negative energy.

Discipline yourself and make it habit to attune with your mind. There is a relationship that exists between you and your mind. It has become common for people to "COMPROMISE" their mind for the sake of "flowing with the current", or "trying to fit in" and upholding the status quo. Studying relationships in the world today, you will notice that "COMPROMISE" is promoted as one of the KEY factors to sustain a relationship. Without further due, allow me to inform you that COMPROMISE means giving up what you desire. Well giving up what you desire is the basis for permanent unhappiness. Moreover, direct that perspective towards your relationship with your mind.

You are the master of your mind, thoughts, and destiny. Do not compromise your dreams, visions, desires or goals for the sake of being pleasing unto others, to assure that you have someone to agree with you or to assure someone else's life is in order. By doing so, you are compromising your destiny, which unfolds itself to you through your thoughts.

Quotes

People who succeed in obtaining FREEDOM have one quality over the average human. They have a MINDSET and they fill their mind with stories, quotes, and beliefs that harmonize with their desired outcome. Some of these stories, ideas, or beliefs may seem complex and others simple, but they are used as the fuel which keeps one driven towards their desired outcome.

A list of quotes drawn from success stories abroad is compiled in this section. As you read them, repeat them aloud, survey yourself thoroughly and determine how these quotes, if any, serve the greater good of your life.

Questions and Quotes

"Hustling is a Poverty Mindset"
Wealthy people do not hustle. Wealth is measured by precision and proper planning. Release the need to hustle and relax yourself to a state of allowing concise and well-structured plans to be your focus.
"As long as you are kept ignorant, things will stay the same"
"Transform the way you look at things, then your world will change"
"Life begins on the edge of your comfort zone"
"Beliefs are more powerful than reality"
"Time is not money, Time is freedom. And you will make more when you realize you are worth more than the money you are being paid for your time"
"Truth is not afraid to be questioned. The truth wants to be questioned"
"Beliefs are ideas formed in the absence of the full truth"
Who was your first love?
What's the importance of crying?
Where there are tears, there is COMPASSION, where there is COMPASSION, there is DESIRE, where there is DESIRE, there is the momentum that leads to DESTINY.
Are you a reflection of your past failures or future desires?
Do you believe the sky is the limit?
The sky can't be the limit because the truth is, there is no limit to your greatness. By telling yourself the limit, you're not telling yourself the truth. How can the sky be the limit if there's footprints on the moon?
"The pursuit of wonder builds a genius"
"Distractions leads to the wrong turn, and some turn and never turn back"

"Our minds operate like computers. Therefore, you must have a hard drive"

If your life was a fortune cookie, what is your message?

"You can't do it is the highest standard to someone with low expectations"

"Just because it has worth, does not mean it's worth it"

"Marry yourself, then Engage the world"

"Emotions are poverty"

"Be selfish now so you can be generous later"

"Be For Real or Be Forgotten"

"Leverage is the most powerful force in the Universe"

"Make decisions based on system, structure and fundamental analysis"

"College and traditional education teach us to be employed, not become WEALTHY"

"Stop being curious and get serious"

"Leaders are Readers"

"Stop trying to make money and make money work for you"

"Mitigate risk, maximize time and profit"

"Your #1 resource is your health and your #2 resource is time"

"The trend is your friend"

"Learn emotionally, but make decisions systematically"

"Don't have a backup plan because a backup plan is backed up by FEAR"

Who has the power, the customers or the business?

What is your Mission, Vision, and Plan?

What is your truth?

Can you give a person a million dollars if you don't have it?

"Less is more, more is less"

"To know nothing means to know everything"

"Blend in but don't get attached"

"The heart can't be broken; it is the toughest muscle in the body"

If you tell someone to go to hell, where do you have to be in order to observe if they make it?

Be careful what you say. If you say negative things or think negatively, you must be in a negative state of consciousness to observe if your words are coming true.

"Your gift has very little to do with you, more with others"

"Paperwork determines seriousness"

"To be our Healthy self, we must learn to Heal-thyself"

"Your body is a house where our heart and mind lives, chaos occurs where they sleep in different rooms"

"Because you want to make money, that's why you are Poor"
You can't make money, only the printing machine can do that. Your
duty is to earn it through creating plans to accumulate it.
"Because you can see, that's why you are blind"
"Because you change, that's why you stay the same"
Can you be ready, but not prepared?
"Options create misery, simplicity creates measurable results"
"Be the opportunity you desire to see"
Power Recharger and Your Energy Recharger
Prayer and meditation are tools to remind you of your power.
"A ship only sinks because they have allowed what's going on the
outside to get inside of them"
"Treat yourself how you wanted to be treated by others"

Building a mindset is an important part of freedom. A mindset is created through the effort emitted through the habits which are required to manifest your desire. As a human family, why do you think a mindset has become so uncommon? The answer is because we prefer not to face the thoughts in our minds because of the FEAR of discomfort that some of them create. Unaware that by living in FEAR of our thoughts, we are DENYING ourselves and equally depriving ourselves of experiencing our own truth.

Denial is deeply rooted in the human mind. The habit of denial is not an easy habit to break, especially when we've become intelligent but equally foolish enough to justify and rationalize reasons why we don't deserve to be happy, why we can't come together, why we can't be wealthy, why we can't overcome poverty, why we can't conquer our fears or whatever other FEAR is rooted in the mind.

Keep this in mind, "A lie is when you don't tell someone else the truth, but DENIAL is when you're not honest with yourself." Understanding denial was always a challenge for me. Why people spend so much time denying themselves of their future, by creating responsibilities that only exist to cover up their weaknesses? In preparing to close this book, I turn the attention to some KEY points of emphasis. Do not allow ANYTHING or ANYONE to limit your greatness. Do not neglect who God has created you to be because your purpose, given by God, is the only thing that makes you different. Remove your tolerance of people in associations that tolerate negative energy and approves DISHONESTY.

History repeats itself because it has become the norm to practice denial. However, allow me to inform you that when you deny the truth, it doesn't go away. It just finds a safe place to hide until it resurfaces again.

The key to freedom is a life marked by NO DENIAL and total acceptance of the "PERFECT BEING" called "YOU" that God created. It is you that has the power to create in your own mind, the thought-form that leads to freedom. Finding that thought pattern and surrendering to it, in action, is the key. The key is inside of you.

There is a price that ALL must pay in order to experience their freedom. The peace and joy that comes with freedom are permitted to those who have discipline and are willing to be honest with themselves and others, despite the price that it may cost.

I conclude this book with this final truth that is essential to all who desire FREEDOM. In doing so, I declare that "nothing is free except energy."

www.ingramcontent.com/pod-product-compliance
Lightning Source LLC
Chambersburg PA
CBHW060759110426
42739CB00032BA/1833